Showing
My Color

Showing My Color

Impolite Essays on Race and Identity

Clarence Page

HarperPerennial

A Division of HarperCollins*Publishers*

A hardcover edition of this book was published in 1996 by HarperCollins Publishers.

HarperCollins books may be purchased for educational, business, or sales promotional use. For information please write: Special Markets Department, HarperCollins Publishers, Inc., 10 East 53rd Street, New York, NY 10022.

First HarperPerennial edition published 1997.

Designed by R. Caitlin Daniels

The Library of Congress has catalogued the hardcover edition as follows:

Page, Clarence, 1947–
    Showing my color : impolite essays on race and identity/Clarence Page.—1st ed.
        p. cm.
    Includes bibliographical references.
    ISBN 0-06-017256-8
    1. Racism—United States. 2. Afro-American—Social conditions—1975–   3. United States—Race relations. 4. United States—Social policy—1993–   I. Title.
    E185.615.P28   1996
    305.896'073—dc20   95-46274

ISBN 0-06-092801-8 (pbk.)
    00 01❖/ RRD 10 9 8 7 6 5

To Grady

and

to Maggie Page (1911–1984)

In memoriam

Contents

Acknowledgments

While I was writing this book I received word that David
Roth, a pioneer in the interethnic relations that have come to
be known as multiculturalism, had lapsed during a heart
operation into a coma from which he never recovered. He was
fifty-five. As director of the American Jewish Committee's
Chicago-based Institute for American Pluralism, David
devoted his life to perfecting techniques for helping various
racial and ethnic groups understand, appreciate and share
each other's ethnic experiences. His work helped lead to the
White House office on ethnic affairs and to the alliance that
won redress for Japanese-Americans who were sent to intern-
ment camps during World War II. He was an endless source
of wisdom and inspiration to me in forming the views collected in this book.

The world and I will miss him.

My endless gratitude also goes out to:

The editors of *The Chicago Tribune*, my professional home
since 1969, except for a few years in local Chicago television
news in the early 1980s. I am particularly grateful to Jack
Fuller and Jim Squires, who had the good faith to grant my
wish for a column and a seat on the editorial board. I hope
their faith has been rewarded.

I would also like to thank Howard Tyner and Don Wycliff,
for allowing me the time and encouragement to work on this
book, to Tribune Media Services for picking up my column
for national syndication and to WGN-TV and the
MacNeil/Lehrer NewsHour (now called *The NewsHour with Jim
Lehrer*) for graciously allowing me the time to work on it.

My agent, Rafe Sagalyn, for his faith, guidance and support.

Wendy Wolf and Janet Goldstein at HarperCollins for teaching this newspaper scrivener how to write a book.

Eric Steel at HarperCollins for understanding so quickly what I was trying to say and helping me to say it.

Frederick Alan Maxwell, my tireless sleuth of a research assistant, who always brought back more than I needed, and our able intern Sean Roberts.

Others who aided immeasurably in my education included Salim Muwakhil of *In These Times*, Robert C. Woodson of the Center for Neighborhood Enterprise, Zach Richter of the Center for Educational Radio and Television, James Whalen of Ithica College, author Gary Rivlin, Ron Takiki of the University of California at Berkeley, Frank Watkins and the Rev. Jesse Jackson of the Rainbow Coalition, Mrs. Mary Kindell, Fred and Saundra Ross, Paul and Sunny Fischer, Leah Witherspoon, Teresa Wiltz, my late grandmother Carrie, and Joe Eszterhas, the first to teach me that there would be more to my journalistic life than the "inverted pyramid."

And, lest I forget, my wife, Lisa, who had no idea what she was getting into.

1

The Rudeness of Race

An Introduction

The Negro leader of today is not free. He must look to white men for his very existence, and in consequence he has to waste a lot of his energy trying to think white. What the Negroes need is leaders who can and will think black.

—H.L. Mencken

Race has long had a rude presence in my life. While visiting relatives in Alabama as a child in the 1950s, I first saw water fountains marked "white" and "colored." I vaguely recall being excited. I rushed over to the one marked "colored" and turned it on, only to find, to my deep disappointment, that the water came out clear, just like the water back home in Ohio.

"Segregation," my dad said. I'd never heard the word before. My southern-born parents explained that it was something the white folks "down home" practiced. Some "home." Yet unpleasant experiences in the North already had taught me a more genteel, yet no less limiting version.

"There are places white people don't want colored to go," my elders told me in their soft southern accents, "and white people make the rules."

We had plenty of segregation like that in the North. We just didn't have the signs, which made it cheaper and easier to deny. We could look out of my schoolhouse window to see a public swimming pool closed to nonwhites. We had to go across town to the separate-but-equal "pool for colored." The steel mill that was our town's biggest employer held separate picnics for colored and white employees, which seemed to be just fine with the employees. Everyone had a good time, separately and unequally. I think the colored folks, who today would be called the "black community," were just happy to have something to call their own.

When I was about six years old, I saw a television commercial for an amusement park near the southern Ohio factory town where I grew up.

I chose to go. I told my parents. They looked at each other sadly and informed me that "little colored kids can't go there." I was crushed.

"I wish I was white," I told my parents.

"No, you don't!" Mom snapped. She gave me a look terrible enough to persuade me instantly that no, I didn't.

"Well, maybe for a few minutes, anyway?" I asked. "Just long enough for me to get past the front gate?" Then I could show them, I thought. I remember I wanted to show them what a terrific kid I was. I felt sorry for the little white children who would be deprived of getting to know me.

Throughout our childhood years my friendships with white schoolchildren (and with Pancho from the only Latino family in the neighborhood) proceeded without interruption. Except for the occasional tiff over some injudicious use of the N-word or some other slur we had picked up from our elders, we played in each other's backyards as congenially as Spanky, Buckwheat, and the rest of the gang on the old Hal Roach *Our Gang* comedies we used to watch on television.

Yet it quickly became apparent to me that my white friends were growing up in a different reality from the one to which I was accustomed. I could tell from the way one white friend happily discussed his weekend at LeSourdesville Lake that he did not have a clue of my reality.

"Have you been?" he asked.

"Colored can't go there," I said, somewhat astonished that he had not noticed.

"Oh, that can't be," he said.

For a moment, I perked up, wondering if the park's policy had changed. "Have you seen any colored people there?" I asked.

My white friend thought for a moment, then realized that he had not. He expressed surprise. I was surprised that he was surprised.

By the time I reached high school in the early 1960s, LeSourdesville Lake would relax its racial prohibitions. But the lessons of it stuck with me. It taught me how easily white people could ignore the segregation problem because from their vantage point it was not necessarily a problem. It was not necessarily an advantage to them, either, although some undoubtedly thought so. White people of low income, high insecurity, or fragile ego could always say that, no matter how badly off they felt, at least they were not black. Segregation helped them uphold and maintain this illusion of superiority. Even those white people who considered them-selves to have a well-developed sense of social conscience could easily rationalize segregation as something that was good for both races. We played unwittingly into this illusion, I thought, when my friends and I began junior high school and, suddenly thrust into the edgy, high hormonal world of adolescence, quickly gravitated into social cliques according to tastes and race.

It became even more apparent to me that my white friends and I were growing up in *parallel realities*, not unlike the parallel universes described in the science fiction novels and comic books I adored—or the "parallel realities" experienced by Serbs, Bosnians, and Croatians as described years later by feminist writer Slavenka Drakulic in *The Balkan Express*. Even as the evil walls of legal segregation were tumbling down, thanks to the hard-fought struggles of the civil rights movement, it occurred to me that my reality might never be quite the same as that experienced by my white friends. We were doomed, I felt, to dwell in our parallel realities. Separated by thick walls of prejudice, we would view each other through windows of stained-glass perceptions, colored by our personal experiences. My parents had taught me well.

"Don't be showin' yo' color," my parents would admonish me in my youth, before we would go out in public, especially among white folks. The phrase had special meaning in Negro conversations. Imbued with many subtle meanings and nuances, the showing of one's "color" could be an expression of chastisement or warning, admonishment or adulation, satire or self-hatred, anger or celebration. It could mean acting out or showing anger in a loud and uncivilized way.

Its cultural origins could be traced to the Africa-rooted tradition of "signifying," a form of witty, deliberately provocative, occasionally combative word play. The thrill of the game comes from taking one's opponent close to the edge of tolerable insult. Few subjects except perhaps sex itself could be a more sensitive matter between black people than talk about someone else's "color." The showing of one's "color," then, connoted the display of the very worst stereotypes anyone ever dreamed up about how black people behaved. "White people are not really white," James Baldwin wrote in 1961, "but colored people can sometimes be extremely colored."

Sometimes you can still hear black people say, in the heat of frustration, "I almost showed my color today," which is a way of saying they almost lost their "cool," "dropped the mask," or "went off." Losing one's cool can be a capital offense by black standards, for it shows weakness in a world in which spiritual rigor is one of the few things we can call our own. Those who keep their cool repress their "color." It is cool, in other words, to be colorless.

The title of this volume, *Showing My Color*, emerged from my fuming discontent with the current fashions of *racial denial*, steadfast repudiations of the difference race continues to make in American life. Old liberals, particularly white liberals who have become new conservatives, charge that racial pride and color consciousness threaten to "balkanize" American life, as if it ever was a model of unity. Many demand that we "get past race." But denials of a cancer, no matter how vigorous they may be, will not make the malignancy go away.

No less august a voice than the Supreme Court's conservative majority has taken to arguing in the 1990s for a "color-blind" approach to civil rights law, the area of American society in which color and gender consciousness have made the most dramatic improvement in equalizing opportunities.

The words of the Reverend Martin Luther King, Jr., have been perverted to support this view. Most frequently quoted is his oft-stated dream of the day when everyone would "not be judged by the color of their skin but by the content of their character." I would argue that King never intended for us to forget *all* about color. Even in his historic "I Have a Dream" speech, from which this line most often is lifted, he also pressed the less-often quoted but piquantly salient point about "the promissory note" America gave freed slaves, which, when they presented it, was returned to them marked "insufficient funds."

I would argue that too much has been made of the virtue of "color-blindness." I don't want Americans to be blind to my color as long as color continues to make a profound difference in determining life chances and opportunities. Nor do I wish to see so significant a part of my identity denied. "Ethnic differences are the very essence of cultural diversity and national creativity," black social critic Albert Murray wrote in *The Omni-Americans* (1970). "The problem is not the existence of ethnic differences, as is so often assumed, but the intrusion of such differences into areas where they do not belong."

Where, then, do they belong? Diversity is enriching, but race intrudes rudely on the individual's attempts to define his or her own identity. I used to be "colored." Then I was "Negro." Then I became "black." Then I became "African American." Today I am a "person of color." In three decades I have been transformed from a "colored person" to a "person of color." Are you keeping up with me?

Changes in what we black people call ourselves are quite annoying to some white people, which is its own reward to some black people. But if white people are confused, so are quite a few black people. There is no one way to be black. We are a diverse people amid a nation of diverse people. Some black people are nationalists who don't want anything to do with white people. Some black people are assimilationists who don't want anything to do with other black people. Some black people are integrationists who move in and out of various groups with remarkable ease. Some of us can be any of the three at any given time, depending on when you happen to run into us.

Growing up as part of a minority can expose the individual to horrible bouts of identity confusion. I used to think of myself as something of a *transracial man*, a figure no less frustrated than a transsexual who feels trapped in the body of something unfamiliar and inappropriate to his or her inner self.

These bouts were most torturous during adolescence, the period of life when, trembling with the shock of nascent independence from the ways of one's elders, the budding individual stitches together the fragile garments of an identity to be worn into adulthood. Stuttering and uncooperative motor skills left me severely challenged in dancing, basket shooting, and various social applications; I felt woefully inadequate to the task of being "popular" in the hot centers of black social activity at my integrated high school and college. "Are you black?" an arbiter of campus militancy demanded one day, when he "caught" me dining too many times with white friends. I had the skin pass, sure enough, but my inclinations fell well short of his standards. But I was not satisfied with the standards of his counterparts in the white world, either. If I was not "black" enough to please some blacks, I would never be "white" enough to please all whites.

Times have changed. Choices abound for black people, if we can afford them. Black people can now go anywhere they choose, as long as they can pay the bill when they get there. If anyone tries to stop them or any other minorities just because of their color, the full weight of the federal government will step in on the side of the minorities. I thank God and the hard-won gains of the civil rights revolution for my ability to have more choices. But the old rules of race have been replaced in many ways by new ones.

Today I live a well-integrated life in the suburbs. Black folks still tell me how to be "black" when I stray from the racial party lines, while white folks tell me how to be "color-blind." I still feel as frustrated in my attempts to transcend race as a reluctant lemming must feel while being rushed over the brink by its herd. But I find I have plenty of company in my frustration. Integration has not been a simple task for upwardly mobile African Americans, especially for those of us who happen also to be parents.

A few years ago, after talking to black friends who were raising teenage boys, I realized that I was about to face dilemmas not unlike those my parents faced. My son was turning three years old. Everyone was telling me that he was quite cute, and since he was the spitting image of his dad, I was the last to argue.

But it occurred to me that in another decade he would be not three but thirteen. If all goes well, somewhere along the way he is going to turn almost overnight from someone who is perceived as cute and innocent into someone who is perceived as a menace, the most feared creature on America's urban streets today, *a young black male*. Before he, like me when I was barred from a childhood amusement park, would have a chance to let others get to know him, he would be judged not by the content of his character, but by the color of his skin.

When our son was four years old he arrived home from his day care center to announce to his mother, "I want to be a white policeman." Mom was somewhat shaken by this proclamation, she told me later. Where had he picked this up? We had dutifully stripped our conversations of all talk of race in his presence. When it couldn't be avoided, we spelled out the words ("Is she b-l-a-c-k . . . ?") as if discussing an X-rated movie. She was incapable of responding to his announcement other than to ask "Why?" He did not have a definitive answer. He simply thought it would be "cool," the kids' universal stamp of approval.

I quietly inched over to a bookshelf and brought down a copy of a book by two black psychiatrists on raising black children. Like a black parental catechism, it quickly offered up a question uncannily similar to our own—*What do you do when a four-year-old says he wants to be white?*—and an answer: *Relax*.

Don't panic, the book said. It is quite normal for children to begin to notice color at age four, but they don't attach the same meaning to it that we, their older folks, do. They are looking for role models, people they like enough to want to be like, until someone tells them otherwise. It is not limited to blacks, the book said. Sometimes young white children want to be brown or black like their favorite sports heroes.

There, I assured my wife. It is normal. As my parents used to say, it's a phase. Let the lad work it out. If we didn't make a big deal out of it, we figured, neither would he. Still, we did not forget it. A week or so later at a local outdoor folk festival, his mother introduced our son to a police officer who happened to be quite visibly a brown-skinned black man. He cheerfully presented our son with his own "junior officer" badge. Our son never again said he wanted to be a white police officer. He didn't say he wanted to be a black police officer, either. He didn't say anything but "Thank you." Still, his mother and I were relieved. Another little life-warping trauma seemed to be averted. For now.

Perhaps we make too much of these little concerns, but we are not alone. We find ourselves commiserating earnestly with other middle-class black parents about issues other parents almost never confront. (*Are white media feeding the ancient and pernicious rules of race to our child through subliminal messages? Did Disney have to give cackling black and Latino voices to the lazy, shiftless, and still extremely dangerous hyenas in* The Lion King? *Does it matter that the noblest voice, that of the father king lion, happens to be that of an African American, James Earl Jones, Hollywood's favorite voice of God? Does it matter that he also voiced the baddest bad guy in outer space, Darth Vader? Why were there no black people in the first* Star Wars? *What happens to black people in white people's future?*)

To educate one's children, who tirelessly produce "Why?" questions about everything, in the rules of race (*Is a little enough? Is more too much?*) is to try to make sense out of nonsense. I quickly gained a new appreciation for what my parents went through when my son, at age five, blurted out while we were on a family drive, "Mom, why do you call yourself black? You look white. Dad looks black."

"It's a figure of speech," I said calmly, keeping my eyes on the road, as though I were not the least bit rattled. "Black means your family can be traced back to Africa."

Pause.

"Do you remember where Africa is?" I asked.

Silence. Perhaps our exchange suddenly was sounding too much like academic work. Yet, once again, he got me to thinking. Children do not imbue race with much meaning, and they remind us, however briefly, that we adults shouldn't, either. Instead, we adults pass on our prejudices to our children under the guise of setting them straight. Rather than teaching them that different is not necessarily better or worse, we teach them how to make difference the basis for abuse, privilege, and exclusion.

His kindergarten classmate Eddy offered an unsolicited example. We were driving to an indoor playground called the Discovery Zone, a national chain where for a few dollars children have an opportunity to wear themselves out and spend their parents' money on coin-operated amusement machines and great mouthfuls of popcorn, cotton candy, ice cream, and pizza. Eddy, who happens to be black and the child of a struggling single mom, had never been to this little corner of children's paradise. As I was driving us to it, he asked somewhat skeptically, "Do they have any black people at this place?"

I assured him that they would. I understood his concern. Even adults are apprehensive of unfamiliar places, and almost every place in the world still was unfamiliar to young Eddy. Even at age five, he already was feeling the impulse that causes many of us African Americans, whenever we walk into a strange roomful of people, to look around and see how many other black people are there.

I felt obliged to help liberate Eddy from his racial anxieties, to help him get over the daunting hump of hesitation that causes black people to avoid integrated situations out of fear of some ominous possibility of racial hurt. It's a daunting task, but someone has to do it, for the sake (as James Baldwin once wrote) of our future generations and the bills they must pay.

My mom is gone now, after helping set me up with the sort of education that has freed me to make choices. I have chosen to move my father to a nice, predominantly white, antiseptically tidy retirement village near me in Maryland with large golf courses and swimming pools. It is the sort of place he might have scrubbed floors in but certainly not have lived in back in the old days. It has taken him a while to get used to having so many well-off white people behaving so nicely and neighborly to him, but he has made the adjustment well.

Still the ugly specter of racism does not easily vanish. He and the other hundred or so African-American residents decided to form a social club like the other ethnically or religiously based social clubs in the village. One night during their meeting in the main social room, someone scrawled "KKK" on little sheets of paper and slipped them under the windshields of some of their cars in the parking lot. "We think maybe some of the white people wanted the blacks to socialize with the whites, not in a separate group," one lady of the club told me. If so, they showed an unusual method for extending the arms of brotherhood.

I live in a community that worships diversity like a state religion, although individuals sometimes get tripped up by it. The excellent Spanish "immersion" program that one of

the county's "magnet" schools installed to encourage middle-
class parents to stay put has itself become a cover for "white
flight" by disgruntled white parents. Many of them, despite a
lack of empirical evidence, perceive the school's regular
English program as inferior, simply because it is 90 percent
minority and mostly composed of children who come from a
less-fortunate socioeconomic background. So the Spanish
immersion classes designed to encourage diversity have
become almost exclusively white and Asian American, while
the English classes have become almost exclusively—irony of
ironies—black and Latino, with many of the children learning English as a second language. Statistically the school is
"diverse" and "integrated." In reality its student body is
divided by an indelible wall, separate but supposedly equal.

In another example, two biracial kindergarten girls whose
parents are white and Asian have been denied transfer to the
French immersion program at another school. The move,
school officials say, would leave the remaining Asian children
too "racially isolated." The Chinese-American mother of one
of the girls, who went to preschool with my son, found that
insulting and absurd. "I went to school in Minnesota with
maybe three or four other Asian students in my entire town,"
she said, "yet to the best of my knowledge none of us wound
up in the penitentiary."

Fortunately, after their story received a mini-blizzard of
national publicity, the two families had their right to choose
restored as quickly and as devoid of official explanation as it
had been earlier taken away. At least their little crisis was
solved, but other such crises were reported to be percolating
around the country. How ironic, I thought, recalling similar
choices denied to me in my childhood, that the remedy for
years of choices denied on the basis of skin color would be
the denial of more choices on the basis of skin color.

Despite all these color-conscious efforts to educate the county's children in a color-blind ideal of racial equality, many of our children seem to be catching on to race codes anyway, although with a twist suitable to the hip-hop generation. One local junior high school teacher, when he heard his black students referring to themselves as "bad," had the facts of racial life explained to him like this: They were not talking about the "bad means good" slang popularized by Michael Jackson's *Bad* album. They meant "bad" in the sense of misbehaving and poorly motivated. The black kids are "bad," the students explained, and the white kids are "good." The Asian kids are "like white," and the Latino kids "try to be bad like the blacks." Anyone who tried to break out of those stereotypes was trying to break the code, meaning that a black or Latino who tried to make good grades was "trying to be white."

It is enough, as Marvin Gaye famously sang, to make you want to holler and throw up both of your hands. Yet my neighbors and I hate to complain too loudly because, unlike other critics you may read or hear about, we happen to be a liberal community that not only believes in the dream of integration, true diversity, but actually is trying to live it.

We reside in Montgomery County, Maryland, the most prosperous suburban county per capita in the Washington, D.C., area. Each of the above-mentioned controversies has been reported in the pages of the *Washington Post* and other local media, right under the noses and, in some cases, within the families of some of the nation's top policy makers.

But when it comes to wrangling with the vagaries of racial prejudices and perceptions, we are not special. These scenes characterize middle-class America wherever parents like us, wedged between the black inner city and the white outer suburbs, try to hang on to the best aspects of racial integration and quality education at the same time. It is not easy, but it is a choice we decided to make, for as long as we can hold on.

Elsewhere, I see my own spin on what civil rights law professor Lani Guinier calls "a nation in denial about race." Black folks deny how far we have come, while whites deny how far we have to go.

We see icons of black success—Colin Powell, Douglas Wilder, Bill Cosby, Oprah Winfrey, Bryant Gumbel, the two Michaels: Jordan and Jackson—not only accepted but adored by whites in ways far removed from the arm's-length way white America regarded Jackie Robinson, Willie Mays, Lena Horne, and Marian Anderson.

Yet, while the media show happy images of blacks, whites, Asians, and Hispanics getting along, amicably consuming the good life, a fog of false contentment conceals menacing fissures cracking the national racial landscape.

Despite the growth of the black middle class, most blacks and whites live largely separate lives. School integration actually peaked in 1967, according to a Harvard study, and has declined ever since. Economic segregation has proceeded without interruption, distancing poor blacks not only from whites but also from upwardly mobile blacks, making the isolation and misery of poor blacks worse. One out of every two black children lives below the poverty line, compared to one out of every seven white children. Black infants in America die at twice the rate of white infants. A record-setting million inmates crowd the nation's prisons, half of them black. The black out-of-wedlock birth rate has grown from about 25 percent in 1965 to more than 60 percent (more than 90 percent in the South Bronx and other areas of concentrated black poverty) in 1990.

The good news is very good, but the bad news has become steadily worse. Economically, we are still playing catch-up. In

1865, newly freed from slavery, African Americans controlled 3 percent of the wealth in America, United States Civil Rights Commissioner Arthur Fletcher tells me. Today we still control just 3 percent of the wealth. After all this time, we have become free, more often than not, to make other people wealthier. The decline of industrial America, along with low-skill, high-pay jobs, has left much of black America split in two along lines of class, culture, opportunity, and hope. The "prepared" join the new black middle class, which grew rapidly in the 1970s and early 1980s. The unprepared populate a new culture, directly opposed not only to the predominantly white mainstream, but also to any blacks who aspire to practice the values of hard work, good English, and family loyalty that would help them to join the white mainstream. The results of this spiritual decline, along with economic decline, have been devastating. While more black women go to college than ever before, it has become a commonplace to refer to young black males as an endangered species. New anti-black stereotypes replace the old. Prosperous, well-dressed African Americans still complain of suffering indignities when they try to hail a taxicab. The fact that the taxi that just passed them by was driven by a black cabby, native-born or immigrant, makes no difference.

By the 1990s, even an icon of integrationism like Bill Cosby, at a Television Academy lunch honoring him, would complain of the "drive-by images" Hollywood still uses to portray black life, as if the writers just "drove by" the houses and neighborhoods of the people they depict. The National Association for the Advancement of Colored People, the nation's oldest and largest civil rights group, would be split over whether to form a working partnership with Nation of Islam minister Louis Farrakhan, the noted black supremacist. A black man would be run out of a white public housing development in Texas because of Ku Klux Klan harassment, only to be killed within days by a black mugger in his new neighborhood, a Houston ghetto.

And Rosa Parks, often called the mother of the modern civil rights movement, survived being arrested by white men for defying segregation on buses in Montgomery, Alabama, in the 1950s, only to be mugged in her own home by a black man in Detroit in the 1990s.

At the same time, affirmative action in the 1990s shows how innocent and even victimized white Americans now feel compared to how insecure and embattled black people continue to feel. Many whites blame blacks, complaining that we still don't work hard enough or try hard enough to meet standards set by whites. Critics complain that even middle-class blacks, who share so much else with their white counterparts, still persist in segregating themselves, to which many blacks respond, "It didn't begin with us."

It is fashionable in today's America to behave as if we have, at last, transcended race, as if we could all just forget about it and get on with our "color-blind" ways if only a few loudmouthed ingrates would just shut up about it.

Then a major racial eruption exposes the raw bones of American bigotry and prejudices, and immediately we are sent into fevered, anguished bouts of finger-pointing. There was the 1989 gang rape and near-murder in Central Park of a twenty-eight-year-old woman, a stockbroker, by a pack of "wilding" black and Hispanic youths out of East Harlem. There were George Bush's so-called Willie Horton campaign and the televised Supreme Court confirmation hearings of Clarence Thomas, each of which had the races arguing over what was really racist and what was really good for black Americans. There were the murders like those of Charles Stuart's wife in Boston and Susan Smith's little boys in South Carolina, when the impulse to blame a black man sent our horrified nation, blacks included, on wild-goose chases before we discovered the terrible, painfully embarrassing truth.

"The problem of the twentieth century is the problem of the color-line—the relation of the darker to the lighter races of men in Asia and Africa, in America and the islands of the sea," W. E. B. Du Bois wrote in *The Souls of Black Folk* in 1903. Almost a century later, the scholarly black historian John Hope Franklin would write, "The problem of the *twenty-first* century will still be the color line." Little in today's news would tend to refute his dire prediction.

"Each person's life is lived as a series of conversations," writes Deborah Tannen, a specialist in gender communication gaps. The biggest tragedy that has happened between the races since the 1960s is our loss of honest conversation across racial lines. In contrast to the 1990s, when every crackpot you hear on a call-in radio show talks as if he or she has a lock on the answers, we seemed in the 1960s to be much more concerned with the questions.

Race as a topic of conversation seems to have become very much like sex. Everyone knows it holds an important presence in our lives, just about everyone feels proudly expert at it, yet we are reluctant to discuss it in mixed company or in front of the children. Most of our knowledge of it is gathered through the prism of our own personal experiences, which makes race a particularly vexing problem, since everyone's experiences are so different.

In race talk, as in sex talk, candor often is corrupted by our own defensive need to protect our racial egos and insecurities. No race holds a monopoly on the demons of vulnerability or victimhood, whether they are real, imagined, or threatened. We are unable to agree even on the language that we use. One person's "little slight" is another person's "institutional racism," so we tend to argue past each other.

Reduced almost to a form of prurient interest, race can be easily sensationalized by news media to what I call "racial pornography," and often it is. A Chicago television station for which I was reporting in the early 1980s went so far in the quest for ratings as to charter a private airplane to fly me and a crew to Indianapolis to cover a routine speech by that Bob Guccione of racial porn, Nation of Islam minister Louis Farrakhan.

We had to have it on the air that night, I was instructed, even though the speech was nothing extraordinary. Although the young white news producer did not say it, I know why she sent me. She was hoping the Nation of Islam leader would say something outrageous. Other black leaders that very day were saying things that were interesting, amusing, inspired, and even enlightening. But that wasn't good enough for my producer. Time was short, competition was stiff. She wanted outrageous.

Racism is not easy to talk about in racially mixed company. It is often considered downright *impolite* to bring it up. Too many demons of guilt, resentment, and vulnerability are tied up in it. Unfortunately, it usually takes a racial eruption like a riot or the Clarence Thomas confirmation hearings or the O.J. Simpson trial to get Americans to acknowledge their racial differences in public and talk about them, at least for a while, before clamping the lid of denial back down.

Behind our questions of race lurk larger questions of identity, our sense of who we are, where we belong, and where we are going. Our sense of place and peoplehood within groups is a perpetual challenge in some lives, particularly lives in America, a land where identity bubbles quite often out of nothing more than a weird alchemy of history and choice. "When I discover who I am, I'll be free," Ralph Ellison once wrote.

As I embarked on the writing of this book of reflections on racial change in America since the 1960s, identity emerged as an important recurring theme, resonant in *African*-American life simply because it is so important in *American* life. In my travels, the very American question, "What are you?" invites different answers in different places. Some people identify with a race or a place, with their country or their gender, their profession or their favorite pastime. In Chicago, where I have heard it often, it invites an ethnic answer. In the District of Columbia, the nation's capital, it invites a political answer. In Cambridge and other college towns, it invites a scholarly answer. In Manhattan, it invites an occupational answer. In Los Angeles, it invites a lifestyle answer. In Miami, it invites an ethnic nationality answer. In the rural South, it invites a religious denominational answer. Identity is all these things and more within the dark recesses of the individual human soul, pulled and tugged by a society that reveres the opposing human values of individuality and the need to belong. "Trying to define yourself is like trying to bite your own teeth," author Alan Watts once said.

The rules of identity, like the rules of race, can be a complicated affair; yet, once learned, they are rigorously obeyed. I have been fascinated, for example, since my college days to see black students give one another a hard time for dating outside the race, yet dutifully exempt the community's jocks, black football and basketball stars who, by virtue of their heroic gladiator status, seem to be all but expected to have a perky Caucasian cheerleader at their hip, just like the white jocks.

Identity is so much a part of human nature that its significance is too easily minimized. Nowhere is this tendency to take identity for granted more dramatic than in the touchy area of race. As a social commentator in newspapers and on the airwaves, I see it in my mail. "I am not a Euro-American," one writer protests. "Why do you insist on calling yourself African American?" objects a caller to a CNN broadcast. "Why can't we all just be American?"

There is usually a hint of frustration in the inquirer's voice. Why, I respond, should I limit myself? Frankly, I think most African Americans, if given a chance, would have chosen to be "just Americans" ever since the first of us was brought here to Jamestown colony in 1619, a year before the *Mayflower* landed. But that choice has never been left up to us.

Their real message: "Racial identity serves no purpose for me, and I reject whatever purpose it serves for you!" Their will to color blindness sounds to my black ears uncomfortably like a desire to render black folks invisible. Their discomfort with their own European heritage sounds to me like a deeper discomfort with the legacy of Europe's adventures in Africa. They would rather not think of that, or the debt it implies. They are offended that I would deign to remind them of it, that I would not be sporting enough to let bygones be bygones and just melt into the melting pot.

When we experience acute anxiety, disorientation, and role confusion, especially as adolescents, as a result of conflicting pressures and expectations, we are said to be suffering an identity crisis. Americans, always going through adolescent changes, suffer a perpetual identity crisis stemming, I believe, from incorrect or obsolete expectations of themselves. Much of it arises from inappropriate metaphors like the melting pot.

I reject the melting pot metaphor. People don't melt. Americans prove it on their ethnic holidays, in the ways they dance, in the ways they sing, in the culturally connected ways they worship. Displaced peoples long to celebrate their ethnic roots many generations and intermarriages after their ancestors arrived in their new land. Irish-American celebrations of St. Patrick's Day in Boston, Chicago, and New York City are far more lavish than anything seen on that day in Dublin or Belfast. Mexican-American celebrations of Cinco de Mayo, the Fifth of May, are far more lavish in Los Angeles and San Antonio than anything seen that day in Mexico City. It is as if holidays give us permission to expose our former selves as we imagine them to be. Americans of European descent love to show their ethnic cultural backgrounds. Why do they get nervous only when black people show their love for theirs? Is it that black people on such occasions suddenly remind white people of vulnerabilities black people feel quite routinely as a minority in a majority white society? Is it that white people, by and large, do not like this feeling, that they wish nothing more than to cleanse themselves of it and make sure it does not come bubbling up again? Attempts by Americans to claim some ephemeral, all-inclusive "all-American" identity reminds me of Samuel Johnson's observation: "Sir, a man may be so much of everything, that he is nothing of anything."*

Instead of the melting pot metaphor, I prefer the mulligan stew, a concoction my parents tell me they used to fix during the Great Depression, when there was not a lot of food around the house and they "made do" with whatever meats, vegetables, and spices they had on hand. Everything went into the pot and was stirred up, but the pieces didn't melt. Peas were easily distinguished from carrots or potatoes. Each maintained its distinctive character. Yet each loaned its special flavor to the whole, and each absorbed some of the flavor from the others. That flavor, always unique, always changing, is the beauty of America to me, even when the pot occasionally boils over.

On the flip side, some people use pride in their identity, their membership in a larger group, as a proxy for lack of pride in their own individual selves. This impulse is acted out in dangerously pathetic ways in militant "black identity" and "white Christian identity" movements that use their

---

*Quoted in James Boswell, *Life of Samuel Johnson* (1791; reprint, London: Oxford at the Clarendon Press, 1936, p. 176), 1783 entry.

sense of racial or religious identity to vigorously demean other races or religions. Instead of showing strength of character, their overinvestment in identity displays little but a pathetic weakness.

I would argue that color does not operate irrespective of my character but very much in connection with it, although in unpredictable ways. Recognition of this unpredictability is important to dispel the dangerous notion that color predicts any significant aspect of character, a notion that forms the very definition of prejudice, which is prejudgment based on insufficient evidence.

The law should be "color-blind," the Supreme Court's conservative majority tells us. Yet our society is not. We Americans must deal with that sad fact or it will forever deal with us.

In my youth, repressing our "color" kept our masks straight and our lips buttoned to keep the peace. But it also hid uncomfortable truths, perpetuated the beliefs that "the coloreds are really happy" and "segregation is best for everybody." Today, repressing our "color" slows progress toward a resolution of deeply rooted conflicts that keep our American mulligan stew in danger of boiling over.

"There is an oversimplification of the Negro," Zora Neale Hurston said in a 1944 interview with the New York *Amsterdam News*. "He is either pictured by conservatives as happy, picking his banjo, or by the so-called liberals as low, miserable and crying. The Negro's life is neither of these. Rather, it is in-between and above and below these pictures."

The world has changed much since then, but the oversimplification of the African American persists. We are either victims, as Jesse Jackson portrays us, or just "vulnerable," as Shelby Steele describes us, with not much in between. We hate ourselves, as a consequence of having been indoctri-

nated and convinced by white racist standards of beauty and
intelligence, or we love ourselves too much, a consequence of
overcompensation for our "woundedness."

Our reality is far more complicated, more complicated
than even most black people realize. Too many of us speak
and behave, for example, as if there is only one way to be
"black." In fact, there are many ways. It is only our sense of
insecurity that attempts to suppress the individuality of those
who would wander off the plantation.

Black people, like other people, come in all varieties, and
we go through changes. There are, for example, the racial
innocents, who have little or no sense of racial identity. They
are what black politicians often like to call themselves in front
of white audiences: Americans who "just happen to be black."

Racial innocents are individualists, perfectly happy to
assimilate in an accommodating way with whites, a bargain
that essentially places all obligation for racial harmony solely
on blacks. They make no demands of whites except to be fair,
and even then, the innocents allow the white people pretty
much to determine the standard for fairness. People who "just
happen to be black" may not think blacks have much that
white people should trouble themselves with learning about,
anyway. They may on occasion be heckled by passing car-
loads of young yahoos yelling racial epithets. They may on
occasion suffer the indignity of being tailed in a department
store or passed over by a taxicab. But they casually shrug off
these offenses as "little slights," as a white person might.

Americans who "just happen to be black" can be perfectly
happy with their lives, but they usually are young, inexperi-
enced in the world, and ripe for a bold conversion. It usually
comes after the individual has encountered racism in a way
that makes the person feel constantly exposed, vulnerable to
racial shame, susceptible to hurt. An accumulation of events,
a series of abuses or slights by white society can be, as Lu

Palmer, an African-American activist in Chicago, likes to say, "enough to make a Negro turn Black!"

The beginning of what some would call "true blackness," but I would call one of several versions of blackness, comes with a defensive withdrawal, a retreat into group identity and to borrow Alice Walker's marvelous phrase, the temples of the familiar. The group shelters the individual, soothes the individual's pain, and protects the individual from hurt, real or imagined. The person who had been racially neutral or even self-hating may suddenly become "Afrocentric," intellectually and emotionally centered on Africa—or, at least, on a mentally manufactured ideal of what Africa ought to be.

Testing new self-images, individuals may overcompensate to prove their blackness, mostly to themselves. They may change their names to something in Swahili or Arabic, festoon themselves with new clothes, "natural" hair, flags, national colors, code phrases, party lines, ten-point programs, and blacker-than-thou ideologies.

The "superblack" phase is so attractive, comfortable, and safe that some people never leave it. Group identity relieves them of such burdensome obligations as independent thinking. As Richard Hofstadter, author of *The Paranoid Style in American Politics*, might say, one no longer needs complicated explanations for a seemingly chaotic, threatening world. The paranoid view is enough. The group's joys, fears, and prejudices do quite nicely. They become one's own.

The new believers are the truest believers; propelled by astonishment and guilt over their own ignorance and how much they had been blinded—*duped!*—by the enemies of blackness into missing its beauty, they passionately immerse themselves in all things black to make up for lost time. It is not always an easy transition. Self-consciousness over one's own discomfort can lead to even more vocal rage directed against white racism and black "Uncle Toms."

"It is a paradox of social change that the most dramatic displays of the new Black image are often exhibited by those least at ease with their new identity," writes Temple University psychologist William E. Cross, Jr., in his book *Shades of Black: Diversity in African-American Identity* (1991) which details identity changes like those described above.

As blackness—"nigresence," as Cross prefers to call it— becomes a measure of one's self-esteem, every nonconformist to it becomes a direct insult, a sign of disrespect against blackness itself, and the new zealot takes it personally. Small wonder, then, that Malcolm X and other revisionist Muslims have been targeted by fellow Muslims. The heretic is always far more threatening than the complete nonbeliever.

Stridency cools over time, writes Cross, and the individuals reencounter themselves. This period of reassessment is often brought on by some great disappointment or revelation. It is a crossroads. Some individuals may turn back to an earlier stage of identity development. Some may stumble instead down a path toward spiritual or mental breakdown, even suicide. A new and unpleasant eye-opener can cause other individuals to drop out of their new blackness as decidedly as they dropped in. Many gravitate to pragmatic, grass-roots, results-oriented approaches to black issues—mentoring groups, block clubs, voluntarism, or elective office, for example.

They may regress to their earlier stage of "just happening to be black" or, embittered by their experience, experience a new, better-informed self-hatred. Or they may become so embittered by white society that they fixate in *hyperblackness*, the highest state of black rage, locking on to extreme anti-white attitudes and bitter nihilism. They can become the casualties of racism, the walking wounded who drop out dis-enchanted, or they can bottom out and turn up a new path to self-awareness and stability in which the individual *tran-scends* race. Instead of embracing race as the central focus of life, a security blanket, they use it instead as a platform, a base of operations from which they can venture forth to deal more effectively with the larger world.

I think this transcendent stage marks the mind's true liberation, an exhilarating leap away from spiritual weakness to true independent strength. Malcolm X offered an excellent example when he returned from Mecca after his break with the pseudo-scientific Islam of the Honorable Elijah Muhammad. Though he was still committed to black people, his vision had expanded to that of the true *transracial man*, for whom blackness was not an end, but a beginning, his point of departure in opening himself to the larger world of ideas, cultures, and experiences. Only then had he transcended his own vulnerabilities, after a lifetime of racial hurt, enough to open the door to white people in his Pan-African movement. If they were willing to assist the struggle of blacks, they were welcome, he said. But he would not let them lead. Some wags might have heard lasting prejudice in this, but, in light of other ethnic struggles, it made perfect sense. The international black liberation movement could no more reasonably be led by whites than the St. Patrick's Day parade could be led by blacks.

Unlike those who relax into a nihilistic state of inactivity during the group identity, the "superblack" phase, Malcolm X provides an effective model for breaking beyond angst, torpor, and frustration to redemption, liberation, and transcendence. Malcolm found release from racial vulnerability through the discovery of distortions he had been taught, internal and external, about Elijah, Islam, and white people.

"It is often assumed that ethnicity acts as a barrier to humanism," Temple University's Cross writes, "but in its highest expression black identity functions as a window to the world."

African Americans are as diverse as other Americans.

Some become nationalistic and ethnocentric. Others become pluralistic or multicultural, fitting their black identity into a comfortable niche among other aspects of themselves and their daily lives. Whichever they choose, a comfortable identity serves to provide not only a sense of belonging and protection for the individual against the abuses of racism, but also, ultimately, a sturdy foundation from which the individual can interact effectively with other people, cultures, and situations beyond the world of blackness.

"Identity would seem to be the garment with which one covers the nakedness of the self," James Baldwin wrote in *The Devil Finds Work* (1976), "in which case, it is best that the garment be loose, a little like the robes of the desert, through which one's nakedness can always be felt, and, sometimes, discerned. This trust in one's nakedness is all that gives one the power to change one's robes."

The cloak of proud black identity has provided a therapeutical warmth for my naked self after the chilly cocoon of inferiority imposed early in my life by a white-exalting society. But it is best worn loosely, lest it become as constricting and isolating for the famished individual soul as the garment it replaced.

The ancestral desire of my ethnic people to be "just American" resonates in me. But I cannot forget how persistently the rudeness of race continues to intrude between me and that dream. I can defy it, but I cannot deny it.

This book attempts to examine the garments of race and identity to loosen their camouflage and constraints on the naked self, on its strengths and its vulnerabilities, so that we might trust more confidently our naked selves. Only then, beyond the confining fashions of race and nationalism, can we express the full rainbow of our true humanity.

I feel like "showing my color" today. My true colors.

2

Who Killed Integration?

The New Apartness

Every Friday evening you can see the young professionals
and postgraduates line up at two bars at Seventeenth and L
streets. The bars sit on diagonally opposite corners just down
the street from the office building where I work in downtown
Washington. The two crowds are almost identical—young,
well-dressed, and well-educated—except in one very notable
respect: One bar's crowd is white. The other's is black.

The white crowd gathers at the Ha'Penny Lion, a faux-
English restaurant by day, a beer garden by night. Blacks
gather across the street at the Ascot, a large walk-down disco.
Together they illustrate a paradox of the post-1960s era.
Segregation is back, except this time it's voluntary.

"Integration is morally right, and the Negro is your
brother," Martin Luther King, Jr., wrote in his historic "Letter
from Birmingham Jail" before today's twenty-somethings
were born. King used to call eleven o'clock on Sunday morning, the church hour, "the most segregated hour of the week."

If so, one might gather from the Friday night sight at Seventeenth and L that "happy hour" must run at least a close second.

It is hardly unusual for blacks and whites to gravitate to different gathering spots or different neighborhoods after work. Outside the workplace, the races live such separate lives that few of us think much about the separateness. Still, I cannot recall when I have seen two such racially opposite saloon crowds situated so close to each other, almost directly across the street from each other, although I also am sure they are not unique. Someone who did not know better might think Jim Crow segregation was still alive and well in the nation's capital. Not quite, say the patrons. It just looks that way.

Normally there are two sets of reasons for self-segregation. One is to be with people who are like you. The other is to get away from people who are not like you. When Laura Blumenfeld, a *Washington Post* reporter, asked the patrons of both bars about the irony of their social apartheid, she heard both types of reasons, but the line between the two was blurred.

"You spend the whole day being diverse," said one young white woman at the white bar.

"They dance over there, don't they?" said another.

"It's Friday and the game is over," a forty-year-old black woman said. The "game," she said, was "assimilation in a white world." Having been through "BS" all week, she said, "You don't want to be stared at now."

The scenes ring with familiarity to me. Hardly a day goes by that I am not reminded of how much, despite the good news of racial progress Americans have made in many ways since the civil rights reforms of the 1950s and 1960s, the races still live largely separate lives.

I was startled to hear that some of my fellow black alumni of Ohio University have formed their own alumni chapters. Then I found out that colleges across the country actually have encouraged such groups, separate but equal to the white chapters, who had little or no success in attracting blacks to their meetings. Elsewhere, national networks of black organizations have survived the age of forced segregation, holding huge conventions and raising millions of dollars. Old-line groups like the Links, the Elks, and the Prince Hall Masons have been joined by new-wave "buppie" (black upwardly mobile professional) organizations like the National Black MBA Association and the National Association of Black Women Entrepreneurs. Applications to historically black colleges and universities also began to grow in the late 1980s, and such schools produce a much higher percentage of black graduates than white campuses do.

Friends invited my wife and me to a New Year's Eve party with the caveat that we should not let a white couple who are mutual friends know about it. "This is going to be a black party," we were advised. Such caveats, spoken or unspoken, appear to be common in modern middle-class black life.

Still, a startling irony and a hint of danger hover like a strange aroma over this new genteel apartheid. Had my alma mater decided on its own to declare separate alumni organizations, there would have been protests, headlines, and lawsuits. But since the black alumni started it, there is a yawn here, a sigh of relief there, and separate meetings and social events popping up everywhere. It is becoming the modern way of American life.

"Guess Who's Not Coming to Dinner?" blared a headline on the cover of the *Washingtonian* magazine in November 1989. If integration was going to work anywhere, it should have worked in Washington, which has the largest concentration of well-educated, middle-class blacks in the country. Yet, by the 1980s, more blacks were living in its suburbs than in the city. The typical black family in four area counties— Montgomery, Prince George's, Fairfax, and Prince William— earns more than the average white family in America. Yet the fifteen-page article quoted numerous prominent, affluent, well-educated black Washingtonians for whom the dream of integration has all but died—largely, they said, because of the reluctance of *white* people to include black people fully in their lives.

Particularly wearying for many middle-class blacks is a pervasive sense of loss, loneliness, alienation, and a broken bargain. Like a beleaguered partner in a bad marriage, they lament constantly having to *do all the work in the relationship.* As my friend Sam Fulwood, a reporter in the Washington bureau of the *Los Angeles Times*, put it, "I'm tired of chasing white folks."

I hear a similar fatigue expressed when other young black professionals tell me they are "tired of being the office expert on black folk," "tired of being pigeonholed," "tired of buttoning my lip when they [whites] ignore what I say anyway," "tired of having to know everything about them and their people while they can get along just fine without having to know anything about me and my people."

"It is not their ignorance of blacks that I mind," said one young black reporter. "It is their *indifference* to blacks that enrages me. I don't expect them to know much about black folks, but I do expect them to make at least an attempt to learn. We have to learn everything about them in order to make it, but they don't have to know anything about us."

Well-meaning white folks sound no less weary of it all. "We are encouraged to be more sensitive to the views and concerns of women and minorities so we can have more dialogue," one editorial page editor told me. "But, instead, everyone is so afraid of offending someone else that we have less dialogue, not more."

Working against the integrationist impulse is the affinity impulse, the desire to spend time with those who share your background and values. You miss the old familiar. You miss the "bull sessions" and "hen parties."

A tension builds up between the two. Fatigue sets in. The races retreat to opposite corners, opposite worlds, staring back at each other with a sense of apprehension across the chasm.

At the roots of resegregation are a set of *parallel realities*, each defined by decidedly different ways of looking at the world. "Like two sets of people riding two sets of escalators, both heading down," was the dreary description National Urban League president Hugh Price gave to it in a conversation with me one day. Culture makes a difference, but so do interrelated patterns of social psychology: The view of the historical oppressor vs. that of the historically oppressed, the victimizer vs. the victim.

Social critic Shelby Steele broke significant ground in our national conversation about this imbalanced relationship when he mused eloquently in *The Content of Our Character* (1990) on our "racial vulnerability," the woundedness we African Americans still carry around in our heads as a result of our racial oppression. It is "our continuing openness to inferiority anxiety and to racial diminishment and shame," he wrote. As the stresses of freedom have increased since the mid–1960s, so has our vulnerability, he writes, leading us "to claim more victimization than we have actually endured."

He makes some significant points, but does not explain why white Americans show so little enthusiasm for crossing the line to mix with blacks, either. Interestingly, Blumenfeld later described to me how one young white woman she interviewed followed her across the street into the black bar to plead for anonymity in the article Blumenfeld was writing. "I could lose my job," she said. She glanced around at the black crowd with a look of surprise and terror. She had never been there before, she said, and she quickly left. Did she not feel vulnerable, too? Would she find any comfort in being told it was all in her head? Should blacks?

Integration fatigue results partly from an inherent filial impulse we feel toward those who are much like us, xenophobia toward those who are not, and anxiety over our hidden need to comply strictly with the rules of modern racial etiquette. Men and women have new gender rules in the workplace, too, but I think men and women, for all our eternal conflicts, get along better than the races do. The genders, after all, are far more intensely, feverishly motivated to get along. Our survival as a species, not to mention a myriad of jolly good times, depends on it. We are nowhere near as motivated toward racial mixing, nor is it essential to our survival. Quite the contrary, after all these years racial integration still carries with it the profound implications of racial mixing, the gradual and eventual disappearance of the races and their cultures as we have known them, an amalgamation process toward which Americans continue, whether they admit it or not, to harbor a deep-seated ambivalence. This ambivalence is felt no less intently by blacks at century's end than it is felt by whites. Just as black Americans were beginning to revive a sense of pride in their peoplehood in the 1960s, whites were only beginning to crack open their doors to integration. Timing is everything.

"White America is de-tribalizing, while black America is re-tribalizing," media guru Marshall McLuhan said in response to a question during an appearance on my campus in 1968. I could see why so many called him a prophet. His words seemed to encapsulate precisely an era of "black power" and heightened black consciousness that had followed the desegregating civil rights reforms of the 1950s and early 1960s. Freed to choose, many blacks chose to stay with other blacks. Blacks and whites who sat at separate tables before desegregation continued to sit at separate tables. The first black man to be invited to join a white fraternity, the "Tekes," on our campus was socially ostracized by other black students, the "community," and quit the fraternity. Black rage roared against "racist institutions," which in many minds quickly became a catch-all demonizing phrase to describe virtually all aspects of American life, as a new generation of "revolutionaries" put the "white man" on notice. Demands for black dormitories and "black studies" abounded and continue today.

As racism has become less visibly obvious since the 1960s, it has become easier for those not directly victimized by it to ignore it, and at the same time, it has become more difficult for those who are its targets to distinguish actual victimization from vulnerability, the possibility (some would say the certainty) of being victimized. "Being black in America is like being forced to wear ill-fitting shoes," a fifty-year-old African-American life insurance broker told author Studs Terkel in his book *Race: How Blacks and Whites Think and Feel About the National Obsession*. "Some people adjust to it. It's always uncomfortable on your foot, but you've got to wear it because it's the only shoe you've got. . . . Some people can bear the uncomfort more than others. Some people can block it from their mind, some can't. When you see some acting docile and some acting militant, they have one thing in common: The shoe is uncomfortable."

The easiest way for the black patrons of the Ascot to protect themselves from potential racial hurt is to avoid the

potential perpetrators of it. Yet one suspects that the patrons
of the Ha'Penny inflict some measure of hurt anyway,
whether they know it or not, without making a move, simply
through their absence. By turning up their noses at such a
popular and easily accessible hangout of their black counterparts, they help confirm in the black mind that white people
really don't want to meet black folks halfway after all. The
white folks, for their part, have no reason to think anything
else of the blacks who decline to make the short hop across
the street and mingle, legally protected as minorities seeking
service in a public accommodation. For both crowds, integration has become a combined joy and aggravation, an attractive nuisance to be tolerated, if not thoroughly enjoyed.

Compromise is a part of success in any organization, but
when compromises must be made with one's fundamental
principles and sense of self, it can bring on a sense of having
sold out. Worse, the very act of constantly dividing one's per-
sonality between a predominantly white world of work and a
predominantly black home community can be wearying,
even damaging to one's sense of identity, especially when
one begins to lose touch with whether one has become a
good role model or "just another flunky for the white power
structure." "Actin' white," a sadly misguided put-down
among some black youngsters for peers who try to get ahead,
also emerges among affluent blacks to describe their peers
who have gotten caught up in shifting gears between the
standards of two quite separate worlds.

Integration, the dilution and amalgamation of one group's
identity into that of another, lost saliency in the sixties for
blacks bent on self-discovery. Even longtime white allies
were cast out of left-progressive civil rights organizations like
the Student Nonviolent Coordinating Committee by the new
black power advocates. Even liberal whites, it was believed,

could not resist the ill effects of living all their lives in the cocoon of a white world, insulated from the stigmatizing world in which most blacks live.

"Liberal whites often say that they are tired of being told 'you can't understand what it is to be black,'" Stokely Carmichael and Charles V. Hamilton wrote in *Black Power: The Politics of Liberation* (1967). "They claim to recognize and acknowledge this. Yet the same liberals will often turn around and tell black people that they should ally themselves with those who don't understand, who share a sense of superiority based on whiteness. The fact is that most of these 'allies' neither look upon the blacks as co-equal partners nor do they perceive the goals as any but the adoption of certain Western norms and values."

But the new black movements also cast out or limited to subservient positions even those white radicals who agreed that Western norms and values ought to be scrapped, if only to make way, in some cases, for the values of Marxism, Leninism, and Maoism. In this, the new black radicals followed the model of Malcolm X, who even in his post-Muslim days insisted that white people "can work with us, but not lead us," paving the way for a sometimes healthy, sometimes unhealthy skepticism among young and impressionable blacks for years to come.

Black people never really wanted "integration" in the first place, wrote James Baldwin. What black people wanted, he said, was "desegregation," the right to go anywhere we could afford or were qualified to go, the same as whites, but not necessarily together with whites.

No question that racism is alive and well or that its pernicious impact continues to be apparent. Statistics continue to show all black Americans constituting something of an economic underclass, a parallel world, separate and unequal.

Even on the Supreme Court, where almost all the white justices in recent decades have been millionaires, the two black justices might best be called "hundred-thousandaires," judging by disclosure reports. Although some gaps are closing, corporate hierarchies continue to be dominated by white males, and the wealth and income of blacks at all levels hover below those of their white counterparts. Federal Reserve Bank studies show blacks less likely to receive loan approval than whites with similar credit histories.

Books like *The Rage of a Privileged Class* (1994) by Ellis Cose describe the enduring complaints of black professionals who, freed by civil rights reforms to bolt into the middle class in record numbers, still run up against the hesitancy of white society and the white power structure to accept them. Others describe the durability of the late community organizer Saul Alinsky's observation, "A racially integrated community is a chronological term timed from the entrance of the first black family to the exit of the last white family."

Some of the most fortunate blacks have broken into the country club set and into high-ranking, decision-making positions at deep-pocket corporations or other places where big deals are made. But their numbers remain small, and progress has been agonizingly slow. In 1990, for example, the *National Law Journal* found that the 250 largest law firms in the country had 23,195 partners of which only 210 were black.

Even those who have "made it" at various levels feel a persistent insecurity and a nagging fear that somehow, any minute now, they will be wounded again by some new and demonic evidence of outsidership, second-class status in a white world. As a social "underclass," even if not always an economic one, black Americans are, on the whole, less able to determine their destiny for themselves and their families, less familiar with the ways of white folks and their "system," and thus more likely at every age and income level to feel threatened ("last hired, first fired") and vulnerable.

Such realities are harsh, yet they need not be debilitating. Our forefathers and foremothers survived and, in some cases, prospered under conditions far worse. The biggest, most enduring tragedy of modern black life is that many African Americans fail to take advantage of opportunities out of the sincere belief that they are defeated even before they begin.

It is in response to just such pain that many follow their impulse to pull back into the family, the "community," or the tribe. It is normal and quite often healthy. I find it downright therapeutic every year to attend the National Association of Black Journalists convention. Please let it be known that, contrary to the braying of a few white skeptics I have known, I do not attend such events because I have something against white journalists. Nor do I have anything against blacks who are *non*journalists. I spend every working day and much of my social life surrounded by journalists, most of whom are not black. I go home to a world mostly made up of black people who are not journalists. Once a year it simply "feels good," as one young female NABJ delegate eloquently put it, to spend a few days surrounded by hundreds of people who happen to be *both*.

The most important question black Americans must answer for ourselves as the nation faces a new century is: How best can we cope with the pain in ways that help liberate us from the tribal mindset, break through the walls of social apartheid, and enhance our choices as individuals, the prize on which civil rights marchers ostensibly kept their eyes?

Everyone who tries to succeed in life faces pressures, but

blacks are more likely to feel them coming and going: the resistance of the establishment vs. the pull of the familiar. Race, ethnicity, or occupational networks are powerful identities around which to organize your life, but they are not life, although for many African Americans, blackness comes remarkably and, I would submit, hazardously close. Taken to excess, they can also be limiting, forming the boundaries of a new plantation. Group identity—*the tribe*—provides a soothing, healing balm for the pain of being black in a white world, but it also shoots a chastening jolt of guilt into the flanks of those who would dare bolt out of the pack or challenge the party-line "groupthink." Any dissension from "unity in the community" or any "airing of dirty laundry" in public threatens the group, which is held together by its mutually felt sense of vulnerability.

At worst, the soothing balm of group identity is only a placebo that feeds a mindless paranoia. A *New York Times*/CBS poll found in 1990 that 25 percent of blacks believe the government "deliberately makes sure that drugs are easily available in poor black neighborhoods." Similarly high percentages thought the spread of AIDS and the availability of guns in black neighborhoods were caused by outside conspiracies. To many of us it would appear that, if such plagues are caused by conspiracies, then those of us who purchase the drugs, guns, and AIDS-infected needles must be coconspirators in our own undoing. But, to those who feel vulnerable enough, it does not matter whether the outside threat is real. It is felt nevertheless, although in different ways by different people.

Paranoia is hardly unique to black Americans. Historian Richard Hofstadter was describing mostly white people when he wrote in his 1964 essay, "The Paranoid Style in American Politics," that the paranoid disposition is mobilized by social conflicts that "bring fundamental fears and hatreds, rather than negotiable interests, into political action," and that the situation becomes worse when representatives of a particular interest "cannot make themselves felt in the political process. Feeling that they have no access to political bargaining or the making of decisions, they find their original conception of the world of power as omnipresent, sinister and malicious fully confirmed." When powerlessness breeds paranoia in a world run mostly by white movers and shakers, black people easily identify with the moved and shaken and do not easily rub elbows with the offspring of their historical oppressors. Unequals make nervous partners.

I saw a television news report not long ago about a modern militialike Ku Klux Klan rally somewhere in the piney woods down South. Like most such rallies since the 1950s, it was sparsely attended. What caught my eye in this report was a souvenir stand that displayed T-shirts, bumper stickers, and baseball caps for sale that read in bold letters, "It's a white thing; you wouldn't understand."

On the contrary, I understand quite well. The phrase is a take-off on the other nose-thumbing slogan, "It's a black thing; you wouldn't understand." The shirt, in its black or white versions, expresses a silent cry for help: "Please don't hate me because I am vulnerable." It is a statement of backlash, which is appropriate to the occasion of a Klan rally. It says that black people do not have a lock on racial vulnerability. Many white people also carry with them a continuing openness to inferiority anxiety, racial diminishment, and shame. Demagogues of all sorts are eager to transform their woundedness, through the magic of eloquent rhetoric, into racial oppression and help them to claim more victimization than they have actually endured. Two can play that game, except white people don't need to turn to organizations like the Ku Klux Klan for relief anymore. They can turn to the Republican Party.

"If at first you don't succeed, redefine success," I once heard a psychiatrist quip.

Many who call for integration really are calling for *assimilation*, the process whereby a minority group gradually adopts the customs and attitudes of the dominant culture, with little reciprocity from the dominants. A minority that never has been allowed the luxury to feel secure in its own home culture does not easily let go of it to adopt the customs and attitudes of the mainstream culture, especially when much of that mainstream has showed a decidedly lukewarm enthusiasm for welcoming them. As a result, we have had less integration than simply *desegregation*, the breaking down of barriers to free choice, which may be the best we're going to get.

Perhaps the much-touted, widely cherished 1960s goal of a color-blind society is not possible. As long as we remain sighted, we remain inexorably color-conscious, and that is not totally bad. The self-segregation we see today may be the early vision of a new, pluralistic, multicultural century that will see blacks become a part of the economic and political mainstream but, like Jews or Mormons, maintain their cultural integrity and identity.

For us to get along in it, whites must recognize their own culpability for the discrimination that persists, and blacks must persist in keeping up the pressure for equal opportunity, holding conservatives as well as liberals true to the promise on which all can agree, "equal opportunity, not necessarily equal results."

To accomplish the job of national unification, it is not enough merely to be "nonracist." It is not enough merely to oppose racism in the abstract. Hardly anyone outside radical white identity movements admits to racism anymore. One must take the extra step of becoming *anti-racist*. For us truly to get along, as Rodney King asked, we need, as the ancient Native American wisdom suggests, to walk in other people's moccasins, to reach out in our day-to-day lives and be an *ally* to others, whether it is a new black or Hispanic in a predominantly white workplace, or a white or Asian at a "black table" on campus.

I detect that guilt helps. Guilt has taken a bad rap lately as an emotional weakness that leads us sometimes to make dire mistakes with the best of intentions. But, fundamentally, guilt is good. It is nature's own self-policing mechanism. Americans often seek feel-good solutions when they really have something to feel guilty about.

Black Americans also must give their children the moral and emotional grounding to understand that being "black" is not incompatible with either success or individuality, and to act on it. Black America can ill afford to let racial insecurity stunt the intellectual growth or economic aspirations of another generation.

Finally, we need to relax. Much has been said about "political correctness," but the "PC" that concerns me is the "politeness conspiracy," the tag coined by Chicago diversity consultant Tom Kochman, author of *Black and White Styles in Communication*, coined for our aversion to speaking candidly about racial differences across racial lines for fear of offending one another. It describes the self-silencing that prevents us from bringing up the questions, gripes, and concerns we have for fear of offending someone and being called a "racist," a "sexist," or a "whiner." Politeness is a virtue programmed into us from childhood, but when it causes us to dodge racially touchy topics, it may lead us to avoid racially mixed situations entirely, just to escape discomfort. Instead, we keep our thoughts to ourselves to be brought out only in safe situations, when we are talking to others of the same race and, more often than not, of the same point of view. Instead of finding answers, we cultivate our frustrations and resentments.

We need to work a little less at taking offense and a little more at building bridges. The races, like the genders, need to break through the politeness conspiracy and reintroduce ourselves to each other. We need to launch efforts as individuals and communities to rebuild helpful alliances across racial lines.

Blacks can be prejudiced, too, but white prejudice is more pernicious. White people are in a better position than black people to help discourage the stereotypes, prevalent in media and popular culture, that portray blacks as irredeemable outsiders—a stereotype that leads to a reality of fear, distrust, and resentment that puts blacks at odds with whites.

At the same time, we black Americans need to recognize who our real enemies are. As the late Supreme Court justice Thurgood Marshall said at his last press conference, when asked if he wanted to be replaced by another African American, "There's no difference between a black snake or a white snake. They both bite." African Americans can ill afford to paint too broad a brush of condemnation and repeat the errors of white racists who, by holding down blacks, held themselves back, too.

True integration, unlike assimilation, is a two-way street. It involves *cultural sharing*, a genuine respect and interest in difference, not cultural submergence by one party to please another.

It is popular, yet naive, to say, "I don't see color. I try to see everyone the same." To me, such a denial, always well-meaning, defies common sense. My initial visceral reaction is to presume the speaker is either lying or blind. How else, I wonder, could they not see something as blatantly obvious as my color? Why, for that matter, would they *not* want to see my color? Why, I wonder, should I be flattered to hear that my color and all that it represents in the crucible of America's complicated history is to be regarded like some sort of blemish, like a wart on the nose or spinach in the teeth to be graciously ignored, even when it most obviously has a significant presence?

French journalist Michael Feher says we should be "'color-curious' rather than color-blind or color-bound." The latter, "color-bound," imbues differences with *too much* significance.*

The treachery of group identity, as it armors and energizes the individual, is that it also works to censor individuality, whether that of its enemies (real or imagined) or in its own ranks. As it sets agendas and becomes a proxy for independent thought, it shuns outsiders and censors alternative views within the group. As a result, it holds on to group solidarity at the price of individual renewal and growth.

Many groups can be quite dangerous. Others can be quite wonderful. One enslaves the individual. Another liberates. Ultimately the individual must face the self. Group connections may occupy an important place in the individual's heart, but they should be liberating, not stifling.

I believe the way out of our racial impasse is to be found through a vigorous cosmopolitanism, the quality held by those who are sophisticated enough to be at home in all parts of the world and conversant with many spheres of interest. Color should be neither exalted to all-important status nor reduced to something viewed as having little or no importance.

When students asked me for a model for cultural sharing, I had to stretch my imagination a bit. The "white Negro," as

---

*Reprinted in English in *Blacks and Jews: Alliances and Arguments*, edited by Paul Berman (New York: Delacorte, 1994).

Norman Mailer dubbed the jazz age hipsters and 1950s beat-niks, offer examples of reverse assimilation by whites into black culture. But the cultural avant-garde dwells too far out on the margins of society to provide much of a model for the mainstream.

Closer to the mainstream and on the opposite side of it from the hipsters is the subculture created by the United States Army. This thought occurred to me during a conversation with sociologist Charles Moskos of Northwestern University, a leading expert on intergroup relations in the military. Speaking of how much soldiers of African, European, Asian, Latino, and Native American descent freely borrow and embrace the language, nuances, and cadences of one another over time, the Greek-descended Moskos was moved to comment in an aside, "You know, we're *all* part black, aren't we?" My own two years in the army during the Vietnam era brought daily examples of farm boys from Tennessee or "brothers" from the Bronx or Polish kids from Chicago unselfconsciously embracing one another's communication styles in their camaraderie. The military has a special culture all its own. It is a mulatto culture.

Subcultures often have much to teach the mainstream. Until Americans are willing to show a little more genuine curiosity about the joys and pains of one another's ethnic and racial experiences, we will continue to build walls between one another, and true integration will continue to be nothing more than an elusive dream.

3

Survivors' Guilt

The Discreet Angst of the Black Bourgeoisie

Intellectual alienation is a creation of middle-class society. What I call middle-class society is any society that becomes rigidified in predetermined forms, forbidding all evolution, all gains, all progress, all discovery. I call the middle-class a closed society in which life has no taste, in which the air is tainted, in which ideas and men are corrupt. And I think that a man who takes a stand against this death is in a sense a revolutionary.

—Frantz Fanon, *Black Skins, White Masks*

We wear the mask that grins and lies.

—Paul Laurence Dunbar, African-American poet

One of the most difficult acts for African Americans is to give themselves permission to make money. I don't mean chump change. I mean *serious* money. *White people's* money. Instead of honoring those whose enterprise has taken them to somewhere within shouting distance of white people's money, we belittle them for even daring to think they can improve their condition, as if the imperatives of black solidarity precluded any of us from making an honest buck.

Few were torn by this conflict more than my first wife, Leanita McClain, an African-American, ghetto-to-Gold-Coast success story whose upward climb was stopped only by the torment of her inner conflicts, made worse by clinical, and ultimately fatal, depression. She eventually gave up. She killed herself on Memorial Day in 1984. Had we still been married, it would have been our tenth wedding anniversary.

A product of a South Side public housing ghetto, she became the first black woman columnist and first black editorial board member at the *Chicago Tribune*, one of the nation's oldest and largest newspapers. She won awards, made speeches, and was beginning to appear as a guest on television chat shows, local and national.

Privately she was a portrait in walking woundedness. "I was born on Wednesday," she would say. "Wednesday's child is full of woe." She was also full of grace and fair of face. Her light freckled complexion, her naturally strawberry-blond hair, and her bright green eyes caused some people to wonder whether she was biracial. Of course, like most African Americans, she was. Somewhere in her family background, some tributaries of white and Seminole blood flowed into the stream of Africa, but not very recently.

"I have a foot in each world," she wrote in an anguished essay for *Newsweek*, which headlined it "The Black Middle Class Burden."

"I am a member of the black middle class," she wrote, "who has had it with being patted on the head by white hands and slapped in the face by black hands for my success."

She went on to describe the personal conflicts of coping with a white world that often seemed too reluctant or too ignorant to accept her as an equal, and a black world that was rapidly dividing right before her eyes between haves and have-nots, with many of her old friends and relatives slipping down the losing end. A boy she had a crush on as a child back in the projects was serving a life sentence for murder. A childhood girlfriend, once bright and lively, now resigned herself to a lifetime on the dole, a single mother on welfare back in the projects. "Jive hustlers" from the old neighborhood still tried to put the moves on her for money. While boarding the bus in the morning with brigades of other mostly white briefcase-toting yuppies, after returning from a trip to Paris, she ran into an aunt who was arriving to clean the condominium of our white neighbor. One of her sisters, "wearing her designer everything," is nevertheless taken to the back door of the lakefront high-rise where she lives by a taxi driver who just assumes, because of her skin color, that she is an employee.

"I am burdened daily with showing whites that blacks are people. I am, in the old vernacular, a credit to my race . . . my brothers' keeper and my sisters', though many of them have abandoned me because they think that I have abandoned them. . . . I assuage white guilt. I disprove black inadequacy and prove to my parents' generation that their patience was indeed a virtue.

". . . Some of my 'liberal' white acquaintances pat me on the head, hinting that I am a freak, that my success is less a matter of talent than of luck and affirmative action. I may live among them, but it is difficult to live with them. How can they be sincere about respecting me, yet hold my fellows in contempt? And if I am silent when they attempt to sever me from my own, how can I live with myself? . . . "

Her loyalties to the "'hood" tugged at her: "As for the envy of my own people, am I to give up my career, my standard of living, to pacify them and set my conscience at ease? No. I have worked for these amenities and deserve them, though I can never enjoy them without feeling guilty."

*   *   *

Our friends called us the "golden couple" until our divorce. Our marriage broke up in 1982, brought on by her worsening bouts with depression. We remained friends. We even went out together a few times, without much success at rekindling the old flame. She hoped that getting rid of the things she loved, like her marriage, might make her feel better. It didn't. Two years after our divorce, home alone on a stormy Memorial Day, she took an overdose of a powerful anti-depression medicine and went to sleep. She did not wake up. In many minds her suicide was an instant paradigm for the discreet angst of America's new emerging black bourgeoisie. Her "generic suicide note," as she curiously titled it, fed that notion and shaped her legacy: ". . . Happiness is a private club that will not let me enter. . . . Please let me go the way I choose. Do not try to pull me back into this world. I will never live long enough to see my people free anyway."

"An investigation of McClain's suicide is an investigation into the pressures on black professionals in white America today," wrote *Washington Post* reporter Kevin Klose in a post-mortem profile a couple of months after her death. "These racial pioneers may possess special reservoirs of eloquence, as did McClain. But they must withstand enormous strains of isolation that whites seldom encounter in achieving similar success."

She withstood all that and more, for a while. Her metaphorical image of happiness as a "private club" that would not let her in was vintage Lea. Happiness became a subject of long, sad, late-night hand-holding sessions between us, either in person or over the telephone. "When will I be happy?" she would ask in tearful moments. She talked about getting to happiness the way a dieter talks about reaching a goal weight.

In response, I had nothing to offer but sentimental bromides. Happiness, I have since discovered, is not a destination. It is a process, like the weather or peace in the Middle East. Every time you think you have it pinned down, its contours shift like desert sands, especially if you are black.

"A black person learns very early that his color is a disadvantage in a world of white folk," George Schuyler, a conservative voice of the Harlem Renaissance, began his autobiography. "This being an unalterable circumstance, one also learns very early to make the best of it. So the lifetime endeavor of the intelligent Negro is how to be reasonably happy though colored."

As the children of "working poverty," we made it our lifetime endeavor, instilled in us by industrious, fiercely religious parents, to "make it."

Growing up in Chicago's Ida B. Wells public housing projects, she would later write, "wasn't paradise. There were purse snatchings, burglaries, domestic rows, gang fights. . . . [But] for me, it was a decent place to live, built to last an eternity, dependably heated, with abundant hot water. . . . Above all, the projects were a stopover. In my family, we were brought up knowing we would not have to raise our children there. . . . the object was to get out, and get out we did."

In surviving the ghetto, she felt conflicting feelings of guilt, shock, denial and blame, including self-blame—the same emotions that were felt by those who survived her suicide.

She called herself a "poverty snob," fiercely proud of surviving the crucible of the ghetto and prospering with the street savvy "those pampered suburban kids" could only read about in books. She insisted that it was *they*, not she, who were culturally deprived.

Yet she was torn between her sentimental affection for the 'hood—it was, after all, home—and her hatred for what it does to people.

An episode of urban terrorism changed her mind about following her two older sisters, Leatrice and Anita (from whom her name was derived), into school teaching. One day, while she was at Chicago State University, she received word that Leatrice, the eldest, had been shot. She had walked out the door of a South Side high school where she had been teaching all day and—*blammo!*—right into the blast from a shotgun in a street gang shootout. Fortunately, most of the blast missed her. She was injured in one arm. But it was enough to frighten Leanita into changing her career plans. A professor offered her a suggestion. It was the early 1970s. The media were looking, at long last, for reporters "of color." Surely she could find scholarship money at a prominent, well-endowed place like, say, Northwestern University's Medill School of Journalism, only an elevated train ride away in north suburban Evanston. She did. When the $6,000 scholarship award arrived in a lump-sum check in her family's mailbox, her father was visibly astonished. He grabbed the check in his rough hands and sat down at the family's tiny Formica-top kitchen table in their cramped little kitchen to examine the check in long silence. Never before had he held so much money in his hands. It would take him at least a year of hard labor to make as much.

We met in the *Tribune*'s newsroom as young black reporters at the very white newspaper. Like most other major news operations across the country, the *Tribune* had not opened its newsroom doors to blacks until the mid-1960s, the era of civil rights and urban riots. In 1969, fresh off the campus, I was one of the first three black reporters the newspaper had hired in its then 122-year history. Lea was hired in 1973, fresh out of Northwestern. A year later, we were married.

Newsroom marriages are common in our business. Reporters and editors don't get out much, I guess. But this bonding of black talents was a first. Friends and relatives showered us with admiration. We were the "keepers of the dream," the first generation to make the long, perilous climb out of the ghetto and master the "game" as it is played in the predominantly white world of downtown corporations.

We, the "golden couple," seemed to flourish in it. We dressed for success. We vacationed in Europe. We attended lavish parties on Lake Shore Drive. We threw racially integrated parties in our two-thousand-square-foot condominium on the city's affluent North Side, overlooking scenic Belmont Harbor and Lake Michigan, but we lived without the designer labels, thank you. She considered them too bourgeois.

Our career ladders were behaving like escalators, moving us up faster than we expected while we tried desperately to hold on, to keep our balance and our heads for fear that some overzealous white manager was not wittingly or unwittingly programming us for failure. We held on. I moved up from general assignment to the rewrite desk, briefly to foreign correspondent for a series on southern Africa in 1976, then assistant city editor, then on to WBBM-TV to become community affairs director, documentary producer, talk-show host, and, finally, general assignment reporter.

Lea, too, moved up in ways neither of us expected. While she was still a copy editor, she put her ambivalent feelings down on paper and submitted it to *Newsweek*'s "My Turn" column. The magazine published it in its October 18, 1980, edition under the headline "The Black Middle Class Burden."

Response to the piece was electric. More than a hundred letters came to her from as far away as South Africa. Black women called to say, "Right on, sister." White people wrote to ask, "You're still not happy? What more do you people want?" An editor at a magazine aimed at black women called to beg her to write "more, more, *more*" for them. Hollywood agents called to talk about film rights.

Most important, her own newspaper's editor, James R. Squires, was impressed enough to fast-track her to a column and the newspaper's editorial board, where she was its first black woman. Lea was dumbfounded. Her pain had brought her fame.

Then it all fell apart. The first casualty was her state of mind, then our marriage. Chronic, clinical depression overcame her like a gathering "brainstorm," as William Styron called his. It seems an appropriate metaphor. Her bleak moods spun around inside her head slowly at first, then gathered speed so furiously that one day she grabbed her own head in her hands and shrieked tearfully, "What's happening to me?"

When she asked for a divorce, she told me not to take it personally. She said she had troubles she had to work out, and she could not work them out with me.

After a couple of years of unsatisfying bouts with marital counseling and a brief separation, we split. The legal part was easy. No children. No fault. No contest. No problem. The emotional part was a different matter.

It did not bring the happiness she sought. She called me one night not long after she moved out. She was sobbing so hard I could hardly make out what she was saying, except that it sounded as if she said she had just tried to kill herself. I rushed right over. She had found a modern one-bedroom Lake Shore Drive apartment in a high-rise overlooking Lake

Michigan, with a view that looked like a postcard from Rio de Janeiro. She was miserable. The window was open. We were more than twenty stories up. A cold wind whipped the curtains. She had guzzled an entire bottle of sparkling wine and swallowed a small bottle's worth of nonprescription sleep aids. She had opened the window, but she could not bring herself to jump. She stripped herself naked, grabbed a razor blade, and climbed into a hot bath, but could do no more than nick her wrist before she called me to cry for help. I took her to a nearby hospital to have her stomach pumped and called her mother and sisters. She assured them she would get help. She did. But it wasn't enough.

Her second suicide threat that I know of occurred while she was visiting with me in our old condo to sort out details necessary to sell the place. Suddenly, while looking at some papers, I heard her say, "Good-bye." I turned to see her holding a gun to her head. Tears were streaming down her cheeks. I told her to give me the gun. She turned and darted to a distant bathroom, holding the gun to her temple and crying loudly all the way. I chased her. She finally gave me the gun. I took out the bullets. They were hollow-points, intended to explode outward on impact. The thought of the damage one would have done to her head chilled me. We took the gun back to the suburban gun shop where she bought it.

Looking back on that episode, I still marvel sadly at the rapidity of her mood swings. One moment she was quite cogent and businesslike. The next, she was a weeping bowl of jelly with a gun in her fist. As soon as I took the gun from her hand, she was sternly businesslike again. First she demanded that I give it back to her. When I refused, she argued that it cost a lot of money. I agreed to help her get her money back, but I would not allow the gun back into her hands.

I later found out, thanks again to inquiring reporters after her death, that she broke up with a boyfriend, a computer salesman in his late twenties; had an abortion; made up with him; and bought a house for the children she said she wanted, a nine-room Victorian structure near the University of Chicago campus, closer to the heart of the black community she knew best. But she broke up with her boyfriend again, and within twenty-four hours after closing her purchase of the house without him, she told her real estate agent that she wanted to put it on the market again. She tried to get back with her boyfriend over New Year's Day, 1984. They had an argument. She fired a shot from a nickel-plated revolver, according to friends, causing him to flee for his life.

Two months after the March 1984 issue of *Glamour* magazine named her one of its top ten career women of the year, she told her mother she was going to be spending Memorial Day in the suburbs. Instead, she stayed home. A wild storm lashed the city, washing out picnics and rattling windows across the metropolitan area. Judging by the clues she left behind, she put a Barbra Streisand album on her phonograph, arranged a stack of carefully handwritten suicide notes on a night table by her bed, and swallowed a lethal overdose of amitriptyline hydrochloride (Elavil), a powerful tranquilizer that was supposed to ease her chronic bouts with depression.

It was May 28, 1984. She was thirty-two years old.

Chicago Tribune foreign editor Jim Yuenger, who would die of a heart attack in 1995 at age fifty-six, captured the substance of her mask in an eloquent eulogy at her funeral: "Leanita was quite an accomplished actress, you know. . . . More than most of us, Leanita inhabited several worlds . . . of blacks and whites, of poor and affluent, and the hectic, competitive world of metropolitan journalism. [She moved] back and forth among them. . . . Perhaps it was the heavy burden of that constant movement that impelled her to create a separate world of her very own [that] she was not able to let any of us enter."

Of all the demons that tortured her private world, I think the most curious was her ambivalence toward upward mobility. It haunts the African-American mind. We want economic success as much as any other group of people do, but experience has taught us better than to expect too much from it.

"One of the chief frustrations of the middle-class Negro is that he cannot escape identification with the Negro race and consequently is subject to the contempt of whites," wrote E. Franklin Frazier in his classic study of America's black middle class in the 1950s, *Black Bourgeoisie* (1957). Despite having invested in "wealth" as a universal solvent for racial discrimination, middle-class blacks were outraged at the insults and exclusion from participation in white society they still had to endure. Many would "resort to any kind of subterfuge in order to avoid contact with whites," Franklin observed. Even paying bills by mail to avoid degrading contact with whites was not uncommon among the more prosperous blacks of the South, he found.

Instead of openly expressing their anger, they would repress it with rationalizations, take it out on other minorities, including Indians and Jews, or threaten, as one middle-class professor did, to "break loose" one day and tell white folks what they really thought. More likely, said Frazier, such frustrated blacks would express their aggressions by other means, such as "deceiving whites and utilizing them to their own advantage."

The vulnerability to which Franklin refers persists, despite the rapid growth in wealth and opportunity for blacks since the 1960s. The only difference, I would submit, is that instead of feeling frustrated over being "subject to the contempt of whites," today's black middle class is frustrated over simply being subject to contempt, not only from whites, but also from a variety of other sources, including other blacks.

I admire the late, great Reginald Lewis. He leveraged his way to the top of Beatrice Foods in the mid-1980s, making himself the first African American to take over a billion-dollar corporation. His lifelong slogan was instructive. It became the title of his posthumously published, ghost-written autobiography, *Why Should White Guys Have All the Fun?* (1994).

Why, indeed? The very fact that Lewis raised the question is testament to how much the prevailing black community wisdom holds just the opposite, that white guys *should* have all the fun, that it somehow defies all that is natural in the universe for black people to *acquire wealth*, improve their socioeconomic status, and actually *have fun* doing it.

A new conventional wisdom of racial romanticism emerged right behind the civil rights movement in the late 1960s and displaced it. It was immediately embraced by the college-educated advance guard of what soon would become the new black middle class. The new racial romantics would have us believe that class essentially does not exist in the black community. Anyone who believes otherwise is quickly and resoundingly denounced and dismissed as some sort of a bourgeois conceit. We are *all* an underclass, say the racial romantics. For black Americans, James Baldwin told National Public Radio in the mid-1980s, there is only one class, "the black class." Any contrary argument, say the racial romantics, threatens unity in the black community. Why kid yourself? the racial romantics will tell you, for white America has never recognized us as being anything but black anyway. Just as racial romanticism has no room for blacks who dissent from its way of universally imposed innocence, neither does it allow for whites who fail to fit its universally imposed guilt. Instead of denouncing and opposing the white racist's propensity to prejudge the character of individuals according to their race, the racial romantic embraces it as his or her principal weapon in a struggle between the races as power groups.

I flirted for years with the tenants of racial romanticism. How tempting it is, after years of oppression and humiliation, to believe that one's oppression has imbued one's self, through no effort of one's own, with a certain indelible nobility. It has always troubled me to hear certain high tribunes of black community "groupthink" employ racial prejudice as a vehicle to fight racial prejudice. It has not troubled me enough, I hasten to add, to call for the immediate dismantling of all affirmative action or diversity efforts. I agree with the white Supreme Court justice who said that, to remedy the past abuses of race, we must take race into account. Nevertheless, I also believe the role of race, like the famous premature announcement of Mark Twain's death, has been greatly exaggerated compared to the role played by class. The passing of anti-discrimination laws made class differences more important arbiters of opportunity than racial differences. Only guilt and a vigorous, unhealthy dose of denial would prevent us from seeing it as we drive our children to private schools in our Volvo station wagons and Armani suits.

In light of this obvious contradiction, I have seen a new black middle-class culture grow up since the 1960s. It has its own neighborhoods, organizations, magazines (*Essence,*

Emerge, Image, etc.), social circles, and grievances.

Still, there is guilt. We, the new black middle class, bristle at the notion that we constitute an "elite," for that implies we believe in a crass, aloof elitism, which we insist we do not, even when our affluence seems to tell a different story. This often leaves us caught in an apparent contradiction: We are victims in a privileged class. It is hard to preach rebellion while raising your children with values that are quite assimilationist.

Many of us compensate by identifying excessively with our less fortunate brethren left behind in the ghetto, despite better judgment imbued by our own parents, few of whom would have put up with the likes of Ice T, Ice Cube, or Snoop Doggy Dogg. Yet this identification is itself a futile attempt to rekindle our own rebellion against our parents' values. My own parents were typical of others who parented the success stories of my generation. They believed in hard work, strong families, religious devotion, and personal responsibility. They believed in a strong role for government, which often has been the last resort for blacks who always were the last hired, first fired in the private sector and therefore the biggest victims of private sector vagaries. But, whether the government helped or not, they believed individuals were ultimately responsible for themselves and their families. Their early admonitions against "showing your color" and the like were just another way to say, Don't behave like *those* Negroes, those loud, lazy, godless, shiftless, doo-rag wearing good-for-nothings who hang out on the corner and get themselves into trouble. Today those same figures in the persons of gangsta rappers are exalted in the new ghetto romanticism. Criticize them, distance yourself from them, and risk ostracism as a tool of the white power establishment's oppression.

Still, in turning one's back on ghetto thugs, one runs the risk of ignoring the conditions that produced them—conditions that have flourished partly because so many of the bracing role models like my parents, freed by the civil rights reforms of the 1950s and 1960s, have moved to more prosperous neighborhoods, often leaving it up to others to tackle the most serious problems facing black America, problems that have more to do with economics than complexion.

Still, the complexities of complexion persist. All black professionals who have been ignored by a taxi, rejected for a bank loan, charged exorbitant insurance rates, or passed over for a promotion in a white company know the pain of *not knowing* for sure whether they have been discriminated against because of race, but suspecting on some level that they have.

While visible contempt for blacks has declined rapidly since the days of segregated water fountains, our susceptibility to it has not. When middle-class African Americans say, "We have slipped backward" since the 1960s or "We were better off" under legal segregation, this is a large part of what they are talking about. How frustrating it is for those who think they have reached the dream of equal opportunity, dignity, and acceptance, only to discover it fading into a nightmare of guilt, fear, suspicion, and resentment. Whether we actually are *subjected* to contempt or not, we are enraged by the very vulnerability that makes us forever *subject* to it.

Leanita's story continues, postmortem. After a respectful month or two of mourning—an eternity in newspaper time—the newspaper asked me to fill her empty seat on the newspaper's editorial board. And I accepted. I inherited her column space, too. Little did I know that the opportunity to do what I wanted most in life, which was to write a newspaper column, would come only after I lost the person I wanted most in life, which was she. I imagined grim Lea getting a hearty last laugh out of that. "Be careful what you ask for," she used to warn me. "You just might get it."

Now I knew what she meant. For years I had daydreamed of having a newspaper column of my own. But columns are hard to come by. When the opportunity came, the circumstances forced me to face head-on the feelings of envy I felt years earlier when Leanita got a column before I did. Now she was gone, and I had survived, to pick up the mantle like a good soldier in the revolution that black professional life still seemed to be in during the 1980s, especially in Chicago, where Harold Washington, the city's first black mayor and a committed reformer, was still fighting stormy political battles with the white-ethnic machine aldermen who still held a majority of the votes in the city council. Picking up the fight, which Leanita had championed passionately and elegantly in print, I felt mixed emotions. My ambivalence brought a troubling flashback to mind, the indelicate label Vietnam combat grunts during my army days attached to promotions inherited from someone who had been killed: "blood stripe." My boss, himself a Vietnam veteran, blanched at the comparison. But it was the most appropriate one my troubled mind could make. Besides, I reasoned, carrying the combat metaphor a step further, who was better qualified than I to continue the column in a way that would do justice to Leanita's sense of mission? Other friends and colleagues agreed. They were quite supportive. Still, there were whispers:

"Is that weird!" Dr. Alvin Poussaint, Harvard psychiatrist and a consultant at the time to "The Cosby Show," was quoted as saying when the *Washington Post* told him the news. "A clear pattern of tokenism. The black gets knocked off, put in another black."

Weird? Tokenism? Say, what? As an old vaudevillian might say, I resemble that remark. I had paid my dues. What would Poussaint prefer? No blacks on the editorial board?

Even so, the remark touched a nerve in me, a wrenching similar to survivors' guilt, the odd guilt that comes to the fortunate who have survived some calamity. Another version of it tormented Leanita as she witnessed terrible fates met by her former playmates back in "the projects."

Like no other form of death, suicide sends the close friends and relatives of the person who killed herself on a wild ride into the dark night of disbelief, denial, anger, guilt, and blame. Once the truth sinks in, you find yourself asking, Why? *Why did she do it? She had so much to live for*. The question is inevitable, although pursuit of it seldom satisfies, at least not right away. Suicide, like depression, grows out of a constellation of causes, few of which modern science has much of a handle on. Peeling back its layers reveals it to be something of an artichoke. One leaf always leads to another leaf. Even when you reach the heart of it, you find it also is composed of many layers, many facets.

Still, people try, and because Leanita was a public figure, the mysteries of her self-destruction became a subject of public autopsy, turning her in many minds into a poster child for what I call the discreet angst of America's new black bourgeoisie. *Time* magazine's "Milestones" column reported her suicide with graceful simplicity: "Friends say she was distraught over the pressures of being a role model." That was true enough. "Wednesday's child," she always had her grim side, too grim with self-deprecation to see herself comfortably as anyone else's role model.

She might easily have withstood the pressures had her dispiritedness not been complicated by the isolation that, beneath the glossy image of success, ran common in the first generation of black professionals to penetrate the predominantly white world of corporate America.

"Despite the tinsel, glitter and gaiety of the world of make-believe in which middle-class Negroes take refuge, they are still beset by feelings of insecurity, frustration and guilt," wrote Frazier. "As a consequence, the free and easy life which they appear to lead is a mask for their unhappy existence."

Much has happened since the 1950s when Frazier was writing. From 1960 to 1975, buoyed by civil rights reforms, the "black middle class" grew from 13.4 percent of black workers to 30 percent, and the black "skilled working class" grew from 25.7 percent to 30 percent, according to sociologist Bart Landry of the University of Maryland in *The New Black Middle Class* (1987).

But the silver lining has a cloud. Measured broadly, says Landry, middle-class blacks tended to be bunched in the lower-middle class, and the new black middle class was more likely to be living hand-to-mouth compared to whites who had accumulated more wealth in the form of savings, stocks, bonds, and property. Black middle-class families ended up with higher debts and less disposable income after expenses. "The optimism of the mid-1970s, then, grew out of the *relative* [emphasis his] gains blacks had experienced during the previous ten years in access to restaurants, hotels, theaters, lunch counters, and other community facilities as well as in greater access to jobs and the resulting rise in real income," Landry wrote.

The black middle class continued to grow through the 1980s, but more slowly with each decade, Landry said. Other studies indicate that social acceptance by whites has improved, but still remains an elusive brass ring. A 1994 study by Andrew Beveridge of Queens College for the *New York Times*, for example, found that the household income of blacks in Queens, home of the fictitious Archie Bunker, actually had grown to exceed that of white households. But here, too, there was a catch. Blacks were more likely than whites to have more than one member of the household working, and much of the reason for high black income relative to white Queens households was that more affluent whites already had moved farther out to the suburbs, where far fewer blacks lived.

A certain awkwardness permeated reaction to Leanita's death. Suicide is disparaged severely in some ethnic communities, and the black community is one of the most severe. Black people in my experience pride themselves on being survivors, an ironic counterpoint to young black male homicide rates. "We don't kill ourselves, we only kill each other," Leanita joked morbidly during peaks of manic humor between "brainstorms." In an actuarial sense, she was right. Suicide is statistically a white man's burden. At the time of her death, white men led the suicide tally at the National Center for Health Statistics in Atlanta, with 20 suicides per 100,000, followed by black males with 10.2. White women came in third at 6.2. Black women were lowest of all, with only 2.4 such deaths per 100,000, almost ten times less than the figure for white men.

The more power, it appears, the more suicides. There was widespread speculation in social psychological circles at the time that Leanita's death might be an early sign of a rapid climb in black female suicides as black women rose in the career world dominated by white men. But, ten years later, I found it was black men whose suicide figures had increased—to more than 12 per 100,000 from 10.2. The low rate of black women had remained essentially flat. Experts still say their numbers have nowhere to go but up, but so

far, black women continue to be remarkably successful survivors. One black woman I know guessed black women are
"too busy raising children and taking care of homes" to
have time for such contemplations.

Yet a closer look reveals that the suicide rate among blacks
tends to increase along with income. The white man's psy-
chic burden seems to accompany the white man's lifestyle.

And there very well could be a black suicide undercount, I
was told by Dr. Derek Miller, head of psychiatry at Chicago's
Northwestern Memorial Hospital, particularly among adolescent black males. Miller suggests that much of the street
violence young black males bring upon themselves by step-
ping into hazardous situations with don't-back-down street
macho may be "suicide by other means." They may refrain
from killing themselves outright, but they don't try very hard
to avoid getting killed, either.

Those who take their own lives in response to overwhelmingly oppressive social conditions commit "reactionary suicide," Black Panther leader Huey P. Newton wrote in
Revolutionary Suicide, a chic book among the radicals of my
youth. Newton was quite taken with French social scientist
Emile Durkheim, who attributed suicide to the social environment. By contrast, said Newton, "revolutionary suicide"
is committed in the course of overthrowing those social conditions. "Revolutionary suicide does not mean that I and my
comrades have a death wish," he wrote. "It means just the
opposite. We have such a strong desire to live with hope and
dignity that existence without them is impossible."

Newton eventually died without much hope or dignity,
gunned down in a gangland-style killing amid reports in the
leftist and mainstream press alike that the remnants of the
Black Panther movement had turned into a little Oakland-
based drug mafia. By all appearances, Newton, the great

Panther leader, did not, in the end, try hard enough to avoid
getting killed.

> *Turning back to me he recalls a time when he became*
> *utterly depressed and was complaining to a woman he'd*
> *met who had been through the Holocaust. "She slapped me*
> *and said, 'I want you to remember this all your life.*
> *Suffering is normal.'"*
>
> —Interview with the son of a suicide, as described by
> Rita Robinson, *Survivors of Suicide*

Suffering is normal. When we see someone less fortunate
than we are, it is natural for us to be overtaken by a shock of
sobering recognition. Even the most stone-hearted disciple
of hard work and discipline has to agree that, as much as
we like to think we deserve whatever fine things we have in
life, success is only partly a matter of merit. The rest is a
matter of luck. Blind, stupid luck. Or, if you prefer, God's
plan.

Even the language that we use—"less fortunate," "under-
privileged"—reveals our fundamental belief in the fickle cru-
elty of fate, that much of one's success or failure in life is
beyond one's control. As a corollary, the proper etiquette of
noblesse oblige obliges us, the more fortunate and overprivi-
leged, to "give back" or "reach down" to help those who may
not be able to afford what James Baldwin called the "price of
the ticket."

At the same time, we are cautioned by our time-honored
American ambivalence to avoid prescribing the wrong remedies, for they can make bad matters worse. Handouts, lowered standards, wringing our hands, blaming others for inac-
tion, or simply giving up can lead to more dependency, more
resentment, and ultimately disaster.

To spread the joys of good fortune, we must do more than

pin the tail on white racism or call for a redistribution of the wealth black Americans are only beginning to accumulate. We must follow the more difficult path, which is to take a hard look at the sources of good fortune as we have in the past examined the causes of poverty. The creation of poverty is no mystery. It's easy to become poor. It is more difficult, but immensely more satisfying, to develop the skills, values, and discipline that lead to success and to share them with others.

The best antidote to racism is excellence. The best way to prevent genocide is to make yourself essential. The best cure for survivors' guilt is to help others to survive and prosper. First, the survivors must acknowledge and somehow accept the cruel normality of suffering in order to recognize and normalize their own lives.

In retrospect, I think Leanita's great tragedy was not that she, as I, was born poor, black, and a social pariah in a racist society, but that in her pathological torment she embraced a philosophy that refused to allow her to appreciate her basic humanity, her immutable personal assets, or her marvelous ability to achieve.

"True guilt is guilt at the obligation one owes to oneself to be oneself," British psychiatrist R.D. Laing wrote. "False guilt is guilt felt at not being what other people feel one ought to be or assume that one is."*

By accepting the theology of guilt, she accepted the thoroughly unsupported allegation that she had something to feel guilty about. On some cerebral level, she had accepted the unreal and conflicting stereotypical roles into which she was cast by a needy, but misguided, public. Some wanted her to be the militant. Some wanted her to be the good little col-

*R.D. Laing, *The Self and Others* (New York: Pantheon, 1961), ch. 10, p. 133.

ored girl. Some wanted her to be the fiery feminist. Others wanted her to be a self-centered bourgeois toady to white power. It must have seemed to her in her final hours that everybody wanted a piece of her and nobody wanted to accept, deliver, and protect the whole her. She chose to believe these unreal characterizations were real and could not be transcended. In fact, her greatest tragedy is that she gave up the fight.

"I'll never live to see my people free anyway," she said in her suicide note. None are so blind, my hometown minister used to say, as those who refuse to see. The contradictions of her life terrorized her. Her struggle up from triple victimization as one who was poor, black, and female exposed her wounds and her susceptibility to being wounded again. Her conflicts distanced her from others, breaking her connections with those who might have served as sources of spiritual strength.

I believe that we in the black community who have "made it" have an obligation to reach back, not with condescension, but with genuine concern, to help those who have not. Lea enjoyed working with young people, but it was not enough, leading me to conclude that her problems ran far deeper than such mundane issues as politics or economics. They were psychological, which struck an important nerve in the black community. Our problems are as much a matter of our psychological self-doubts as they are a matter of politics or economics. This psychological aspect of our problem is seldom addressed, partly because it is so mysterious and partly because, no matter how much of it can be blamed on white people, it cannot be solved by them. It will require deep retrospection and dialogue among ourselves that will have to be far more honest than the conventional anti-bourgeois wisdom has allowed.

Looking back, I see with greater clarity the freedom Leanita had at her disposal, whether she was willing to realize it or not. She did not have to march for it, fight for it, or crusade for it. All she had to do was something that for many of us has been infinitely more difficult: to accept it. I am sorry she couldn't bring herself to do that. I'm sorry that she decided to let the white guys and gals have all the fun.

4

The R-Word

"When I use a word," Humpty Dumpty said in rather a scornful tone, "it means just what I choose it to mean— neither more nor less."

—Lewis Carroll, *Through the Looking-Glass*

Sympathy for victims is always counter-balanced by an equal and opposite feeling of resentment towards them.

—Ben Elton, British author and performer

Racism is a sensitive word. Americans often avoid mentioning it, even when it is relevant. For example, the word "race" was used dozens of times in major media stories following the 1992 Los Angeles riots, but never "racism," according to a computer database search by the University of Florida's Joseph Feagin, author of *Living with Racism*.

It is a sensitive word because it exposes so much, institutionally and personally. It is a Rorschach word, a linguistic inkblot test. How you define it reveals something important about you, how you see the world and your place in it.

A lawyer for Rockford, Illinois, public schools told *USA Today* in the early 1990s that his district's policies could not possibly be racist because "Racist to me is a conscious attitude, like running around with hoods and white sheets." He did not see racism despite the fact that the school board he was defending had just been cited by a federal judge for deliberately dodging desegregation "with such subtlety as to raise discrimination to an art form." The judge said the district's "ability tracking" had somehow managed to track white students with below-average ability into "high-ability" classes and blacks with high ability into low-ability classes. As if that was not enough, the almost all-white "gifted" classes used separate classrooms, separate bathrooms, and sometimes even separate entrances from minority-dominated classes. Minority schools received used textbooks while white schools got new ones. But, alas, as the lawyer correctly pointed out, there were no hoods or white sheets in sight. So, if those are your criteria, there was no racism, either.

It follows, then, that if no one outside the Ku Klux Klan hoods or sheets is to be considered racist, actual bona fide Klan leaders inevitably will trade their sheets for business suits, stir up the masses, and suck up to the ruling class. Klan membership dropped sharply in the early 1980s, according to researchers for the Anti-Defamation League and other Klan-watching groups, as many found a new, satisfying voice and vehicle in Republican Party politics. Enter David Duke. Years before he earned a startling 60 percent of Louisiana's white vote as the state's unsuccessful Republican gubernatorial candidate, he had been test-marketing hot-button issues like "crime, welfare . . . school choice . . ." and racial "quotas" as racial code words, which were easily picked up by conservative political campaigns. "I think racism has reversed," he said, meaning it is now blacks who have the edge, thanks to affirmative action, while whitey gets the shaft. No one wants to be called a racist, even when he or she is one.

Competing definitions of the R-word illuminate the boundaries of America's racial divide as brightly as landing lights on the landscape at night. White people, in my experience, tend to believe the definition found in most dictionaries, which, as it happens, are written mostly by white people.

Mine* defines it as "discrimination or prejudice based on race" or "the belief that race accounts for differences in human character or ability and that a particular race is superior to others." It is a pleasing definition because it is personal. It emphasizes "belief," not practice. It makes racism a strictly personal sin, which makes its absolution a strictly personal matter. Change your beliefs—or, at least, espouse changed beliefs—and you do not actually have to do anything. Absolve yourself of racist attitudes and instantly absolve yourself of oppressor status. Instead, you might even be able, in this day and age, to claim instant victim status. "I didn't own any slaves," says the innocent white person. "Why penalize me?" Small wonder, then, that 62 percent of white people think black people complain too much about racism, according to a poll by the Anti-Defamation League of B'nai B'rith in 1993. As one annoyed Rush Limbaugh fan in Texas put it more pointedly in a newspaper column by Molly Ivins, "I agree with Rush that racism is dead. I just wonder what the niggers are going to come up with next."

What many black intellectuals have come up with is a broader definition of racism than most dictionaries offer. They see it as less a personal belief than a public practice, a "power relationship," a set of social, historical, traditional, and institutional habits of mind that are deeply imbedded in the national psyche and work as active agents to impede equal opportunity for blacks.

And here's the rub: For blacks, the beauty of defining racism as an institutional tool of the oppressor is the instant innocence it offers to the oppressed, a direct contradiction of the instant innocence whites have grasped off the shelf in their dictionaries. If you are white and you believe the black

---

*The American Heritage Dictionary of the English Language, Third Edition, copyright © 1992 by Houghton Mifflin Company. All rights reserved.

definition of racism as an *institutional* flaw, it does not matter what you think as an individual. The system already was set up long before you were born to give you advantage and penalize blacks. Don't take it personally, the black speaker is saying, it's bigger than both of us.

Yet, not too surprisingly, many do take it personally. The R-word is too powerful of an epithet, less a conversation maker than a conversation breaker. "I have just about given up on meeting with the black community to improve race relations," said a liberal white friend in Chicago. "I can't ask a question without being called a racist. I don't like to be called a racist, especially when I'm trying to help."

Black filmmaker Spike Lee, a master at stirring up self-promoting controversy, succeeded perhaps beyond his own wildest dreams after he said in a *Playboy* magazine interview that "black people can't be racist." That was all it took for Spike to make headlines in gossip columns and entertainment pages of the mainstream, which is to say white-owned, media. I had seen or heard the same statement written or spoken for years among black folks as notable or prominent as James Baldwin, Dick Gregory, Spellman College president Johnetta Cole, former Detroit mayor Coleman Young, and Nation of Islam minister Louis Farrakhan. But it had not been said very much in the mainstream media, which made it news to white people, which made it important news: a fact of life and an endless annoyance to black people who are accustomed to living with racism.

Nothing annoys black people more than the hearty perennial of black life in America, the persistent reality of having one's fate in America decided inevitably by white people. It is an annoyance that underlies all racial grievances in America, beginning with slavery, evolving through the eras of mass lynchings and segregated water fountains, and continuing through the age of "white flight," mortgage discrimination, police brutality, and the "race card" in politics. Ironically, tragically, it is an annoyance that actually works against the normal operations of America's traditional assimilative processes, the fabled melting pot that in the past absorbed Asians, Latinos, Jews, Irish, Italians, Poles, and other groups that, at one time or another, were as despised and taboo as blacks are today. But no other immigrant group was held back for more than a generation or so. Blacks were held back for two centuries of slavery plus another century of legally sanctioned subjugation and humiliation. One does not, as President Lyndon B. Johnson once said, hold some people back that long, then tell them they are free to run the race the same as everyone else. Accordingly, because the assimilative process was denied to blacks for so long, many now resist it with ferocious tenacity. Liberal blacks respond by calling for affirmative action to force whites to face up to the lingering effects of racism. Black conservatives and nationalists respond by calling for various forms of independence, self-help, and separatism from dependency on whites, even white largesse. Either way, whether the reformers happen to be a bell hooks or a Clarence Thomas, the ultimate goal, black self-determination, and the motivating force, white dominance, are the same. Both want to free the destiny of blacks from the power of whites.

Most of which tends to be, in my experience, a complete mystery to most white people. Privilege is least apparent to those who have it. When they hear suddenly that, lo and behold, they have too much of it, they tend to take it personally, the way many of Spike Lee's critics did. I did not take it personally, since it was not directed at me, but I criticized Spike anyway in my nationally syndicated column. I felt it was important for some black person to take a public stand for the nobler impulses for which Martin Luther King, Jr., died. Sure, we as black people have suffered the sting of a racism far more wide-reaching and complicated than most white people are willing to comprehend, I said, but it does us no good to pose as if we are somehow so morally superior as to be biologically incapable of committing the same sins if we were in charge. Tell, for example, the East Indians who were expelled from Uganda by Idi Amin that black people can't be racist. How "racist in reverse," it was, I said, for Lee to make such a statement.

Well, why did I say that? From Oakland to Brooklyn, the angry mail and telephone calls flowed to my desk from black folks who wanted me to know that Spike Lee was right and that I had missed the point. Whether black people ever could get the power to be racist was irrelevant as long as white people have the power and we can't even see a light at the end of the tunnel leading toward the day when we are going to get it.

That's what I get for believing dictionaries. Black people may read dictionaries, but many see them as instruments of white supremacy. They have a point. Dictionaries define what is acceptable and unacceptable in the language we use, as defined by the ruling class. Since English is an open language, its gates are routinely unlocked to accept new words from other languages, dialects, and subcultures, you dig? But the gates ultimately are controlled by white people. The dictionary's pleasant synonyms for "white" ("free from moral impurity ... *innocent* ... *favorable, fortunate* ...") and unpleasant synonyms for "black" ("... thoroughly sinister or evil ... *wicked* ... condemnation or discredit ... the devil ... sad, gloomy or calamitous ... *sullen* ...") are alone enough to remind black people of their subordinate position to white people in Anglo-European traditions and fact.

It soon became apparent to me that to understand what

many black people are thinking, it pays to listen to what Spike Lee was trying to say. He was not denying that black people could be *prejudiced*, but he did not want to let white Americans off the hook by agreeing with their attempts to regard simple prejudice and the much more sweeping racism as the same thing. "Racism is when you have laws set up, systematically put in as a way to keep people from advancing, to stop the advancement of a people," he said. "Black people have never had the power to enforce racism, and so this is something that white America is going to have to work out themselves. If they decide they want to stop it, curtail it, or to do the right thing . . . then it will be done, but not until then."*

The difference between the "white" and the "black" definitions of racism is, I believe, the difference between perceived guilt and the quest for innocence. White people define it in very narrow terms, so narrow that it could not possibly apply to them. Black people, by contrast, tend to define it quite broadly, broad enough for it to apply to almost everyone *but* them.

Racism, it has been said, is America's original sin. You will not hear much argument about that now. There is only disagreement over how much it continues to be the national sin, who should be responsible for it, and what can be done about it. Instead of working it out, conversation across racial lines has broken down since the 1960s. Instead of talking honestly, candidly, and nationally, we deny that a problem exists, except maybe in somebody else's head, somebody who simply cannot be talked to. When everyone is a victim, no one is left to accept the blame. We are, as someone once said of the British and the Americans, divided by our common language.

*Interview with critic Elvis Mitchell in *Playboy,* July 1991.

The Roots of Racism

Americans like to think of racism as some sort of deviation from the norms of a fundamentally rational society. I would argue that racism is the rational result of a racially imbalanced society.

Racism is the belief *or practice* that devalues other races as biologically and morally inferior. It is not just an internalized personal belief or attitude. It is also an externalized public practice, a power relationship that continually dominates, encourages, and reproduces the very conditions that make it so useful and profitable.

It has been called America's original sin. It is. But it was not invented here. America only gave it peculiarly American nuances. Its roots can be found in the very concept of group identity itself, dating to the cradles of tribal organization, in the xenophobic impulses that showed themselves with humanity's earliest declarations of "us" and "them," "our people" and the "other." Hatred starts at home. The family grows into the clan. The clan grows into the tribe. The tribe becomes an ethnic group. The very act of pulling together for purposes of survival, however rationally motivated it may be, leads inevitably to competition with other groups for food and choice territory. Or, as I once heard radical author-professor Michael Parenti say, "With brotherhood comes *Other*hood. With ethnic identity comes the risk of ethnocentricity," the belief that the world can best be viewed through the lens of a single ethnic group's experiences.

The uplifting of pride in one's own ethnic group does not necessarily mean an attack on others, but quite often it does. While it is possible to cultivate a color-blind, cosmopolitan, universalistic view of others and hold one's other-hating impulses in check, there is always, as Parenti suggests, a risk. The human animal's more basic impulse is to compete with other groups, whether for food, cheap labor, or empire. Ethnocentrism can quickly, almost imperceptibly devolve into xenophobia, even between people of the same stock. Examples abound of groups who appear to outsiders to be virtually indistinguishable, yet turn ferociously hostile to each other, whether they are the Catholics and Protestants of Northern Ireland, the Serbs and Bosnians and Croats of the Balkans, the Tutsis and Hutus of Rwanda and Burundi, the Hatfields and McCoys of Appalachia, or the Crips and Bloods of Los Angeles.

Groups tend to get along not so much because such accord is natural as because they perceive a common foe. The fall of that common foe can reignite ancient animosities, bringing all manner of tribal hatreds to the surface. The lifting of colonialism reignited ancient ethnic conflicts in Africa. The lifting of the Iron Curtain released ancient tribal conflicts in Yugoslavia and Azerbaijan. The lifting of apartheid unleashed ancient conflicts between the Zulu and other black South African ethnic groups.

Even within the same race in the same society, such as black people in the United States, cultural differences can create powerful tensions. African Americans often quarrel with one another over skin tone or family lineage. Those of us whose family line goes back to the slavery generations quarrel with more recent arrivals from the West Indies or Africa. The same kinds of tensions occur among white ethnics. Misunderstandings mount into major disagreements with "those people over there who don't behave the way we do."

Slavery codified racial supremacy into law. It would have been a simple matter after the Civil War for Americans in the North and the South to have welcomed freed slaves as fellow Americans, as it welcomed other immigrant groups. The Thirteenth, Fourteenth, and Fifteenth Amendments to the

Constitution were enacted for that very purpose. But the will
to racial justice was lacking. Instead there were rollbacks in
the North and South, including lynchings, disenfranchisement, and Jim Crow segregation in the South, and housing
covenants and de facto discrimination in the North.

Modern capitalist society puts racism to work, wittingly or
unwittingly. It populates a surplus labor pool of last-hired,
first-fired workers whose easy employability when economic
times are good and easy disposability when times go bad
helps keep all workers' wages low and owners' profits high.

Racism has populated a seemingly "permanent underclass" that performs society's least desirable work, whether
shucking crabs in coastal Virginia or sweeping floors in St.
Louis. In many cases they compete for jobs with immigrants,
legal and illegal, who also serve to keep labor costs low.

Racism helps keep working classes fragmented and disor-
ganized. Owners and bosses are safest when they keep workers fighting among themselves.

Racism helps keep voters fighting among themselves
along racial and ethnic lines. Otherwise unproductive politicians also are safest when they can play the "race card" and
manipulate the xenophobic fears and suspicions of voters to
their advantage. Race is one of many nonclass issues, such as
busing, affirmative action, or flag burning, that diverts attention from pocketbook issues that might unite voters across
racial lines.

Racism helps panic-peddling real estate agents stir "white
flight" among homeowners who are fearful of racial change,
causing them to sell their homes at low prices so the houses
can be resold to blacks at higher prices.

Racism thrives on fear, and there is plenty to go around.
White people fear black uprisings, which may explain why
black wrongdoers tend to be prosecuted more vigorously and

punished more severely in the criminal justice system than whites for similar crimes. Black people, at the same time, fear that white people, unsure of what to do with us now that all the cotton is picked, may be turning to quiet forms of "genocide" and population control to eliminate us as a concern. Each side's suspicions feeds the other's.

And racism always rationalizes itself. Since tribal times, the alien has been perceived as something less than morally equivalent to one's own people. Ideologies are fashioned to justify the horrors that are imposed. Once the Nazis had dehumanized the Jews, nothing stopped the Holocaust. American GIs gathered scalps and skulls of Japanese soldiers and ears of enemy Vietnamese soldiers on those two battlefronts, but not so much in Europe, where the enemy bore greater physical resemblance to America's dominant race and was less easily demonized.

Even the wisest white males have not been immune to identifying so closely with the ruling class of which they are a part that they can rationalize the most barbaric behaviors. Parenti reminds us that Aristotle in his *Politics*, written in the fourth century B.C., rationalized thus: "Some men are slaves by nature and others are free men. By the condition of their souls some are inferior to others. This being so, it is advantageous to both parties for this man to be a slave and that to be a master. It is good and just that some should be governed and others govern in the manner that nature intended."

Aristotle called this view "mutual utility." It was best for everybody, he said, slave and master. Similarly stark class distinctions are justified today as working out for the best for everyone, an inevitable manifestation of nature itself, not of the family into which one is born. Long before *The Bell Curve* attributed black poverty and IQ scores to genetics, Robert Fogel and Stanley L. Engerman published *Time on the Cross*

(1974), which argues through highly selective emphasis that slavery could not possibly have been all that bad because it would have been irrational for slave masters to have been unnecessarily cruel to their human livestock. Slaves actually increased their skills and bettered their condition, they argue. *Gone With the Wind* presented similarly sugar-coated portraits. Fortunately, we have the surviving first-person accounts of the slave narratives to show that rationality often was put aside to impose bitterly inhuman cruelties upon slaves, including murder, rape, mutilations, and permanent family separations to keep them subdued and their masters safe.

The "white" and "colored" signs of racial apartheid are long gone, but news accounts of discrimination continue. A study by the Boston Federal Reserve Bank, for example, found that black applicants were more likely to be turned down for home loans, even when they shared similar or slightly better credit histories than whites who were approved. CBS's "60 Minutes" sent out job "testers" to do office work and found whites more likely to be hired and enthusiastically processed than blacks who had the same or slightly better job qualifications. So much for meritocracy. Black New York City police officers threatened to stop working plainclothes after one of their mates, while lying on the ground, was shot repeatedly by a white officer who mistook him for a suspect during the summer of 1994.

Internalized Racism

Sometimes the victims of racism embrace the very values that have victimized them. Black people don't like black people very much. Continued affronts, abuse, and reminders of racial inequality cause some to internalize the values that have oppressed them for so long, if only to throw them back in the faces of the white power structure. Young blacks will ridicule their peers as "talking white" or "acting white" just for trying to speak proper English or make decent grades. Light-skinned blacks will shun their darker brethren and vice versa. A color caste system will be imposed, as described in the street poem I learned during my childhood in the 1950s, back when we were still "colored," back when "black" was still a fighting word:

If you're white, it's all right,
If you're brown, stick around,
If you're yellow, that's mellow,
But, if you're black, get back, get back, get back!

The "black power" black consciousness movement of the 1960s was a direct rebuttal to those deeply ingrained white standards of beauty. Its most significant messenger was Malcolm X, who was slain in 1965, but not before he impressed a new generation with the importance of self-love. For a few years, just about everyone in my generation of college students was growing "naturals" and "Afros" and wearing African garb. "Black is beautiful," was the slogan, which made many white people nervous, as any show of positive black racial identification tends to do, which became its own reward for many blacks.

Fashions changed. The Afros were trimmed and the dashikis went back into the closet. But the central vexation, the control white America continued to exert over the fate of black America, continued to irritate. Just as racism could be internalized by its victims, so could the sense of victimization itself, even by those who had few tangible targets to complain about. Black skin in itself became sufficient evidence for some to claim grievance and demand retribution or revenge. In this way, the noble status of victim became, in many ways, corrupted and devalued not only by America's historic victims but also by interlopers.

Take, for example, Colin Ferguson. On December 7, 1993, he opened fire with a Ruger 9-mm semiautomatic pistol aboard a Long Island Railroad commuter train, killing six passengers and wounding nineteen. His radical media-savvy defense attorney, William Kunstler, who previously had defended such movement luminaries as Martin Luther King, Jr., H. "Rap" Brown, and the Chicago Seven, said Ferguson went on his bloody rampage because of "black rage," a psychological condition brought on by daily life as a black man in a predominantly white racist society. Various critics, black and white, blasted the argument. Even the Jamaican-born Ferguson in an interview with a Jamaican newspaper repudiated that defense, saying it would "cause serious setbacks to the civil rights movement." He eventually argued his own case, without the "black rage" defense, and lost.

Yet a poll in the *National Law Journal* before the trial found that more than two-thirds of the blacks and an impressive 45 percent of the whites surveyed found the black-rage defense to be, in general, compelling.

Real victims still can be found, sadly enough, but their proper place in the public's narrow aperture of attention and sympathy has been crowded uncomfortably by dubious interlopers. Books have been written about the Menendez brothers, whose trials resulted in hung juries in Los Angeles after they blamed their father's alleged molestation of one of them for their decision to murder both their father *and* their mother. Or there's the case of Lorena Bobbitt, who received a light sentence after she blamed her husband's physical and emotional abuse for her decision to cut off his penis while he slept. Or there's the case of the woman who was awarded $2.9 million from McDonald's for burns she suffered after spilling coffee on herself in her own car.

But, sobering or amusing as these cases may be, discussions of modern victimania inevitably lead to the subject of race. Ultimately they raise troubling questions about the right of nonwhites to continue to claim group victim status in America. They even raise disturbing questions about the seriousness of white racism itself as a modern social problem in the era of the "angry white male."

The modern victim explosion feeds on a spirit hijacked from the civil rights movement. Martin Luther King, Jr., would hardly have approved of the way Colin Ferguson, to name one example, has achieved a dubious hero status in some quarters. Khalid Muhammad, former spokesman for Louis Farrakhan, brings cheers from some black audience members by comparing Ferguson to the slave rebellion leader Nat Turner, even though Ferguson's "enslavement" was all in his twisted little mind. "God spoke to Colin Ferguson and said *'Catch the train, Colin, catch the train,'*" Muhammad told a rally at historically black Howard University, bringing thunderous laughter and applause.

By definition, a victim is someone who has been harmed or made to suffer by some outside person, agent, or circumstance, usually beyond his or her control. The suffering can be current or passed down from past sufferings of one's ancestors, just as guilt can be transferred across generations to the racial or gender descendants of the victimizers of one's ancestors.

Get victimized enough and you move up the hierarchy of victimhood, gaining license with each step to exact some sort of payback from others who are more empowered than you, whether they be whites, males, straights, the abled, or whatever. Rally a community of similar victims and you have a recipe for polarization, self-segregation, and even arrogance in the spirit of the impatiently impudent T-shirt slogan: "It's a black thing; you wouldn't understand."

Or perhaps you will have a full-blown demagogue like

Khalid Muhammad, who, after comparing Colin Ferguson to Nat Turner, tried to one-up the Jews on the victim scale by picketing the Holocaust Museum in Washington because nothing like it stands on the mall to memorialize slavery. Maybe something should, but marching against the memorial built by Jews will not bring it about.

The Anti-victim Backlash

Since white power lets few attacks go unchallenged for long, the victim explosion quickly generated its own backlash. Author Charles Sykes charges in *A Nation of Victims* that America has become just what his title says we are. The result, he says, is a "decay of the American character." The national anthem, he says, has become the "whine." Before Sykes, Shelby Steele, a black California English professor, in his book, *The Content of Our Character* (1988), charged that too many of us, his fellow black Americans, have trapped ourselves in a "victim-focused identity" (my, how the man can turn a phrase), causing us to pass up innumerable opportunities to take advantage of the hard-won victories the civil rights years have brought. In later writing, he has expanded his critique to women, Jews, ACT-UP activists, and other minority group members who have, at various times, claimed what Steele calls the "new sovereignty," using their own victimization as a rallying point to segregate themselves from others and build a fortress around their vulnerabilities. More recently, lawyer Alan Dershowitz devoted an entire book to his own ravings against *The Abuse Excuse.* His argument, in brief: Other victims of (fill in the blank) managed to get along somehow without (killing, torturing, mutilating, suing) others, so why should we excuse it on that basis this time?

Feminists have generated a backlash industry of their very own. Most boisterous is Camille Paglia, author of numerous essays about how Puritans on the Left took all the sexual fun out of the women's liberation movement; Katie Roiphe, author of *The Morning After*, about how women's movement rape paranoia threatens the sexual fun of campus life for women; and Christina Hoff Sommers, author of *Who Stole Feminism*, who says an elite of "gender feminists" has taken too much fun out of life itself, so much so that few mainstream women want to be called "feminist" even when they admittedly believe in most of the movement's basic tenets.

Each of these ladies and gentlemen has provided generous ammunition for political conservatives who are eager to undermine liberal agendas. Yet, interestingly, Steele, Dershowitz, Roiphe, and certainly Paglia, among others, would not necessarily fit comfortably into the conservative label. In common they share only a desire to narrow the way we define victimization and restore the values of King in an age of compassion run amok.

Still, it is significant to note how, in all the critiques that spew out about victimania, few trouble themselves to critique America's newest self-proclaimed victim class: *heterosexual white males*. Mightily empowered by virtue of birth, yet feeling pitifully threatened by a rising tide of women and people of color, many white men, mad as hell and determined not to take it anymore, have taken to fighting fire with fire, claiming a special form of victimization all their own.

They complain of "reverse discrimination," even in the workplaces they dominate. They complain of being put upon by women and minorities and the liberals who support women and minorities. They are confused by the new, ever-changing laws, rules, regulations, and court decisions regarding sexual harassment and hostile workplace environments.

For solace they turn to their own cultural heroes—Rush Limbaugh, Tom Clancy, Newt Gingrich, Michael Crichton, Clarence Thomas, Howard Stern, and Camille Paglia, just for starters. In the words of Archie Bunker's theme song, they long nostalgically for the days when "goils were goils and men were men." As one exasperated white male executive put it, "Geez ... we let the gals into the game and all of a sudden they want to change the rules."

Maybe so. Or maybe the rules *needed* changing.

The Value of Victimhood

Obviously, victimhood has its value. It elicits sympathy, transfers guilt, and provokes favorable action. King's civil rights movement gained mountain-moving moral authority by scrupulously avoiding the use of black victimization as an excuse to avoid personal responsibility. Today King's coalition is in splinters, and so is its compelling moral message. Victimization, real and imagined, has become an excuse in itself for any act by anyone. Victimhood, thoroughly hijacked, is used by some to absolve victims of personal responsibility for improving their condition. Even David Duke has tried to claim it. "Racism has been reversed," he declares. *Victim transferal* confers victim status on larger and larger constituencies.

In victimhood there is a double bind. If anyone can claim it, no one can claim it, and it quickly becomes an agent to protect the guilty. Alice Walker and Ntozake Shange were roundly castigated for breaking racial solidarity with their accounts of abusive black men, although I, an official black man in every way, didn't think their works were any more of an assault on black men than *The Burning Bed*, a true story about an abused wife who got revenge by setting her hus-

band's bed afire with him in it, was an assault on white men.
Anita Hill, who accused Clarence Thomas of sexual harassment, and Desiree Washington, who accused Mike Tyson of
date rape, suffered similar attacks. Never mind their complaints or the guilt or innocence of their accused. The only
important argument to those who depend on racial reasoning
is that black men *in general* have been so put upon that each
of these black men *in particular* should be given a pass.

"Oh, the holiness of always being the injured party," wrote
Maya Angelou.* "The historically oppressed can find not
only sanctity but safety in the state of victimization. When
access to a better life has been denied often enough, and suc-
cessfully enough, one can use the rejection as an excuse to
cease all efforts. After all, one reckons, 'they' don't want me,
'they' accept their own mediocrity and refuse my best, 'they'
don't deserve me."

If anyone has a legitimate claim to victimhood, it is
Angelou. Yet her best-selling, lyrically recounted stories from
her hard-luck childhood and hard-knocks climb to glory lift us
up with their spirit of triumph, of relentless inspiration, per-
spiration, perseverance, and overcoming; they are not just
depressing dead-end tales of woe. That's the tragedy of the
abuse excuse, for it devalues the plight of those who strive quietly but relentlessly against victimhood that is quite legitimate.

No question that black rage is real. But, while rage explains
much black violence, it does not excuse it. In *Black Rage*, the
1968 book by black psychiatrists William H. Grier and Price
M. Cobbs that inspired Kunstler's black-rage defense,
nowhere do the authors excuse violence that erupts from
rage, black or otherwise. Instead they praise the courage and

---

Singin' and Swingin' and *Gettin' Merry Like Christmas* (New York: Bantam, 1976), vol. 3, ch. 9,
p. 75.

tenacity of black Americans who channel their rage into constructive pursuits. "We weep for the true victim, the black
American," they write. "His wounds are deep. But along
with their scars, black people have a secret. Their genius is
that they have survived. In their adaptations they have
developed a vigorous style of life. It has touched religion,
music, and the broad canvas of creativity. The psyche of black
men has been distorted, but out of that deformity has risen a
majesty. It began in the chants of the first work song. It continues in the timelessness of the blues. For white America to
understand the life of the black man, it must recognize that
so much time has passed and so little has changed."

Persistence of Racism

While David Duke and other interlopers reach so eagerly for victim status, it is a curious poignancy of our times that many other
more legitimate sufferers don't want any part of it. You can hear
it in the language they use. Many victims of breast cancer, child
molestation, or other dysfunctions prefer to be called "survivors." Telephone listings for "survivors' networks" or "survivors' support groups" can be found in almost every town for
almost every malady. Some simply call themselves "meetings,"
as popularized by Alcoholics Anonymous, the mother of all
twelve-step self-help programs for various addictions and the
promulgator of the reality school that says, "Don't call me cured,
I'm recovering."

"Call me a survivor or don't quote me at all," one breast
cancer survivor told a reporter for the newspaper where I
work. The reporter complied.

People take their language choices seriously. Like Lewis
Carroll's Humpty Dumpty, when they choose a name for
themselves, it means just what they choose it to mean, nei-

ther more nor less. I learned this the hard way during the
mid-1980s rise of AIDS activism. The new movement formed
by HIV-infectees quickly rejected the labels "patient" or "victim." They preferred to be called "people with AIDS" or
"people living with AIDS," which the gay press sometimes
shortened to "PWA" or "PLWA."

As one who makes his living by putting opinions before
the public, I thought their insistence on this linguistic nicety
was not only nonsense, but dangerous nonsense, a preten-
tious euphemism that needlessly trivialized the tragedy this
deadly virus had brought and diminished the urgency of the
need to find a cure. PWA, I wrote in a newspaper column,
sounds to my ears "like a name for some new airline," not a
name for someone who truly deserves sympathy and support.

I quickly regretted that attempt at rhetorical cleverness.
No sooner did that particular column go to press than the
mail, telephone calls, and icy personal comments flowed in.
Even more hurtful were the second-tier comments from
those who had only heard about my comment out of context
and secondhand. Word soon rolled across Chicago's tightly
knit gay and lesbian activist community that I was a gay
basher. At one point, an embarrassed lesbian friend asked
me to provide her with a copy of the original column that
she could show a gay man who had refused to donate to her
art gallery as long as my name appeared on its advisory
board. I apologized to her and to him for any misunder-
standing.

Suddenly, I felt a taste of what I am sure it is like for white
liberals, brimming with their own sense of innocence, to be
stung by the charge of racism. It is not pleasant.

The episode also taught me an important lesson about
human nature: Attack the labels people have chosen for

themselves and you will be viewed as having attacked them. We don't want your sympathy, I was told. We want understanding. Words like "victim" or "patient" imply a helplessness, passivity, and defeat of which the "HIV community" wanted no part, I was told. "We are not victims," one person with AIDS told me. "We are not giving up. We are defying the illness and, we hope, defeating it."

Little words mean a lot to those whose last best hope lies within themselves and the life-affirming powers of their own positive thinking. Recovery depends on the power of your mind, I was informed. "If I walk around with 'victim' stamped on my forehead, I inhibit my own ability to heal," a person with AIDS told me. Concessions to victimhood also sacrifice self-esteem, motivation, and ambition, he said. Give up all that and you become one of the walking wounded, slipping nowhere but downward to the grave.

Similarly, I think the black community has its walking wounded, too, our moody, touchy casualties. Few ever go off as explosively as Colin Ferguson, but many simmer with a quiet storm inside. Some become so angry, resentful, morose, or spiritually defeated, they simply give up trying to fight the battle. Feeling a pain too painful to articulate, they bottle it up behind the mask of black macho: *Gotta be strong, "hard."* Relinquishing the safety valve of talk, they may act out their frustrations in ways destructive to themselves or others: smoking, drinking, shooting, violently attacking themselves or somebody else. They may take out their rage on somebody close, who may very well happen to be black—a spouse, a lover, a friend, a rival gang member, a stranger who bumped into them on the subway—anyone whose disrespect, real or imagined, drops the last straw on the sufferers' junkpile of self-doubt.

We African Americans often pride ourselves on our relentless survival. We survived the Middle Passage, more than 350 years of slavery, another century of segregation, degradation, and humiliation. Will we survive freedom?

Freedom is not free, the elders of the civil rights movement used to say. It brings burdens and frustrations as much as it alleviates them. When discrimination was outlawed in the mid-1960s, many African Americans were left stranded in an unexpected sense of isolation. Behind them was a ghetto whose colleges, shops, and other institutions had been undermined by desegregation. Ahead was a white community still too steeped in centuries of its own prejudices even to recognize itself as a "community," let alone be very welcoming. I think it was here that many of the young and, therefore, least secure turned away from assimilating into the white establishment and turned instead to a movement that could satisfy their yearning to belong to something larger than themselves. So scores flocked to the black power movement in the 1960s, and two decades later, scores of their children flocked to study Malcolm X or hear Louis Farrakhan.

More violent and tragic is the rage unleashed every day in spousal abuse, child abuse, gang fights, drive-by shootings, or drug addictions. Therapists like Dr. Howard Mabry, a psychologist at Washington's Institute for Behavioral Change, suggest releasing bottled-up rage through family or community intervention and mediation that brings resolution to the patient's concern and helps the patient develop a good self-image and useful coping mechanisms. He does not recommend denial, either for patients or for growing black children. Trying to pretend racism doesn't exist only sets the child up to become a casualty later in life, he says. Survivors come most easily from supportive families that impart to them a strong sense of self-esteem. They know they are worth more than the world wants to tell them they are. They easily and freely talk about it, laugh about it, challenge it, defy it. They become stronger, more focused, and more powerful.

Prescriptions

It is one of our nobler impulses as Americans to exalt the individual and to focus on attitudes. But it is sensible also to remember the larger institutions of structural or systemic racism that influence American life. It does no service to the cause of racial equality for white people to content themselves with judging themselves to be nonracist. Few people outside the Klan or skinhead movements own up to all-out racism these days. White people must take the extra step. They must become anti-racist. They must be willing to open their eyes to the privileges white skin still affords in this society and renounce them as surely as black people must renounce their victim focus. White people need to relinquish their truncated view of "fairness" to pursue true egalitarianism and justice.

In that spirit, the white editors of *Race Traitor: A Journal for the New Abolitionism*, a tiny Cambridge-based magazine, have gone so far as to call on their fellow white Americans to become "traitors to their race" by renouncing white privilege and identifying with the "racially oppressed." Among suggestions co-editor Noel Ignatiev offered in the November/December 1994 *Utne Reader* were: Oppose "tracking" in schools, oppose all mechanisms that favor whites in the job market, and "oppose the police and the courts, which define black people as a criminal class."

If someone utters a racial slur, Ignatiev suggests that whites answer with, "Oh, you probably said that because you think I'm white. That's a mistake people often make because I look white."

Or if someone says people on welfare don't want to work, they just want to stay home and have babies, Ignatiev suggests you answer, "Me, too."

That may sound extreme, but every white person who is not too caught up in his or her own sense of righteous victimization knows that white skin still affords certain privileges in our color-coded society. There may be no easily identifiable "white culture," but there doesn't have to be when the "mainstream culture" is so decidedly white-dominated.

In *Two Nations: Black and White, Separate, Hostile, Unequal*, political scientist Andrew Hacker describes asking white students how much compensation they would request if a visitor told them that, because of a mixup at birth, they would have to live the rest of their lives as a black person. Most seemed to feel $50 million, or $1 million for each coming black year, would not be inappropriate. "And this calculation conveys, as well as anything, the value that white people place on their own skins."

Surviving Racism

In this spirit, I think the "survivors" of AIDS, cancer, abuse, and other plagues offer an important lesson to the rest of us, including us sufferers from the vagaries of racism. We, too, could benefit from replacing our victim identity with a sense of survivorship.

Racism cannot complete its dirty, deadly work unless we serve as its accessories, which we do every time we internalize the second-class-and-helpless image others try to project on us. King knew. In *Bearing the Cross*, historian David J. Garrow recounts how King resisted the urgings of Stanley

Levison, a trusted aide, to delete from his writings references to the need for African Americans to help lift themselves out of poverty. Levison was particularly rankled, Garrow tells us, by "the section on Negro self-improvement. . . . The goal should be to activate and organize people toward the main objective rather than appeal for change of character separated from the pursuit of social goals."

King thanked his loyal and devoted counselor, who was seventeen years his elder, but held fast to his more complicated view, a dual strategy that tied a rigid adherence to self-help ("burning the midnight oil") to direct action against the forces of racism. While others denounced self-help as "blaming the victim," King insisted, "We must not let the fact that we are the victims of injustice lull us into abrogating respect for our own lives."

King believed in self-love, but it was tough self-love. If ever he felt vulnerable or insecure about assuming ownership of our internal social disarray in the black community, he didn't show it. Neither should we. Fear of "blaming the victim" or "washing dirty laundry in public," as if our enemies were not already fully aware of the state of our wardrobes, have prevented black Americans from candidly confronting the horrors that plague us—crime, drugs, slums, and illiteracy. As deeply as the black consciousness movement committed us to defining ourselves, we cannot own ourselves until we own up to our responsibilities.

If we don't take ownership of our problems, we leave them for others to take ownership from us and use it against us. A piquant example is offered by the presumption held by some taxi drivers, store clerks, and ordinary passersby on the street that black people, particularly young black males, are automatically suspect. It is simplest to fault white people or the legacy of white racism for such slights. It is more challenging, but, in the long run, more rewarding, for us to declare crime to be the threat to civil rights that we know it to be, since black people are, by far, the majority of the victims of black criminals. Instead of blocking crime-fighting efforts, black Americans should be demanding to be included in them to assure they will be responsive to black community concerns, not exploited at black community expense.

We African Americans too often flatter white racism unnecessarily by exaggerating the power it holds over our lives. Derrick Bell, for example, in his *Faces at the Bottom of the Well*, argues that racism is so strong as to be permanently imbedded in American culture, a cancer he suggests we relentlessly oppose, but without any hope of vanquishing. He may have a point, but it sounds to me as though he has given up the fight before engaging in the battle. It is, in a sense, a tribute to the notion of white supremacy that we imbue white racism with the power to leave us helpless to do more than chip away at it. Why not spend that energy on other problems, internal problems that cry out for our attention and might genuinely help black self-determination?

So it is with the black community's walking wounded, our listless and lumbering *casualties of racism*, the sad, angry, moody, or confused souls who have been spiritually, if not physically, defeated by it. Their cases are sad not because they see racism everywhere. (Racism, after all, *is* everywhere. To feel it is to know it.) Their cases are sad because they have been debilitated by it. Their energy is sapped. Their spirit is shattered. Their optimism is nonexistent. To them, every silver lining is attached to a huge overwhelming cloud. Racism may not explain all their problems, but it's good enough for them. They might as well have "victim" stamped on their foreheads.

Casualties of racism do not look for any other explanations to life's problems when racism will do. Casualties of racism picket and march against every problem. Since that solution worked so well during the civil rights years, they apply it everywhere. They march against unemployment, march against crime, march against drugs, and march against teen pregnancy. When disrespected by a neighborhood grocer who belongs to another race, casualties of racism do not open their own businesses. Instead, they picket the offending grocer, perhaps driving the store out of business, leaving the community a little bit poorer for the sake of false pride. Casualties of racism may not even bother to look for work. They have given up. Why *bother*? they say. The white man won't let you get anywhere anyway. It is a conspiracy, they may say. If so, it is a conspiracy in which the victim serves as a willing accomplice.

The casualty of racism might even tell you that black people were better off before desegregation came along, and, to them, we were. Racism stood boldly in the schoolhouse door in Birmingham or South Boston, in front of television cameras or behind police dogs, firehoses, and cattle prods. Blatant racism made our enemies easier to spot and relieved us of the burden of making choices, for we had fewer choices to make. Freedom freed white Americans from the burden of trying to control black lives even when they could barely control their own. Today's more subtle institutional racism is harder to detect, easier to deny, and more likely to generate nagging questions of doubt in its victims: *Is my condition my own fault or someone else's fault?* It is no slam to the brilliance or courageousness or accomplishments of Martin Luther King to say that his foe was easy compared to today's enemy, an enemy whom so many black people credit perversely with omniscience, omnipresence, and omnipotence, an enemy who lurks as much within our own minds and spirit as on the streets.

Since the 1960s, black Americans have had more choices than ever before, which eased some burdens by adding others. Racism is real, but a diminishing burden compared to the many others emerging in the challenge of rescuing the large portion of black America the civil rights revolution left behind in poverty and powerlessness. They must be helped to discover the power they have to take charge of their own lives. Casualties of racism have no power because they have given up. Survivors of racism understand that political change can only give us the right to create choices for ourselves, which is the right to take on more burdens individually or as communities, not to pass them off on the government or anyone else. Survivors take ownership of their problems, take inventory of their personal strengths and resources, then use the power within themselves to bring about change. Casualties of racism give up. Survivors carry on.

Yet self-help messages remain a hard sell, unless they are conveyed by Nation of Islam minister Louis Farrakhan or someone of his fiery ilk, attached to a message of generous whitey-bashing and, perhaps for added spice, a dash of anti-Semitism. Those who raise a cautionary question as to whether such irrational ravings are good for black folks in the long run risk being shouted down as "sell-outs" or "Uncle Toms" if they are black and "racists" if they are not. Take your pick. It's a popular game, although tiresome and ultimately useless.

But the work of rebuilding race relations is not for black people to do alone.

Americans of all colors are PLWRs—people living with racism. Sometimes we get it. Sometimes it gets us. It is time we recognized it and did something about it. Dreams have fallen out of fashion in our cynical age. But with a new racial vision for the nation's future, we Americans might yet trade in our current national anthem, the "whine," for the 1970s disco hit, "I Will Survive." It's got a good beat. We can dance to it.

5

A Valentine to Black Women

If there hadn't been women we'd still be squatting in a cave eating raw meat, because we made civilization in order to impress our girl friends. And they tolerated it and let us go ahead and play with our toys.

—Orson Welles

I am a feminist, and what that means to me is much the same as the meaning of the fact that I am Black: it means that I must undertake to love myself and to respect myself as though my very life depends upon self-love and self-respect.

—June Jordan, *Moving Towards Home: Political Essays*

There's such purity in a love that is essential to the loving of one's self.

—Me'Shell NdegeOcello

When the battlegrounds of race and gender overlap, the woman of color is caught in the crossfire.

She may find that her simplest pleas abruptly shouted down amid angry countercharges of "Jezebel," "Sapphire," "Aunt Jemima," or "Aunt Thomasina," the female equivalent of an "Uncle Tom." It happened to Anita Hill, Alice Walker, Michelle Wallace, Ntozake Shange, and Desiree Washington, to name a few, simply for challenging the fabled, cherished, yet somehow always elusive "unity" of the race.

Jezebel, ninth century B.C. Phoenician princess, queen of Israel and wife of Ahab, encouraged idolatry and ultimately was killed for her treachery, according to the Old Testament. In black traditions, rooted more firmly in the Old Testament than the New, she lives as the prophesied embodiment of the evil, scheming, seductive, and betraying temptress. Sapphire, the loudmouthed and short-tempered wife of Kingfish on the old "Amos 'n' Andy" TV series, embodied the shrill and evil shrew. Aunt Jemima, star of pancake boxes, represented the safely sexless nanny and nurturer.

Michelle Wallace touched a raw nerve at age twenty-eight when her *Black Macho and the Myth of the Superwoman* attacked sexism among blacks against black women in the mid-1970s. She was particularly angry at the likes of Eldridge Cleaver, for example, who portrayed rape as something resembling a revolutionary act in *Soul on Ice* and, like other black macho men, attacked James Baldwin's homosexuality as somehow un-black. Ntozake Shange ripped the scab open wider with *for colored girls who have considered suicide/when the rainbow is enuf,* which portrayed women trying to rediscover the secrets of joy in one another's company after having been let down and brutalized by black men. Ishmael Reed, whose fascinating novels have had a tough time rising above cult status over the years, was one of the more prominent black voices who lashed out. Reed, most of whose fiction I deeply admired, saw something quite sinister in white society's eagerness to thrust so many black women to best-seller lists while banishing talented black male writers (like, uh-hmm, himself) to the literary underground. He detected a widespread feminist conspiracy that included the editors of *Ms.* magazine, who introduced Wallace's work to a wider audience; Joe Papp, whose theater staged Shange's play; and anybody else who created or perpetrated popular attacks against black men.

Alice Walker's book *The Color Purple* also portrayed black women supporting one another through the trials and tribulations of black male brutality. Steven Spielberg's Oscar-nominated movie brought Walker's work, along with the black community's gender war, to mainstream attention.

Most prominent black male voices either criticized Walker and Spielberg at the time or were ominously silent. As a new and still-local Chicago newspaper columnist, I took note of *The Burning Bed*, a wildly popular made-for-TV movie starring Farrah Fawcett in the true story of an abused wife who killed her husband. I wrote that I thought "*The Color Purple* was no more an attack on black men than *The Burning Bed* was an attack on white men."

For that sage tidbit of wisdom, I was quoted in a *New York Times* story about the controversy. The *Times* story was read by producers of the "Today" show, who invited me to debate the subject with Ishmael Reed on the morning before Oscar night. I imagined myself making a career out of defending Alice Walker. Reed certainly seemed to be making a cottage industry out of attacking her. He had just published *Reckless Eyeballing*, a thinly veiled attack on Walker, his intellectual target for more than a dozen years, right along with *Ms.* magazine and the rest of what he saw as a conspiratorial white feminist movement.

I would be the first to admit, without much pride, that my performance could have been better. Yet I received grateful telephone calls from black women as far away as the San Francisco Bay area, where Reed and Walker live.

Closer to home, my masculinist friend Asa Baber, *Playboy* columnist and resident men's rights activist, was not pleased. "The male equivalent of Uncle Tomming," he sniffed. Balance, like beauty, is in the eye of the beholder.

Small wonder, then, that I have seen black women, while speaking at rallies for the race, digress a moment to reassure cheering throngs that "I'm black first, a woman second," as if there was only one way to be black, one way to be a woman, and dues cannot be paid to one without taking away from the other.

That's the image we black folks like to carry around in our heads. You can hear its echoes on the community "drum"—black talk radio, barbershops, beauty parlors, dinner parties, and other black gathering spots—in grass-roots black America. The black woman is silenced by community standards the way women often have been silenced by being placed on a pedestal too narrow to allow them much movement, a pedestal that says women don't *need* equality with men, for that would only be a demotion.

It is chic in black conversations to view feminism as a white women's movement, inappropriate for the black community, where women seldom have had the luxury of the male-dependent roles that educated white women have been trying to escape. Maya Angelou once said, "No black American man at any time in our history in the United States has been able to feel that he didn't need that black woman right against him, shoulder to shoulder—in that cotton field, on the auction block, in the ghetto, wherever."*

So goes the popular romantic image. Any evidence to the contrary—rape, abuse, divorce, abandonment—or any plea for power or protection is shouted down by the resounding defense: Women don't need equality.

Or, putting a black spin on it, black women don't need the same type of equality the middle-class white women who led the feminist movement did.

An odd understanding of this peculiar relationship emerges from unexpected sources. Pam Grier, star of low-

---

*A Conversation with Maya Angelou," interview, November 21, 1973. Published in Jeffrey M. Elliot, ed. *Conversations with Maya Angelou* (Jackson: University Press of Mississippi, 1989).

budget, big-breasted black exploitation movies in the early 1970s, understood. In an interview with *New York* magazine at the time, she described a salient truth about male respect: Big boobs remind men of "mama," and there never was a black man born who wasn't afraid of his mama.

The dictionary defines "feminist" as "one who believes in the social, political, and economic equality of the sexes." But, under bombardment from some who are malicious and others who simply are fearful of change, it has come more widely to mean something much more narrow, an anti-family, anti-feminine, anti-heterosexual bunch of bib-overall-and-workboot-wearing man haters. The most extreme voices in the movement have been generalized to stereotype the whole, a smear no more honest than the casting of all Republicans as neo-Nazis.

Many blacks viewed the emerging, mostly white, mostly middle-class feminist movement warily, partly because it arose from the world of white Americans, our traditional oppressors, and partly because some of its most prominent voices, like Susan Brownmiller, author of the landmark *Against Our Will* anti-rape study, targeted black men for particularly pointed condemnation. Because any attack from outside the community triggers a reflexive circling of the wagons around the target, black women seeking a clear, unambiguous voice for their gender grievances declared themselves to be "womanist," believers in women's self-determination but with a special consideration of race and class. If feminist tradition sought to make women more capable of controlling their own destiny, "womanist tradition assumes, because of our experiences during slavery, that black women already are capable," said Alice Walker.

Critics responded with faint praise, which is not dissimilar to condemnation. Black women already have more power than men, went the Africanized spin on an ancient argument. A woman who plays her cards right, it was said, could squeeze whatever she wanted out of the patriarchy. And isn't playing your cards right and squeezing benefits out of the system precisely what men have had to do all along? What, then, is equality all about? I thought of women as having control, more control than they actually had.

"Nature has given women so much power that the law has very wisely given them little," Samuel Johnson once said, revealing a truth we men closely guard: the relationship between men and women is, at bottom, a power relationship. We love each other and fear each other's power. Black women wanted a movement set apart from white feminists, partly because so many black women do not yet trust white women, partly because black women suspect white women do not quite trust black women, either.

Like Pam Grier, Camille Paglia also understands. She pooh-poohs the notion that women are in any way inferior or even equal. "Woman is the dominant sex," she once said. "Men have to do all sorts of stuff to prove that they are worthy of woman's attention." Paglia loves to irritate the women's movement, which makes her delightfully amusing to men. She's one of the boys, an honorary equal in our eyes. "Woman of the year," John McLaughlin called her during one year-end episode of "The McLaughlin Group" in the early 1990s. Unlike the women who strike fear into male hearts, she is neither a tease, an easy piece, nor a stuck-up bitch. She shares our fear of most women.

Men suspect and thus fear the superiority of women from an early age. It is a lurking fear. We do not care for it. We will act to ease it mostly by asserting the trappings of superiority by any means necessary. We will show off our smartness by arguing trivial points with long-winded, astonishingly unembarrassed pomposity. We will overwhelm all opposition with the sheer force of our machismo. And, if the woman gets up in our face, as they say in the 'hood, we gonna *lay the smack down*.

So much for "shoulder to shoulder." Angelou's statement describes the image of ourselves that we ambivalently carry around in our heads, and we often silence anyone, particularly a woman, who question its veracity. Yet many African Americans yearned for a nuanced, nonconfrontational feminism that, unlike the mainstream variety, could bring black men and women closer to one another and secure for black women the very home-centered roles against which white women appeared to be rebelling.

Instead of struggling to get out of traditional home roles and into the workplace, black women dreamed, more often than not, of escaping the workplace and enjoying the luxury of spending more time at home. Many who were employed raising the children of others, for example, yearned to stay home and raise their own. For this, many had found their dreams slipping into a nightmare of deprivation and stigmatization as political whipping girls, "welfare queens" and "teen moms."

While the feminists rebelled against the safe, secure, exquisitely dull "Ozzie and Harriet" life, countless poor black women lusted after that brass ring, simply because it had been denied them for so long.

"Brothers" and the women who would protect them always have the ravages of racism, rightly or wrongly, as a universal solvent for all stains on any black man's permanent record. When Anita Hill charged Supreme Court nominee Clarence Thomas with sexual harassment, she was branded a Jezebel, and the wagons quickly circled around Thomas, with more than half of blacks in polls saying suddenly that they supported him, even though only a fraction of them agreed with his stated conservative views. The nationally televised sight of yet another "brother in trouble" triggered the familiar reflex. The wagons were circled. Hill was roundly condemned on black talk radio by militant macho brothers and their shoulder-to-shoulder sisters who questioned why Hill would hound Thomas on national television, *embarrassing the race* for some routine "trash talking" a decade earlier. Ishmael Reed, in a *Washington Post* op-ed essay, lambasted the white feminist conspiracy for putting Hill up to it.

Not since the Marion Barry cocaine trials, when vendors sold "The Bitch Set Me Up" T-shirts outside the courthouse, had Washington been in such a tizzy about uppity black womenfolk. The nationally televised FBI sting, in which Barry clearly appeared to be seeking something other than cocaine from Rasheeda Moore, the FBI's lure, confirmed for all to see the very image of the nightmare Jezebel. The image would spill over to stain Desiree Washington, Mike Tyson's date-rape victim. Even the murdered Nicole Brown Simpson would not be immune from whispered implications that she must have *asked for it* in some way that would make her life unworthy of the conviction, guilty or not, of a "good brother" like O. J. Simpson.

Why? The black womanist cause reflects a reluctance to be as hard on black men as feminists might like, partly in pursuit of racial solidarity, partly out of a maternal sense that the black man, in the generic sense, has suffered enough, and if the black woman does not serve as his loyal friend, no one else will.

The unity imperative emerged out of a need to remedy the damage left by American slavery and its legacy of turning African Americans against allies, like poor and indentured whites and Native Americans. As legal scholar A. Leon Higginbotham, Jr., judge of the Third Circuit of the U.S. Court of Appeals, writes in *In the Matter of Color: Race and the American Legal Process; The Colonial Period* (1978), colonial justice was dispensed along a racial and gender hierarchy. In statutory and case law, black men were punished more severely for the same offense than black women, who were punished more severely than white women, who were punished more severely than white men. The defiant resiliency of black men against racial humiliation is admired to the point of romanticism. "There is an incredible amount of magic and feistiness in black men that nobody has been able to wipe out," writes Toni Morrison. "But everybody has tried."

Washington Post columnist Donna Britt wrote a valentine to the black man, for which she received many thanks, some of it with flowers, some of it with tears. It felt so good for many of us to hear some kind words in the media for the black men who are not in jail, not in gangs, not strung out on drugs, and not abandoning their families.

I have nothing against women who are not black. Some of my best women friends are not black. They are sisters with black women in more ways than they are not. Inside every woman, there is a Billie Holiday, a Bessie Smith, or an Aretha Franklin screaming to get out.

But the black woman is caught in a special double bind, and out of it she derives a double awareness. Her perceptions are not clouded by the illusion of equality. She is keenly aware of her suppression, not only by the white patriarchy, but also by the black community. She is more likely than her white sister to work longer hours for shorter pay, to come home to face more work, and to do it without the aid of a man. She is less likely to get married, thanks to what black University of Chicago sociologist William Julius Wilson calls the "shortage of marriageable black men" because of unemployment, prison, drugs, bad health, and homicide. The fewer the marriageable men, the fewer the marketable women.

She is beautiful, but her beauty is not sought as eagerly as that of white women. Despite our progress, the Image Award given by the Hollywood chapter of the National Association for the Advancement of Colored People for black women in movie roles has gone unawarded in several recent years, simply because there were too few black women in leading roles to have a contest in that category.

I would like to send a valentine to the black woman. I would like to honor those who have not been Jezebel or Sapphire or Aunt Jemima. They have been Toni Morrison, Anita Hill, Tina Turner, Sojourner Truth, Ida B. Wells, Queen Latifah, Jennifer Beals, Grace Jones, Marita Golden, Dorothy Gilliam, Angela Davis, Alice Walker, Carol Simpson, Chaka Khan, Charlayne Hunter Gault, June Jordan, Sister Souljah, Carol Moseley-Braun, Diana Ross, Diahann Carroll, Lena Horne, Lani Guinier, Bessie Smith, Mary McCloud Bethune, Me'Shell NdegeOcello, Jackie Joyner-Kersee, and every other African-American woman.

They have been black women trying to discover and love their inner selves without hiding from their blackness, but rather using it as a springboard to the mainstream that represents a larger world.

Some people win independence. Others have it thrust upon them. "Some of us are becoming the men we wanted to marry," Gloria Steinem once said. Many black women are becoming, out of necessity, just that.

We need an honest dialogue within our community. We need to discuss what good it does us to gain a thin-skinned semblance of unity that, despite the naysayings of universalistic critics, is not a sign that we love ourselves too much but that we love ourselves too little.

To be black and feminist or womanist does not mean we must subdivide ourselves along gender lines, black man against black woman. It means we must stage a revolution within the revolution. We need to listen to black women whose voices have been silenced or ignored by the imperatives of *nigresence*, becoming black, at the price of losing our humanity. Breaking the silencing of black women is not a source of weakness for the black community. It is essential to our strength.

6

Resistance Motifs

"Bad Niggaz" vs. "Actin' White"

The adolescent . . . however, vacillates between infancy and youth, halting for a moment before the infinite richness of the world. He is astonished at the fact of his being, and this astonishment leads to reflection: as he leans over the river of his consciousness, he asks himself if the face that appears there, disfigured by the water, is his own.

—Octavio Paz, *The Labyrinth of Solitude*

It might have been just another shooting of a would-be mugger by his intended victim, who happened to be an undercover police officer. But this young mugger in the summer of 1985 in the Morningside Heights section of Manhattan turned out to be Edmund Perry, who ten days earlier had graduated from Philips Exeter, one of America's most prestigious prep schools, with a scholarship to Stanford in the fall.

Thus opened one of the great urban mysteries of the 1980s. Perry, a product of the Harlem ghetto, had been scouted by a program that has given scholarships at eastern prep schools to low-income black youths who show high potential. Most have been heartwarming success stories. Why did this one fail? Most important: What did his fate say about the forces that pull so many others back into the maelstrom of ghetto pathologies? What are the cultural factors that cause so many other black youths, particularly young black males, to shun the opportunities that have opened up to blacks since the

1960s and put on the brakes instead? If racism, even the legacy of slavery, plays a part, what is the part, when young black males kill more young black males every year than the Ku Klux Klan did over several decades?

I think an important clue is to be found in their own adolescent values, particularly the quest to be "cool," a mission that occupies ultimate importance in the way most young black males define manhood. In literal translation from black slang, "cool" means "excellent" or "first rate." One speaks of a "cool pair of sneakers" or of hearing "cool jams" at a "cool party." It can also mean self-control, as in "I was cool" in the face of a stressful situation. But on a deeper level, "cool" also describes a pattern of social acceptability and a psychological pose that serves as a coping mechanism for social and psychological survival. In tandem with the daunting, reflexive rejection the larger society imposes on young, poor black males, it describes the pull of the ghetto, a morally debilitating subculture of self-defeating and irresponsible attitudes and behaviors.

Two years after Perry died, a study by two anthropologists, Signithia Fordham of the University of the District of Columbia and John U. Ogbu of the University of California, focused national attention on a major damaging factor in this quest for cool: negative peer pressure that derided academic success as "acting white."

Although the persecution of nerds is hardly a new development in the cultural life of teenagers, it has taken on a particularly tragic manifestation among poor urban blacks in the post–civil rights era. In a study of an unidentified 99 percent black District of Columbia high school, Fordham spent a year interviewing thirty-three students. She found otherwise promising black youths driven to unusual extremes to avoid visible signs of academic success.

A football player identified as "Sidney" had fallen from his earlier A's and B's to mediocre scores on standardized tests to dispel fears of being called "Mr. Advanced Placement," he told Fordham.

"Shelvy," once an honor roll student, also had experienced falling grades to avoid being called a "Brainiac." Most other "Brainiacs" will "sit back and they know the answer and they won't answer it," she told Fordham, "'cause see, first thing everybody say, 'Well, they're trying to show off.'"

More recently, a black seventeen-year-old at affluent suburban Bethesda–Chevy Chase High School was quoted in the *Washington Post* as saying he turned down offers of a place in an honors math class despite his high ability because he did not want to be the only black student in the class. "It would have been hard to relate [to white students]. I wouldn't have been able to relax. . . . I would have been alone and isolated. [But] by the end of the year, I thought geometry was pretty easy. I wish I had taken the honors math."

Cedric, another stunning example of a black District of Columbia teen with bright ambitions despite his bleak background, came to the attention of the *Wall Street Journal* and ABC's "Nightline" in 1994. His mother was a clerical worker. His father was in the penitentiary. By the early 1990s, his neighborhood near Frank W. Ballou High School had become one of the District of Columbia's war zones. In one school year, a student was shot dead by a classmate, another boy was attacked with an ax, a girl was badly wounded in a knife fight—with another girl—and the body of an unidentified man was discovered early one morning in the school dumpster.

Cedric would check in at the school's computer lab every morning, usually before 7:30 A.M., and stay sometimes until dusk, escaping into the electronic community of cyberspace. He was one of only eighty students who can boast an average of B or better at the school, where the total enrollment is 1,350. Yet he was not much honored among his peers, and it was having an effect. Cedric skipped two assemblies at which he was to receive academic honors. He was not alone. Some honorees showed up but refused to stand up until teachers pushed them to the stage. The principal admitted that he had tried to keep the assembly's purpose a secret, because so many honored students had been ridiculed by their peers as "goody" or "nerd," or, worst of all, it seemed, as "trying to act white."

"White" has long meant uncool in the language of black youths. In my youth, "actin' white" was a comparatively innocent critique for anyone who didn't walk, talk, dance, or shoot baskets with sufficient style, grace, or grandiosity. "He shoots like a white boy," we might say on the basketball court of anyone who preferred flat-footed long shots to the more daring running, weaving, and dribbling up close to the basket for a magnificent leaping jump shot. But to today's hip-hop generation, "white" has come to mean something far more sinister: the "enemy."

One friend of Cedric's told the *Journal* reporter that Cedric's attempts to make it in a white man's world are seen as "a type of disrespect to us."

Disrespect? Yes, it is. Ambition shows no respect to those who choose to stay behind. By the 1990s, young black males had become the most feared creatures on America's urban scene. Those who have few other achievements to show in their lives, who have grown up amid poverty and violence and the fear—or reality—of homelessness at any moment, have taken the fear they invoke in the eyes of the straight world—the "white" world—as a badge of honor, a cloak that says, *Yes, at least I am better at something than you are!*

Yet the contradiction endures, most vigorously in the same young minds in which one also finds the deepest despair. Their pride wounded by their abandonment, first by whites, then by upwardly mobile blacks who have followed whites to the gleaming corporate buildings downtown and out to brighter suburbs, they lash back by exalting the world to which they have been confined. They fight back in a cultural war by other means, beginning with the way they talk. Language is an expression of culture. For many in the post-1960s generations of black youths, their self-esteem bombarded from all sides, even from other better-off blacks, language is a way to throw down a marker. It is a way to fight back. It becomes ethnic race war by other means.

"Language is one area in which an ancient cultural warfare between whites and blacks is carried on," said Fordham, who moved to Rutgers University, in a telephone interview.

She called it part of a "resistance motif" that dates to the days of slavery. "The history of black people in America is laced, bludgeoned with a resistance motif," she told me. "It follows a belief that using the master's tools will forever enslave us to the master. One way for us to maintain *cultural space* is to speak our own version of the language. I think we work very hard at it, often unconsciously, even when we otherwise are immersed in standard mainstream English."

Young people carve out cultural space for themselves in many ways, but most pointedly in their language. For black youths, this holding on to street culture in the face of new opportunities in the larger world is not "oppositional," as sociologists call it, it is conservatorial, a tendency to gravitate toward the familiar for comfort. It is a way of presenting and conserving a distinct "black self." Immigrants longing for home often slip into their mother tongue or dialect around close friends to enhance a feeling of kinship and comfort, undiluted by the dominant culture.

The more white people claim a cultural prerogative for standard English, Fordham says, the more some blacks will pull back deliberately into a linguistic code of their own, in accordance with the code of the streets, not unlike the way the Spanish dictator Francisco Franco's attempted repression of the Basque language and culture actually sparked their resurgence.

It being the fervent obligation of every generation to outrage its elders, this generation is doing its part. For those of us who came of age steeped in the pride-enhancing, consciousness-raising "black is beautiful" days of the 1960s, there is painful, heartbreaking irony in the inverted standard that equates success with "white," for what does that leave "black" to mean but failure? Instead of celebrating blackness, they are debasing it.

Black parents traditionally have used the folk image of "crabs in a basket" or "lobsters in a bucket" to warn their children against the hazards of negative peer influences. When gathering crabs in a basket, it is said, you never have to trouble yourself with putting a lid on. If any of the crabs tries to crawl out of the basket, the others will reach up and pull it back in.

So it is with the packs in which young people run. Underachievement loves company and loathes competition. Only in a culture in which the causes of underachievement can so easily and often be blamed on the legacy of racism, as they can in the formation and perpetuation of urban ghettos, can underachievers find not only company but a cult following. Today's noble savage is the "ghetto gangsta."

"Ghettocentricity" is the pointedly appropriate term coined by pop culture critic Nelson George. "If Professor

Molefi Asante's philosophy of Afrocentricity means placing Africa at the center of one's thinking, then ghettocentricity means making the values and lifestyle of America's poverty-stricken urban homelands central to one's being," George wrote in *Buppies, B-Boys, BAPS & Bohos: Notes of Post-Soul Black Culture* (1992).

The ghetto-centered world view dictates ghetto style in manners, dress, language, and values. It lauds ghetto culture as more "authentic," more "real" than the corrupt, oppressive mainstream with its fawning, imitative "Uncle Toms" and "Oreos"— "black on the outside but white on the inside."

Its most immediate victims may be those who are closest to it, the black youths of the lower middle class, where, three decades after the civil rights revolution, as Bart Landry documents in *The New Black Middle Class* (1987), blacks are more prevalent than they are in the upper middle class.

Powerful examples of how the quest for cool "authenticity" among middle-class black youths can become a quest for criminality are offered by three popular black biographies of the early 1990s: *Makes Me Wanna Holler*, by Nathan McCall; *Laughing in the Dark: From Colored Girl to Woman Color—A Journey from Prison to Power*, by Patrice Gaines; and *Monster: The Autobiography of an L.A. Gang Member*, by Sanyika Shakur, AKA "Monster" Cody Scott.

Each book shares in common with the others a powerful first-person account of a kid from a relatively comfortable, middle-class background who shucked it all as less "real" than the lure of the streets, a lure made all the more attractive by anger at white racism.

Gaines describes her rebellion against her parents' values and their disapproval of her boyfriend Ben, a high school dropout who would father her child and turn her on to heroin. Of her parents, Gaines writes: "Their lives were dedicated to uplifting the race by uplifting their own family, and they did not believe Ben could raise one branch of our family tree. But I didn't consider any of this; any hint of elitism turned my stomach."

McCall also rejects the middle-class life after his stepfather, a retired military man, takes a landscaping job in a white suburban neighborhood. "I didn't like the way he humbled himself and smiled when white folks were around," McCall writes. "[He] looked too much like pictures of downtrodden sharecroppers and field slaves I'd seen in books."

Monster, a leader in the Crips, wrote from jail, where he is serving a lengthy sentence for some of the crimes that earned him his nickname. His middle-class upbringing was exposed later by journalists like Mark Horowitz in the December 1993 *Atlantic Monthly*. Neither his godparents, singer Della Reese and musician Ray Charles, nor much of the rest of his family appear in his book. Apparently they conflicted with his need to sound cool and "authentic."

On closer examination, the reader finds that the pernicious impact of white racism in the lives of these writers was far less damaging than their sense of vulnerability to it. Its actual injury was quite effectively offset by the sense of victimization it offered them as a rationale for their mindless drifts into the criminal underworld.

Yet each book sold well in hardbound and paperback, particularly to prisons. This says something about the attractiveness of tales about black pathologies—"an appetite for the pulp of the Negro," as critic Stanley Crouch put it. But it may say even more about the demand African Americans have for what Howard University's E. Ethelbert Miller calls "guides for the race," success stories that can offer badly needed clues to how such pathologies can be overcome, road maps for how young lives that have gone wrong can be set straight.

The most popular example since the 1960s has been *The Autobiography of Malcolm X* (1965), the ultimate paradigm for a black man's rise from young, cool ghetto gangster to a race leader whose relentless individual enlightenment transcended the confines of group identity.

Few other tales can match its spellbinding drama, but a cottage industry in black middle-class confessionals has emerged around the struggle felt by middle-class blacks caught between fear of rejection by whites and the tug of black "authenticity" they don't want to leave behind.

One example, Jill Nelson's *Volunteer Slavery* (1993), became a surprise best-seller for Path Press, a small, black-owned Chicago house, after its rejection by major New York City publishers. Black book buyers made the book a success, I believe, because her often caustic account of black middle-class angst in the white corporate world, while less dramatic than the pathology tales, more closely matched the angst-ridden conflicts of upwardly mobile blacks in the decades since the 1960s.

For example, after landing a prestigious reporting job at the *Washington Post Magazine*, only to see a major protest by prominent local blacks against the magazine's coverage, she laments, "Suddenly I cannot remember if I am Clair Huxtable, Harriet Tubman, or someone else entirely. I have no idea of who I am or where I fit. Am I a freed black who has made it or a slave struggling to free herself and her people?"

Although the roots of "cool" as a definition of black manhood or womanhood often are traced to the oppositional attitudes engendered by slavery, they may go all the way back to Africa. In *The Cool Pose: The Dilemmas of Black Manhood in America* (1992), Richard Majors and Janet Mancini Billson trace it back as far as 3000 B.C. For example, they translate the title *Ewuare*, awarded at the crowning of Nigerian kings in the fifteenth century, to mean literally "It is cool." In the same century, they found a Yoruba leader who took a name that means "Cool and Peaceful as the [native herb] Osun." To be cool under pressure, they conclude, is "akin to exuding a royal demeanor."

Most blacks have tended to define manhood the same way whites do in terms of parenting, providing, protecting, and procreating, say Majors and Billson, but lack of access to the same means to fulfill their best dreams of success cause many to become angry, frustrated, alienated, suspicious, and rebellious against the dominant culture that has humiliated them. From this grows an acute sensitivity to possible hurt in mixed racial situations.

In slavery we find ample evidence of Fordham's "resistance motif." Outright slave rebellions like those of Nat Turner or François Dominique Toussaint L'Ouverture were notably rare, largely because the slaves in the United States were vastly outgunned and outnumbered. But W.E.B. Du Bois describes how quiet rebellions were staged daily in the form of deliberate work slowdowns, theft, and the glorification of the "bad nigger" as a form of small-scale revolutionary. Black historian Orlando Patterson has written of the "slave underclass" that formed around values that made them nearly worthless as cheap labor. The "bad nigger" endured through the folk hero Stagolee, Richard Wright's Bigger Thomas in *Native Son*, and the young street-hustling Malcolm X. Today's glorification of gangsta rap stars like Ice T, Snoop Doggy Dogg, and NWA (Niggaz With Attitude) may have been born on the plantation.

Regardless of its roots, *gangsta worship* is infectious in ways that cross racial and economic lines. White consumers buy two-thirds of rap, marketing experts say, to get the narrow peephole it provides into a counterculture that thrives in neighborhoods no longer safe for white Saturday night tourists.

And the white quest for black authenticity doesn't stop at the record shops. For example, in rural, white upstate Indiana—Dan Quayle and Larry Bird country—a cute clique of white teen girls touched off a monochromatic "race war" at their high school in the early 1990s and made national headlines simply by dressing "black" or, at least, what they thought was black—dark lipstick, baggy pants, big lumber-jack shoes, hair tied severely in gang-color bandannas, big denim coats—the full hip-hop look.

"Wiggers," their angry classmates called them derisively, and, as a confirmation of the desperately sought authenticity that comes with bona fide evidence of oppression, the slur caught on as their badge of honor, reemerging in the jargon and poses of affluent teens in suburban Potomac, Maryland, where, according to a *Washington Post* profile at the time, it was considered cool to walk the walk and talk the talk of a black ghetto that is no closer than the "MTV Raps" programs on local cable television screens.

So there was a new breed of adventurers, urban adven-turers who drifted out at night looking for action with a black man's code to fit their facts. The hipster had absorbed the existential synapses of the Negro, and for practical purposes could be considered a white Negro.

Norman Mailer wrote that in a famous essay called "The White Negro" in the 1950s. Mailer was describing "beat-niks," new existential hipster intellectuals who lived daily beneath the looming mushroom clouds of the nuclear age.

Mailer described how the ravenous desire of this existential hero to "feel" himself—to "know one's desires, one's rages, one's anguish"—caught the glare of the "knifelike" entrance of jazz into the "partially totalitarian" white-bread world of white American culture. The white Negro then followed it backward, in deep admiration and envy, to choose an underclass street style as close to the *authenticity* of the Negro hipster, for whom no experience is casual, for he has lived with danger, ostracism, and oppression that is very real, palpable, and permanent. "The cameos of security for the average white: mother and the home, job and the family, are not even a mockery to millions of Negroes, they are impossible," Mailer wrote. "The Negro has the simplest of alternatives: live a life of constant humility or ever-threatening danger." Mailer's black Negro was a righteously sensuous, rebellious, and spontaneous creature who "stayed alive and [began] to grow by following the need of his body where he could."

And the 1950s hipster begat the 1960s hippie—who enlivened beatnik gloom with the psychedelic surfer's *joie de vivre*—and the hippie begat the inner self-explorers of the "Me Decade," a decade that also begat the "punks," the "new wave" born in Britain's racially integrated labor class, which begat the thrift-shop style of Seattle gloomy grunge rockers half-stepping alongside the authentically in-yo'-face criminal pose of the *fin-de-siecle* "wiggers," deliberately flouting the high caste/low caste boundaries of traditional racial and ethnic identity to discover a truer, more authentic self.

This is the dawning of the age of the *culture shopper*—the white kid in dreadlocks, the black kid in the Izod golf shirt—the identity cruiser who rejects the particularistic notion that race should set the standard for one's life, that pigment is destiny.

But for blacks there is, as always, a catch. The white Negroes can always step back, when the spirit moves them, into the shelter of their pigmentation when the hammer of racial caste inevitably comes down, while the black ghetto-centrics often are left behind, quite stuck with their indelible condition, if it is the only life they know.

If some "cool" whites are striving to emulate a rather narrow ghetto-hip definition of "blackness," the ghettocentric blacks at all economic levels are striving after the same crabbed view.

This quest for authenticity was well expressed by Lisa, a black seventeen-year-old senior at once-black, now-multiethnic Annandale High School, in suburban Fairfax, Virginia. Disapproving of the only two black males nominated for homecoming king, while no black females made the final running for queen, she said to a *Washington Post* reporter, "They are part of the preppy crowd. We want a 100 percent black person."

At the other end of the socioeconomic scale, the worst insult you can give a gangsta rapper is to accuse him or her of being a "studio gangsta," a middle-class *poseur* whose ghetto style was purchased at Banana Republic. The criminal arrests of Snoop Doggy Dogg, Tupac Shakur, and the like serve as authenticators, by this standard, that despite their wealth and fame, they are true, righteous outlaws, role models for modern rebellion against "the man."

But the very values that protected rebellious slaves in a slave underclass are exposing some of their descendants today to the losing end of a widening gap between rich and poor, haves and have-nots, educated and undereducated in a post-industrial information age.

Ghettocentricity takes its most tragic turn in the age of crack, AIDS, drive-by shootings, and post-industrial downsizing when it tugs at the coattails of kids who have the most tenuous grasp on the upward side of the success mountain.

Much has eroded in the inner city since the 1960s. Buildings have fallen, factories have closed, entire blocks have been leveled. But the worst erosion has occurred to dreams, hopes, and aspirations. Poor black kids used to dream of jobs; marriages; homes with green lawns, two cars, and a washing machine. Today's poor kids plan their own funerals. To many of them age twelve is not a time to *act* grown. Age twelve *is* grown. And age twenty? Well, might as well not even talk about that. Even tomorrow is not promised to you, so you might as well not bother to plan on it.

Today's ghetto child looks at the struggles and sacrifices of past generations, knows it has helped some black folks to get ahead, but sees *no payback*. His life remains miserable. He may scoff at those of us who have "made it," left the 'hood behind, for rejecting our roots or trying so hard to join the world of white people who still refuse to give us proper respect, despite our economic achievements. At least on the street he can get respect. He has not lost faith in the system. He has no faith to lose.

Black community life, like that of the larger society, is best understood as operating between two opposing subsocieties: the street and the "straight," the hoodlums and the saints, the no-account layabouts and the hardworking family men, the hustlers and the deacons, the whores and the choir ladies. One is constructed by the values of "decent," hardworking church folks, the other built on the street. In each, the basic goal is the same: respect.

Respect, a need as fundamental as the need to be loved or to belong to something larger than one's self, is taken for granted by those who receive it automatically from a nurturing family and community and is highly prized even in its simplest forms by those who have only immediate goals and no perceived long-range potential. On today's ghetto streets, respect is "juice," for it energizes. It makes things move. It lubricates. It helps oddballs fit in. The quest for respect explains why, in a commercially driven society, a ghetto child will kill another over a jacket or a pair of fancy gym shoes. As University of Pennsylvania's Elijah Anderson, author of *Streetwise* and *The Code of the Streets*, has written, those who already have respect for themselves see a jacket as just a jacket. But those who feel short of respect might see that jacket as a way to reinvent themselves to gain the respect they crave or, at least, the trappings of respect, which, for those who have little else, is close enough.

On the flip side, getting "dissed"—disrespected—is a sin punishable by death, according to the rules of the street. If the individual is "tried" by someone trying to "get up in his face," a gun can equal instant "juice." The possibility of prison is an offer of higher education, a place to "toughen up," get more street juice. The death penalty? No big threat among people who do not feel promised a long life or a natural death anyway. Revered in today's street life is the "O.G."—original gangster, a term created in the culture of southern California Crips and Bloods, a culture that produced the multimillion-dollar folk heroes of gangsta rap: Ice T, Ice Cube, Snoop Doggy Dogg, Dr. Dre, and Warren G, among others.

Anderson calls today's black "street" culture, with all its rap, its violence, and its prison-yard wardrobe similarities, an "oppositional culture" endemic to black society—a "street" culture, as opposed to the "decent" culture of solid, upstanding, hardworking, churchgoing families like the one into which I was born, poor but proud. The straight respect themselves. Those who lack self-respect may seek it in the streets, a powerful lure for the disrespected. Those who respect themselves can take a joke. Respect flows out of our suffering. We take pride in our survivorship against the odds. We take pride in our heroes.

When the doors to economic opportunities opened up in the late 1960s, those who were prepared stepped inside and moved away from the old neighborhoods that nurtured us. Those who were left behind, the group social critics came to call the underclass, hardened our old cultural hierarchy into a pyramid of power that exerts an attraction with terrible force for the young and impressionable hearts and minds who dwell at its base, looking upward and making life-changing choices in a tug-of-war with the bigger and, for many, more forbidding power pyramid of the white-dominated social mainstream.

With fewer middle-class people or middle-class values around, "street" values gain the upper hand over the "straight" among those who were left behind. More unemployed or unemployable men father children out of wedlock and leave the mothers to go on welfare. More teenage girls get pregnant, simply because they have been offered fewer reasons to avoid pregnancy. Fewer children get the time and attention they need. Social service agencies, their tax and contributions base shrinking, are overloaded. More boys and girls join gangs to find love and a sense of affiliation. More deal or use drugs. More commit violent crimes. Family and community structures break down. As life loses value, more lives are lost. A spiral of pathologies sucks everyone down into a maelstrom of sinking hopes. It is most convenient to blame it on racism, but as National Urban League president Hugh Price has pointed out, if racism were to dry up and disappear overnight, it would leave most of them still in poverty, ill-prepared to take advantage of the new opportunities.

Through the ghettocentric view, then, we begin to understand the secret of Nation of Islam minister Louis Farrakhan's success at filling large halls with blacks of all classes. The Nation, in its various incarnations since the 1930s, has always been more effective than any conventional civil rights groups at reaching and converting those who were the poorest, most criminal, and most disconnected from the values of the dominant culture. Their secret: They wrap middle-class values (hard work, thriftiness, enterprise, religious worship, strong family attachments) in the trappings of the *racial outlaw*, the ghettocentric fiercely opposed to and even superior to the dominant white Christian society and power structures.

In short, by taking the ghettocentric view, instead of rejecting it, Farrakhan makes the uncool message cool.

What is to be done? The ghettocentric view turns the 1960s consciousness-raising slogan "black is beautiful" on its head. It narrows and debases the blackness it purports to glorify. After all, it has been noted, if black kids are looking for authentically "black" studies, they should be whizzes at trigonometry, for it began in Africa, with the ancient Egyptians. They should eagerly soak up not only *The Autobiography of Malcolm X* and Ralph Ellison's *Invisible Man* but also *The Three Musketeers* and *The Count of Monte Cristo*, for their author, Frenchman Alexandre Dumas, also was black.

Besides, Frederick Douglass did not let Edmund Burke's skin pigmentation keep him away from Burke's eloquent denunciations of slavery and defense of human rights. Ralph Ellison did not let the complexions of T. S. Eliot, Ezra Pound, Gertrude Stein, Mark Twain, or Ernest Hemingway turn him away from their offerings of "release from whatever 'segre-

gated' idea I might have had of my human possibilities." Nor
did Thurgood Marshall let the slaveholding of the
Constitution's framers prevent him from studying the laws
they laid down, word for word, nuance for nuance, in order
to fling them back at an all-white Supreme Court and win a
war of words that ended a century of legal racial segregation.

There is no reason that the Nation of Islam should have a
monopoly on the constructive values wrapped in the resistance motif. First, we in the more fortunate class must rebuild
bridges lost by the social changes that have ripped the black
community apart since the 1960s.

It is nearly impossible for those of us who work diligently
from paycheck to paycheck to comprehend what the world
looks like to a kid who has never worked, who has grown up
in households where work is not revered, and who lives in a
community where most work takes place in the underground
economy's gray areas or worse.

Today's ghetto child lives a largely "public" life—public
aid, public schools, public housing, and public health services. "The only free enterprise most of them witness is the
drug dealer on the corner," laments Robert C. Woodson,
director of the Center for Neighborhood Enterprise. "These
kids are victims of the poverty Pentagon."

Woodson, a leader in the black conservative movement,
helps organize public housing residents, among others, to
rebuild community support and mentoring for poor black
youths, implementing the West African proverb, "It takes a
whole village to raise a child."

"If you want a kid to care about his health," I once heard a
health professional say, "don't just give him a condom. Give
him a future." The same can be said about getting young
people to care about their mental and intellectual health.
White people can help. But black people are best equipped to

teach black children the true richness, depth, and breadth of the black experience and the guidance it can provide them toward a rewarding life.

One such organization, Concerned Black Men in Washington, D.C., does just that. To "reclaim" black junior high school–aged boys, they organize baseball and basketball games, hold career day–style conferences, and mentor youths one-on-one, involving themselves in young lives and showing them someone cares.

"Education is our passport to the future," Malcolm X once said, "for tomorrow belongs to the people who prepare for it today."

Black America wants white America to reach out to it, but first black America must reach out to itself. Besides passing on the pain, the warnings, and the street savvy of black life in white America, it also must share the tools, spiritually and educationally, that enable individuals to succeed in the world. It must share with its children the enriching diversity of the black experience—the depth of knowledge, the crucible of struggle, and the joy of overcoming that make up the great contribution that the black experience has brought to the human experience.

Then our children can know how to "be black," not as an end in itself, but as a launching pad from which they can go forth to deal with the world as authentically self-knowing, self-assured men and women, not just "actin'."

7

"The Signifyin' Muslim"

Louis Farrakhan's Notions of Islam

What then did you expect when you unbound the gag that muted those black mouths? That they would chant your praises?

—Jean-Paul Sartre, *Anthologie de la Nouvelle Poésie Nègre et Malgache*

Those to whom Evil has been done will do Evil in return.

—W.H. Auden

Minister Louis Farrakhan is an enigma wrapped in a paradox.

He poses as a black-and-proud Afrocentric, yet his espoused views are laced with three of Europe's oldest poisons: anti-Semitism, theocracy, and fascism.

He promotes family values, but with most of the power centered in the men in traditional patriarchal roles.

He preaches numerology, promotes a creation theory that blames an ancient evil wizard for creating the Caucasian "white devil" race to punish the black man and professes the belief that his predecessor and mentor, the late Elijah Muhammad, can pay occasional advisory visits in a flying saucer.

He eloquently denounces white racism, yet blames black economic problems in post-1960s America on black culture

and behavior, the same targets singled out by ultraconserva-
tives like the Hoover Institute's Thomas Sowell or the
American Enterprise Institute's Dinesh D'Souza, whom
Farrakhan devotees most likely would denounce for "blaming the victim."

He cultivates a defiant image but at bottom his separatist
prescription is almost indistinguishable from the turn-of-the-
century accommodationism of Booker T. Washington, whom
today's black nationalists usually denounce for saying the
first priority of black Americans should be basic education
and economic development, not desegregation or political
empowerment.

Farrakhan has reinvented himself into a larger-than-life
figure precisely because television, the big baby of mass
media—the most powerful yet also the most naive, impressionable and childlike medium—is the easiest for him to
manipulate with his clever, commanding, and arrogantly
exotic presence and oratory.

All of this has brought the Nation of Islam leader great
notoriety. It has helped him fill stadiums and draw hundreds
of thousands of black men to a grand historic "Million Man
March" on Washington.

But while Farrakhan's fascinating contradictions have
enhanced his appeal, they also have put profound limits on
it, particularly with America's interested, yet still skeptical
black middle class. At bottom, Minister Louis Farrakhan's
greatest draw, the institution that gives him credibility
among black Americans, is the long legacy of the Nation of
Islam. For more than sixty-five years it has intrigued and
impressed the masses of black community dwellers with its
ability to build and operate its own schools, farms, and businesses and perform miraculous acts of redemption on the
lives of pimps, prostitutes, drug addicts, and other street hus-

tlers and criminals, most notably the brilliant Malcolm X.

The Nation's emphasis on self-help, strong families, and spiritual rigor fills an important gap in black leadership in the post-'60s era, an era in which all people of good will yearn for the liberation of poor blacks left behind more isolated than ever by the civil rights revolution. Yet, as his attempt to fill that gap plays to the qualities that made the late Malcolm X the Nation's greatest spokesman, it also reminds one and all of how Malcolm, once he voiced true independence from Elijah Muhammad's theocracy, quickly became the Nation's most despised outcast and a victim of a murder in which many believe the Nation and Farrakhan played a significant part.

An investigation of the fall and the resurrection of the Nation of Islam is a look into a side of African-American life that Malcolm X called the "nightmare" alternative to Martin Luther King's dream, the flip side of our docile patriotism. Farrakhan is not an aberration. He did not create himself. If all had been going well with American race relations, the Nation of Islam would have died with its founder in 1975. Instead, Farrakhan revived it, restored its multimillion-dollar economic empire, and, aided by new media and the sensationalism of an impresario, the lost-found Nation of Islam draws bigger audiences than ever. It follows a black community tradition that predates the Civil War as a counterpoint to egalitarian integrationism throughout the history of the African in America. We shall see the Nation or something like it flourish as long as African Americans feel insecure and unprotected about their place as a group in American society.

The story of the Nation of Islam begins with a Detroit fabric salesman named Wallace Fard, whom many Muslims call Master Wali Farad Muhammad, a mysterious light-skinned man who claimed to be half-white. He opened a storefront temple of the Nation of Islam in Detroit in 1930 and a second one in Chicago a year later. Elijah Poole, a factory worker and preacher's son from Sandersville, Georgia, became Fard's leading disciple, renamed Elijah Muhammad.

After Fard mysteriously disappeared from public view in 1934, Muhammad took over, then moved to Chicago with his wife, Clara, and six children in a power dispute with rival ministers. At Chicago's Temple No. 2, his new national headquarters, "the Messenger of Allah" founded a newspaper, *The Final Call*, which later became *Muhammad Speaks*. He distinguished himself from countless other black messianic leaders and nationalist organizers by overseeing the building of an economic empire that included a school, a restaurant, stores, houses, trucking services, and a printing company, most of which were in Chicago, and acres of farmland in the South. These impressively visible symbols of success and economic independence formed the beginning of his master plan to establish a separate black nation in America.

He also created what would be the Nation's signature force, the Fruit of Islam, an elite, fiercely disciplined, yet unarmed army of strong black Muslim men easily identified by their conservative suits, bow ties, and closely cropped hair as they sold fish, bean pies, and copies of the Nation's newspaper. For ceremonial occasions he created blue uniforms for "the Fruit" patterned almost identically after the uniforms worn by the men who may have been more respected in grass-roots black America than any others outside the black church: Pullman railroad sleeping car porters. Just as Pullman porters had escorted a flood of black migrants like himself from the rural South to "the promised land" in the urban North, Muhammad promised, so would the Fruit of Islam escort black Americans to a new day in their own promised land, freed from the "white devils."

Despite his many enterprises, Muhammad found time to write to inquiring black inmates in prison, a fruitful recruiting ground. One of his correspondents was a convicted pimp and street hustler named Malcolm Little, who, under the guidance of "the Messenger" (as many called Muhammad), would become Malcolm X.

Malcolm Little's father had been an organizer for Marcus Garvey, the "back to Africa" nationalist who became a model for many others, including Elijah Muhammad. Born in Jamaica in 1887, Garvey founded the Universal Negro Improvement Association in 1914 to foster worldwide unity among blacks and promote the greatness of their African heritage. His brilliant oratory and his newspaper, *Negro World*, made him the most influential African-American leader in the years immediately following World War I. In 1920 he filled twenty-five-thousand-seat Madison Square Garden with a convention of his pan-African movement. But his influence declined after his misuse of funds intended to establish an African-American steamship company resulted in a mail fraud conviction. A young FBI agent named J. Edgar Hoover, sensing either danger or career advancement in organized Negroes, led the drive to arrest Garvey. He was jailed in 1925 and deported to Jamaica, where he died in relative obscurity in 1940.

The same year Garvey was convicted, Malcolm Little was born. He was a bright child who was reared in racially integrated schools in Nebraska and Michigan. A counselor told him that his dream of becoming a lawyer was not a serious goal for a Negro and suggested he try carpentry instead. Malcolm fell into a series of illegal hustles—pimping, burglary, drugs—and was convicted of burglary in 1946 and sentenced to ten years in prison, where he adopted the faith many would call "the Black Muslims." On his release in 1952

he became a Muslim minister and charismatic advocate of
black separatism.

His biting cleverness and charisma are recorded in rare
film clips like the one in the documentary *Eyes on the Prize II*.
The scene shows a rainy day in Harlem in the early 1960s. A
fine misty rain fills the air around a crowd of black faces
gathered at curbside to hear him connect the Nation's exotic
preaching to the urban misery concentrated all around them.
A stoic, stone-faced soldier of Muhammad's Fruit of Islam
holds a sheltering umbrella over Minister Malcolm's head.
Standing like a beacon, stately and cool in his conservative
suit, bow tie, and white shirt, he preaches. The audience
interrupts him with cheers—"*Yes! Yes! Amen!*"—and
applause, to which he instantly plays, rhythmically, lending
his beat a profoundly, lyrically poetic tone:

"They call Mr. Muhammad a hate teacher . . . "
"*Ye-e-e-sss! We-e-e-ell!*"
"Because he makes you hate dope and alcohol!"
"*Awright!*"
"They call Mr. Muhammad a black supremacist . . . "
" *. . . Yes!*"
". . . because he teaches you and me not only that we're as
good as the white man . . . "
" *. . . Oh, yes.*" Anticipation builds.
". . . but *better* than the white man!"
"*Yes, sir!*"
"Yes, *better* than the white man!"
Cheers. Applause.
"You're better than the white man!"
"*All right! Yes, sir. Yes, sir.*"
". . . and that's not saying anything."
"*No, it ain't!*"

"You know . . . where . . . it's nothing just to be equal with him!"

"No, no, no!"

"Who is he to be equal with?"

"No! That's right!"

"Just look at his skin."

"Yes! Yes! Look at it!"

"You can't compare *your* skin with *his* skin!"

Whoops. Shouts.

"Why, your skin looks like *gold* beside his skin."

Louder whoops and shouts.

"You find that ol' pale thing laying out in the sun trying to get to look like you."

Roar.

"That old pale thing."

"Oh, yes."

"Pale, pale thing."

"Yes, sir."

"You find him using *Man Tan!* Tryin' to . . . to look like you."

Explosive roar, shouts and applause.

"That old pale thing. . . ."

There was much competition on those Harlem street corners, but Malcolm always drew the biggest crowds, witnesses say. His influence soon flowed far beyond Harlem. Few others could speak as effectively to the woundedness black Americans carry around with them and replace it, if only for a moment, with a sense of spiritual rigor and strength. "I do not know a Negro so completely adjusted that some part of him did not respond to what Malcolm X was saying," wrote New York columnist Murray Kempton after Malcolm's death, "just as I do not know a Negro so entirely alienated

that some part of him does not respond to what Martin
Luther King, Jr., is saying."

For a people whose self-esteem had constantly been battered
by white standards of beauty, Malcolm's glorification of
Negro features was not idle ego tripping. It was therapy.

It was also comedy, verbal reincarnation of the mythical
West African Trickster, Esu-Elegbara, precursor to Br'er
Rabbit outfoxing ol' Br'er Fox and Br'er Bear, the signifyin'
monkey lightening the black man's heavy load by taunting
the mighty but lumbering lion of white power.

Malcolm's speech resonated with the playfully combative
African diaspora speech form known as "signifying," a form
common to the play of black children and the speeches of
clever black preachers. "Signifying" can be many things. It
can refer to the call-and-response exchange between preachers and their "amen corner" at church meetings, between
speakers and responsive crowds and rallies, to the various
aggressive in-yo'-face games of bravado or insults known as
"woofin'," "the dozens," "selling woof tickets," and
"soundin'," all of which gave rise to modern rap.

It can be cute, mocking, metaphorical, directly insulting, or
slyly hinting, says Thomas Kochman, author of *Black and
White Styles in Conflict*.

It can be "a bit like stumbling unaware into a hall of mirrors; the sign itself appears to be doubled, at the very least, and
[re]doubled upon ever closer examination," writes Harvard's
Henry Louis Gates in his important study, *The Signifying
Monkey: A Theory of African-American Literary Criticism*.

It can appear in the form of the "dirty dozens," a verbal
duel of insults to "yo' mama," as in "Yo' mama's so fat she
got her own area code," or "Yo' mama's so stupid she goes to
the library to get a book of matches."

Or it can appear in more elegant form in the poetry of
Langston Hughes:

And they asked me right at Christmas
If my blackness, would it rub off?
I said, ask your Mama.

But, importantly, Malcolm's mocking speech grew out of
not only American, but also African traditions. Gates tells us
that the roots of signifying stem from the "divine trickster,"
who appears as a powerful and popular image in the artwork
and spoken traditions of Yoruba mythology, as Esu-Elegbara
in Nigeria and Legba among the Fon in Benin, and reappears
in the Americas as Exu in Brazil, Echu-Elegua in Cuba, Papa
Legba in Haiti, and the "signifying monkey" in the United
States, where the image of a tricky monkey outwitting a far
more powerful lion must have been particularly appealing to
the black minority dominated by powerful whites. One
"toast" Gates cites goes like this:

Deep down in the jungle so they say
There's a signifying monkey down the way
There hadn't been no disturbin' in the jungle for quite a bit,
For up jumped the monkey in the tree one day and laughed
"I guess I'll start some shit."

It was not Malcolm's "hate rhetoric" or his apocalyptic
vision that kept the crowds coming. It was his entertainment
value, his playing the role of the grand trickster, the signifier
who tweaks the white power structure, then scampers back
up to Harlem—*"way up high"*—before the power of the lion
can lash back.

The larger world already had begun to learn about Malcolm
X and the Nation of Islam through a 1959 documentary titled

"The Hate That Hate Produced." Louis Lomax of *Jet* magazine and a freelancer to major publications like *Life* magazine, in an era when major media were not yet ready to hire black reporters, approached WNET (New York City Channel 13) correspondent Mike Wallace with a story Wallace found incredible: a sect of militant Negroes who professed superiority over whites. Wallace wanted to do it. But, Lomax pointed out, there was a catch: Elijah Muhammad would not talk to white reporters. WNET got the hint. The station hired Lomax—for the duration of the Nation of Islam report.

The program also introduced the world fleetingly to a young man named Louis X. His voice is heard on the soundtrack saying the lines of the "Prosecutor" in a play he wrote called *The Trial*, in which a stern-faced black jury sits in judgment of a very nervous white man. "I charge the white man with being the greatest liar on earth," the Prosecutor intones. "I charge the white man with being the greatest drunkard on earth. . . . I charge the white man with being the greatest gambler on earth. I charge the white man, ladies and gentlemen of the jury, with being the greatest peace-breaker on earth. I charge the white man with being the greatest adulterer on earth. I charge the white man with being the greatest robber on earth. I charge the white man with being the greatest deceiver on earth. I charge the white man with being the greatest trouble-maker on earth. So, therefore, ladies and gentlemen of the jury, I ask you, bring back a verdict of guilty as charged!"

The jury is polled. The verdict: guilty as charged. The sentence: death.

The defendant is dragged away, loudly protesting his innocence and all he has "done for the Nigra people." The audience roars its approval for several thundering minutes as the players take their curtain calls. The play, a striking lampoon of the way whites sit constantly in judgment of blacks, is a hit. So is the handsome young Prosecutor. Louis X, then the twenty-six-year-old minister of the Boston mosque, staged the play in temples across the nation. A song he wrote, "White Man's Heaven Is Black Man's Hell," became a hit in Muslim circles on a 45 rpm record, advertised in *Muhammad Speaks*. Still, he will not be widely known in the rest of the world until the 1980s, two decades after the "Messenger" Muhammad has awarded him with a new Muslim name: Louis Haleem Abdul Farrakhan.

If Louis Farrakhan has any stories of blatant racial oppression in his life to match those experienced by Malcolm Little, he has been reluctant to talk about them. Born May 11, 1933, in a section of Boston's Roxbury, the young Louis Eugene Walcott was an honors student and track star at racially integrated Boston English High School, a teenage acolyte in the Episcopal church, and a member of the drum-and-bugle corps. He loved music, particularly classical violin, which he would continue to play in private moments into his adulthood. After two years at a Winston-Salem teachers' college in North Carolina, he took to the stage as a calypso singer and musician. His stage names: Calypso Gene and The Charmer.

Farrakhan once told me in an interview that he found out about the Nation of Islam from an old friend he happened to meet on a Chicago street while he was booked to perform at Mister Kelly's, a nationally famous nightclub in the city's Rush Street nightlife district. In those days, black stars could perform in the city's downtown hotels, but were not allowed to rent a room in them. Instead, they stayed in black-owned hotels in the city's South Side "Bronzeville." The friend invited him to come hear Elijah Muhammad. It changed his life, Farrakhan would recall years later. He joined, dropped his "slave name," became Louis X, and soon put his charm and stagecraft to good use. While still in his twenties, he was put in charge of the Boston Fruit of Islam and, later, the Muhammad's Temple No. 11 in Boston.

He became a close disciple of Malcolm X, then minister of the Harlem Temple No. 7. But Malcolm, who became the Messenger's national spokesman in 1963, was ousted later in the year, after his reference to John F. Kennedy's assassination as "chickens coming home to roost" outraged Muhammad. In context, Malcolm had been referring to his earlier, less-publicized warnings to the White House to take action against the rising tide of violence against black civil rights workers in the South, or the violence would return to haunt the White House itself. But, according to Malcolm's autobiography, the Messenger thought the statement would be widely misinterpreted as if the Muslims were dancing on Kennedy's grave, a misconception that would bring more heat than it was worth from a nation that "loved that man."

Following his split with Muhammad and a pilgrimage to Mecca, Malcolm converted to orthodox Islam, became El-Hajj Malik El-Shabazz, and in 1964 founded the Organization of Afro-American Unity, which promoted black nationalism but also invited the possibility of interracial brotherhood, as long as it was under black leadership. He also lashed out at his former mentor for preaching false doctrine and carrying on an adulterous personal life with several "wives" employed as "secretaries." After Muhammad excommunicated the young militant he had recruited straight out of a penitentiary and had regarded as another son, Louis X rose in prominence—with a vengeance: In the December 1964 *Muhammad Speaks*, he wrote, "Such a man as Malcolm is worthy of death, and would have met with death if it had not been for Muhammad's confidence in Allah for victory over the enemies."

Three months later, Malcolm was dead, assassinated in a Harlem ballroom seconds after uttering the Muslim greeting, "As-salaam alaikum [Peace be unto you]." Three Nation of Islam Muslims were convicted of the crime, although some, including Farrakhan, say they believe government agents were involved. No official blame was ever linked to Louis X or other top Nation of Islam leaders, but Dr. Betty Shabazz, Malcolm's widow, made no secret of her belief that he was involved. Farrakhan would later admit, with regret, that he contributed to the "atmosphere" of animosity in which such an assassination could take place. But the controversy would not die, as evidenced by the arrest of one of Malcolm's daughters thirty years later on charges of conspiring to assassinate Farrakhan. Amid countercharges against the FBI informant who set up the arrest, she was released on a plea bargain. She only wanted to put the whole matter behind her, she said.

When the Honorable Elijah Muhammad died of natural causes in 1975, Nation of Islam elders bypassed Farrakhan as a likely successor and chose Muhammad's fifth son, Wallace. Malcolm and other Nation insiders called Wallace the most theologically astute of the "Royal Children of Muhammad." Yet many would agree with a Sepia magazine article by a Muslim author who lavished praise on Farrakhan as "a better orator than the late Dr. Martin Luther King, Jr. He sings better than Marvin Gaye. He's a better writer than Norman Mailer. He dresses better than Walt Frazier. He's more of a diplomat than Henry Kissinger. And he's prettier than Muhammad Ali."

Wallace, by contrast, the author wrote off as "dull, listless . . . a mild-mannered postal clerk."

Nevertheless, Wallace took command of the Nation as if he had invented it—and proceeded to reinvent it. He converted the sect to orthodox Islam, changed its name to the American Muslim Mission, dropped its restrictions against nonblacks, abandoned all talk of "white devils," relaxed its rigid dress codes, disbanded the paramilitary Nation of Islam, sold off Chicago's Salaam restaurant and other unsuccessful businesses (which he revealed had plunged the Nation more than $10 million in debt), and changed his own name and title to Imam (Minister) Warith Deen Muhammad.

"The Honorable Elijah Muhammad used to say that, if we didn't scare black people as much as the white man did, they wouldn't do what they were supposed to do," he told me in an interview in the late 1970s. "I believe our people are better off if they do something because they realize it's the right thing to do, not because somebody forces them to do it."

W. D. Muhammad also transferred Farrakhan from Harlem to Chicago's West Side, where he was offered the post of "national ambassador." Some sources say he sought the transfer so he could keep a closer eye on the young powerhouse, although W. D. Muhammad insisted he only wanted to put Farrakhan's charisma to better use. Instead, Farrakhan broke away, at the insistence of other diehards, to reestablish the former Nation of Islam, complete with Fruit of Islam security, who, Farrakhan said, were to protect him from W. D. Muhammad's orthodox Muslims, a charge W. D. Muhammad dismissed as "ridiculous."

In 1984, few observers paid much attention to the Fruit of Islam bodyguards Farrakhan provided to Jesse Jackson during the early days of his presidential campaign, before he received Secret Service protection. But then Jackson's reference to Jews as "Hymies" and New York City as "Hymietown" in what he thought were off-the-record remarks to Milton Coleman of the *Washington Post*, made

Farrakhan's reaction to Jewish criticism of Jackson into national news. In a late February rally in Chicago, Farrakhan said of Jewish leaders who were upset over Jackson, "If you harm this brother, I warn you in the name of Allah, this will be the last one you harm." The next month, in a radio sermon, Farrakhan tagged Coleman, who is black, as a "traitor." "One day soon we will punish you with death," Farrakhan said, reminding many of his earlier incendiary remarks that had preceded Malcolm's death.

He later told reporters that he was not referring to Coleman specifically but to "traitors in general" and how they would be dealt with when blacks come to power. "The lives of Milton Coleman and his family are sacred to me," he said in a somber tone, closing his eyes and touching his chest over his heart. Nevertheless, Coleman and the *Post* took the remarks seriously enough to hire bodyguards for Coleman and his family.

But Farrakhan would not back down. In later speeches and press conferences he would refer to Hitler as "great," although "wickedly great," and to Judaism as what sounded like a "gutter religion," although he insists he was referring to Zionism as a "dirty religion," as if that made a big difference. He also would accuse Jews of controlling major media as "a wicked cabal that manipulates the mass mind and will not allow either black nor white, Jews nor Gentiles to freely think without the manipulation of the media."

When I asked Farrakhan in a 1984 interview why he singled out the Jews more than any other white ethnic group, he responded, "It is sad that Jewish leaders can be very critical of blacks and black leaders and not be called anti-black. But when blacks have a legitimate criticism of Jewish posture, Jewish behavior, Jewish action, we must do it with our tongue in cheek, lest we be labeled as anti-Semitic.

"When [Jackson's] 'Hymie' remark was released by way of Milton Coleman in the *Washington Post*, the Anti-Defamation League [of B'nai B'rith] passed out a twenty-eight-page document on Jackson which was not for publication, but was just for the edification of persons in the media, so that when Jesse came within their view he could be hammered away at with questions. I felt Jewish people do have a tremendous amount of control in the media."

He sounded conciliatory, saying he wanted "dialogue" with Jewish leaders, but far from apologetic. As a result, Jewish leaders had nothing to gain by holding "dialogue" without receiving from him a renunciation of his earlier remarks, particularly his Jewish conspiracy talk.

I found it astonishing that he would cite as an example of Jewish "control in the media" such a low-yield public relations move as the distribution of a handout background paper on Jackson. Yet, to those whose hopes and dreams were embodied in the quixotic candidacy of Jesse Jackson, any impediment thrown in his path was viewed as the work of a truly "evil cabal," an enemy even if dressed in a friend's clothing. Farrakhan's supporters, young and old, rationalized his reckless moments as the courage of one of history's victims "speaking truth to power." Black people cannot be racist, Farrakhan preached, for they do not have the power to oppress others. Only the white male hierarchy, including the Jews, have such power, he would say, and many others would echo his words.

Yet, as always, Farrakhan's words seemed to defy new realities. Just as he concedes having contributed to the "atmosphere" that led to Malcolm's death, how can he not concede contributing to the atmosphere that could lead to tragedies like the death of Yankel Rosenbaum, an Australian who happened to be killed by black attackers after wandering into the wrong place at the wrong time during the black-Jewish riots in the Crown Heights section of New York City, a city governed at the time by a black mayor?

Malcolm called on black folks to take responsibility for their own lives. Farrakhan, unfortunately, is just as happy to fawn off responsibilities on outside conspirators. Robbed of the blatant racism Malcolm could attack in his day, Farrakhan relies on the same scapegoats of neo-Nazis, Ku Klux Klansmen, and extremist anti-government paramilitary militias—the Rockefellers, the World Bank, the Trilateral Commission, the Queen of England, international drug cartels, secret AIDS scientists, and, that old eternal standby, the Jews. Small wonder that two former Klansmen attended one of his California rallies and, at the end, dropped a few dollars in Farrakhan's plate.

One evening in a South Side Chicago cocktail lounge, Salim Muwakhil, a friend, fellow black journalist, Vietnam-era military veteran, former Black Panther, and former Nation of Islam member, confided that he views Farrakhan as a "tragic figure," a true believer in orthodox Islam who, Muwakhil thinks, is unable to take his offshoot sect closer to the orthodox faith for fear of enraging his own hard-liner associates.

Tragic? What an odd adjective, I thought, to apply to Farrakhan, a man many would say is causing more tragedy than he is experiencing.

Still, tragedy may easily apply to Farrakhan in the sense that it applies to anyone who falls far short of his or her potential for greatness. George Orwell once wrote, "A tragic situation exists precisely when virtue does not triumph, but when it is still felt that man is nobler than the forces which destroy him." Farrakhan lost nobility when he decided to apply the drawing power of a well-targeted scapegoat.

After years of heaving barbs at various white people and institutions, even he appeared to be amazed, delightfully so, at the bonanza of publicity that followed his initial harangues against unnamed Jews. That the publicity was resoundingly negative only enhanced his apparent authenticity as an embattled hero, in black eyes. If white folks were attacking him, it is traditionally reasoned among blacks, he must be doing something good for blacks.

Much is at risk. Farrakhan's popularity has been riding high since the "gutter religion" flap, but there are rivals, other pretenders to Elijah's throne scattered around the country, although none has shown the crowd-drawing appeal of Farrakhan. Even Malcolm in his heyday never filled Madison Square Garden, as Farrakhan did in 1984, matching Garvey's historic feat, or, for that matter, Atlanta's sixty-thousand-seat Georgia Dome in 1992—at $15 a head. Farrakhan has filled his coffers and enabled his reconstituted Nation of Islam to purchase Elijah Muhammad's Temple No. 2, formerly a Greek Orthodox Church on Chicago's far South Side, from W. D. Muhammad's organization; repurchase thousands of acres of farmland; and, in 1995, reopen amid national fanfare a jewel of which Elijah was particularly proud, the no-pork, no-booze Salaam Restaurant.

But I think my friend Salim was talking more about the cross-pressures on Farrakhan, pressures from within himself, as a Muslim scholar, to steer his people toward a more orthodox version of Islam, but stymied by pressures from hard-liners in his ranks who do not want to see him water down the rhetoric of race and paranoia the way Warith Deen Muhammad did.

Farrakhan in the early 1990s began to make furtive gestures that looked more conciliatory. He gave a conciliatory-sounding 1993 interview to *Chicago Sun-Times* columnist Irv Kupcinet, a

Jew who long ago befriended Malcolm X, and he staged a widely publicized performance of Felix Mendelssohn's violin concerto with an interracial, interfaith orchestra at Christ Universal Temple in Chicago. He said he hoped to bring together with music people who had been divided by words. Jewish leaders, some of them noting that Mendelssohn was a Jew who converted to Christianity, were not impressed. They wanted an offense that had been made with words to be corrected with words, in the form of a full, unequivocal apology.

But Farrakhan refused. In an interview in the August 1993 issue of Baltimore's *Jewish Times*, he explained, "Jews want everybody to bow down to them, and I ain't bowing down to nothing or nobody, but God." He did not mention it, but he was receiving other pressures at the time from his more militant supporters who already were accusing him of capitulating to "Jewish racism" with his violin diplomacy.

The next month, Congressional Black Caucus chairman Kweise Mfume astonished many by embracing Farrakhan, verbally and literally, in an announced working agreement during the caucus's annual legislative weekend. Jesse Jackson, also in the group, stood back, uncharacteristically avoiding center stage.

But the deal fell through a few months later when Farrakhan's national spokesman Khalid Muhammad delivered a speech at New Jersey's Kean College that was completely devoid of Farrakhan's charm as he lobbed caustic bombshells at Jews, the pope, and others, including Jackson and other moderate black leaders. Again, Farrakhan was forced to choose: Discipline Khalid, as Elijah Muhammad had disciplined Malcolm's embarrassing remarks, and prove he, indeed, was moderating, or stick by Khalid, reassuring the hard-liners. Farrakhan split the difference. In a lengthy press conference carried live on CNN, he removed Khalid's "spokesman" title but declined to denounce what he called the "truths" of his statements.

"Why," Bertrand Russell once asked, "is propaganda so much more successful when it stirs up hatred than when it tries to stir up friendly feeling?" Perhaps Farrakhan, in his private moments, also asks himself that question.

Initially, at least, his success has been mixed. At a time when other civil rights organizations and leaders are hamstrung in "agenda shock," locked into an array of reflexive civil rights responses to black problems that appear increasingly to be economic in nature, Farrakhan's ability to reach the young and the most alienated and disaffected on America's campuses and in America's ghettos made him a sought-after figure among mainstream black leaders, until he and his former national spokesman, Khalid Muhammad, began bashing Jews.

With that, they instead became targets of blanket denunciations from black leaders as diverse as Carl Rowan, Roger Wilkins, Bayard Rustin, Tony Brown, Newark mayor Kenneth Gibson, U.S. Civil Rights Commissioner Mary Francis Berry, and his former ally Jesse Jackson. He gained publicity and income, but squandered his political, social, and moral capital.

As a separatist, he has fiendishly clever strategic reasons to attack Jews. What better way to separate blacks from whites than to target the Jews, many of whom traditionally have been the closest link black Americans have had to America's white-dominated mainstream. At best, it hastens the day when blacks can be truly separate and independent from whites. At worst, it wastes energies by alienating potential allies—and providing endless amusement to those who don't have either group's best interests in mind.

Farrakhan also may figure that his attacks against Jews

will enhance his prestige among orthodox Muslim political leaders in the Middle East. Libya's Moammar Ghadafy loaned Elijah Muhammad $2 million in the early 1970s to purchase a new mosque, and Farrakhan told me he was seeking "hundreds of millions" more "to begin to do for black people what needs to be done."

How ironic, I thought, to cut ourselves loose from the white man in America only to hold our hand out to Arabs in the Middle East. What does it profit us to escape one plantation to plant ourselves onto another, just as limiting, but calling itself a "black nation"?

James Baldwin, after leaving a sumptuous and surprisingly cordial dinner with Elijah Muhammad and his top aides in his South Side Chicago mansion in the early 1960s, concluded in *The Fire Next Time*, "For the sake of one's children, in order to minimize the bill that *they* must pay, one must be careful not to take refuge in any delusion—and the value placed on the color of the skin is always and everywhere and forever a delusion."

So it is. Black people cannot afford to live in delusions. Increasingly I have learned to appreciate not just the Malcolm who wanted to set up a separate black nation, but also the Malcolm who grew out of all that, the El-Hajj Malik El-Shabazz who, in his final days, renounced his earlier "hate that hate produced" and displayed a self-love that enlivened his view of the world.

Two days before he was assassinated in a Harlem ballroom at age thirty-nine, he would recall in an interview with Gordon Parks an incident included in his autobiography. A white female college student asked him in a restaurant what whites could do to help his Muslims. "Nothing," he retorted, sending her away in tears.

"I've lived to regret that incident," he said to Parks. "In many parts of the African continent I saw white students helping black people. Something like this kills a lot of argument. I did many things as a Muslim that I'm sorry for now. I was a zombie then—like all Muslims—I was hypnotized, pointed in a certain direction and told to march. Well, I guess a man's entitled to make a fool of himself if he's ready to pay the cost. It cost me twelve years.

"That was a bad scene, brother. The sickness and madness of those days—I'm glad to be free of them."

And Malcolm, in the end, was free. Freed of his worst impulses and free to pick his targets more carefully, he realized he no longer had to demean all whites to build up blacks.

He outgrew the conceits of racism, separatism, and hatred. He became more pluralistic. He began to fit his black identity into a comfortable niche in the firm foundation of his life. He put race into its place as a part of his life, but not, by any means, all of it. Nor did he sacrifice in any way his ability to shock, to make noise, to rattle the cages of the complacent. There was much more to Malcolm than his racial identity. At his death, he was only beginning to show us.

By contrast, Malcolm's protégé-turned-rival, Minister Louis Farrakhan, has yet to free himself. He remains tied to the old-style demagoguery, bolstering black innocence by pinning the tail of guilt on devils of various sorts.

His love for the roar of the crowd reveals him to be, at bottom, still an entertainer, still "The Charmer," a modern tribal medicine man whose show is getting an exceptionally long run, and he doesn't want the music to end.

There is always a danger in the game of "signifyin'" when the boundaries between playful aggression and real aggression begin to blur. The game then turns into an eyeball-to-eyeball challenge, unless someone backs down. But danger does not appear to trouble Farrakhan. That's part of his appeal.

As I watched Jesse Jackson address the multitudes at Minister Louis Farrakhan's "Million Man March," I could not help but be struck by the moment's significance in the evolution of black American leadership. It was Jackson who unintentionally had provided the platform from which Farrakhan leaped to mainstream notoriety in 1984. Now Jackson was serving as Farrakhan's warm-up act, just another of many speakers in a day-long procession of VIPs that included Al Sharpton, Stevie Wonder, and civil rights pioneer Rosa Parks. All spoke and were almost forgotten in the building anticipation of the main event, Farrakhan.

Even if you accepted the National Park Services official estimate of 400,000—a widely disputed figure (a University of Boston digital analysis commissioned by ABC-TV would later put the figure at closer to 800,000 and possibly as many as 1.1 million or as few as 600,000) that even the park service would later raise to 600,000—it was the largest black gathering anywhere in recorded history, leading to much speculation as to whether Farrakhan could now be considered the nation's premier black leader. That conclusion was hard to make, since so many of the men who participated in the peaceful and inspiring rally, including me, insisted they were there because of "the march, not the messenger." Almost every one of the dozens of participants to whom I talked that day said they were there not to celebrate Farrakhan, but to come together with other black men who were fed up with the cycle of violence and despair that gripped millions of black lives, seemingly untouched by the civil rights reforms of the 1960s. If nothing else, their presence would help put an image into the national media of black men who were not criminals, gangsta rappers, or hustlers who were abandoning their families and communities. They were the invisible black Americans raging to be visible.

This rage against invisibility was too important a force to be easily minimized by those who would take stock of the event's historical significance. As a regular panelist on a Black Entertainment Television cable network news-panel program, I had seen the march take on a life of its own shortly after Farrakhan announced it. That's how clearly black Americans saw the need for some kind of direct action to complete the last phases of black liberation, the economic and spiritual phase. Farrakhan was not the first to speculate that perhaps a new march on Washington was necessary, a march that would not protest the government as much as it would protest black dependency on it. He was only the first to stick his neck out and put his reputation on the line by acting on it. His instincts proved to be correct. The event was an overwhelming success on several levels. For those of us who were there, it was a reminder of how little black men like one another. It was a measure of how deeply we have internalized the white supremacist notion of black male inferiority and treachery and an illustration of how much we obsessively call each other "brother" precisely because we feel so little genuine brotherhood toward one another.

It was an invigorating relief to be at ease with other black men for a change, to look one another in the eye (normal street etiquette calls for unacquainted black men to avoid direct eye contact, for fear of sending the wrong signals and triggering a violent response) and smile, wink, shake hands, and even hug in a spirit of genuine brotherhood. Spending time with other black men was a massive therapy as love-in, a black reflection of a back-to-primitive-basics machismo out of Robert Bly's *Iron John* or Bill McCartney's Promise

Keepers, which leads stadiums full of mostly white men in Christian fellowship and pledges to reassert traditional male roles and family values. It was, in my view, a time for black men, who usually turn away without looking one another in the eye on the street, for fear of sending the wrong signals, to let down their usual defenses, expose their emotional vulnerabilities for a healthy airing, and catch up in a very moving way with the self-discovery that black feminists and "womanists" (many of whom ironically were decrying the all-male event as "patriarchal") had been exploring for decades.

For the home viewers, it was a stunning television event, a day-long infomercial for Farrakhan that he watered down by talking too long—two and a half hours once he finally took the podium. White America had ignored Louis Farrakhan and the rest of the Nation of Islam for decades. He could not be ignored now. By calling attention to himself, he called attention to the nation's persistent racial divide, an attention for which even many of his opponents in black America were begrudgingly grateful. Had Farrakhan not invented himself, it seemed more than ever that it would have been necessary to create him. The march left widespread speculation as to what Farrakhan would do next. Perhaps a more important question is what will the rest of America do to make the Farrakhans of this world less necessary.

8

Blacks and Jews

A Broken Marriage

I have a friend who tells me she was almost a teenager in her middle-class, heavily Jewish neighborhood before she found out the Yiddish word *Schwartzer* did not mean "maid."

I knew the word was Yiddish slang for a black person and not always the kindliest slang, either. I first heard the word in a monologue by the late black comedian Godfrey Cambridge. He was describing the indignity suffered by every prosperous-looking middle-class black American who has been passed up by a taxi in New York City. "I'm not black," he said he yelled at one taxi as it zipped past, "I'm a *Schwartzer Yiddishe boychik!*"

Throughout my friend's childhood, she had heard the word used in her aunt's house to mean "cleaning lady," as in "Excuse the mess, honey, my *Schwartzer* didn't show up today."

My friend said this to me as something of a personal confession, but I told her not to feel guilty. Looking back, I recalled I must have been almost a teenager before I found out the word "Jew" was not a verb meaning "to bargain," as in "Jew him down." That's how it was used in *my* neighborhood.

I reacted to my friend's story the way I, as a black American, have learned to cope with most of the little insults of life. I laughed. When you are faced with as many insults, big and small, as black people have to put up with, you learn to laugh or go crazy. Laughing off life's lesser insults helps you to conserve your energies to cope with the bigger ones. Perhaps, in some poignant way, such similar indignities help explain why America's black and Jewish communities have produced so many fine comedians. As Julius Lester, a black author and professor who converted to Judaism, once wrote, "Without Jews and blacks, I wonder if there would be laughter in America."

Much has been said and written about how the fabled "special relationship" blacks and Jews built up over the decades fell apart in the late 1960s; how we came together in the labor movements, civil rights movement, and other historical struggles, then parted ways in an era of black power, Palestinian rights, and Louis Farrakhan.

Both of our groups share such strikingly similar victim profiles. Both of us have been regarded as pariahs by mainstream white gentile America. Both are burdened by the special woundedness carried like a persistent weight by historical victims of slavery and emancipation, a memory that is both a burden and a source of pride, empowerment, and peoplehood. Both groups have shared the same neighborhoods when no one else would live with us and worked together when no one else would work with us. When no one else would give black talent a break, it was Jews, more often than not, who teamed up with blacks to help one another make money, particularly in the worlds of entertainment, sports, and publishing.

But behind the rosy, heartwarming scenarios of harmony, our special relationship was heavily fortified, more often than not, by robust and treacherously addictive doses of denial. Our public displays of unity often masked private doubts, prejudices, and resentments even in the best of times. While leaders and activists from both communities intelligently and courageously organized around the many views and experiences we hold in common, our few, yet significantly, conflicting views and experiences were allowed to fester. Today the mask is off, and, ironically, earlier myths of rosy unity have been replaced by new myths of hopeless conflict. Today it is the few incidents of violence, verbal or physical, between us that are widely publicized, masking the many less-publicized examples of cooperation and common ground. News media that once helped accelerate earlier civil rights reforms have tended more recently to accelerate the problem, shedding more heat than light. But others must share the blame. We who work in the media cover the conflict and comment on it, but we didn't create it.

To determine where we are headed, we need to take a fresh look at where we have been. Our "special relationship" predates the Civil War. It appears in the abolitionist movement, reappears frequently in later left-progressive political activism into the twentieth century, most notably in labor unions and the civil rights movement. Jews contributed two-thirds of the funding to Martin Luther King's movement and were two-thirds of the white participants in the 1964 "Freedom Summer" voter registration drive in Mississippi, where two Jewish men—Andrew Goodman, twenty, and Michael Schwerner, twenty-four—and one black man, James Chaney, who was twenty-one, were murdered one night on the backroads by terrorist upholders of the old order.

But, even then, many blacks resented what they perceived as a one-sided condescending relationship, as Jews were welcomed into the upper ranks of black organizations in ways blacks were not welcomed into Jewish organizations. Some blacks may have advocated separatism, it is important to remember, but they didn't invent it.

After the coalition's biggest victories, the Civil Rights Act of 1964 and the Voting Rights Act of 1965, the coalition lost its footing on common ground. Powerful villains never again would surface with the bold audaciousness of the old George Wallace or Theophilius Eugene "Bull" Connor, the Birmingham police official who turned dogs and firehoses on civil rights demonstrators. Instead, racism became more subtle and, in the search to root it out, everyone became more suspect, less trustworthy.

The rise of "black power" and third-world nationalist militants, who sympathized more with Palestinian rights than with the right of Israel to exist, coincided with, among other points of tension, the rise of new Jewish identity movements surrounding the 1967 Six-Day War. Dramatic clashes erupted around New York's 1968 Ocean Hill–Brownsville teachers strike; the rise of affirmative action; United Nations ambassador Andrew Young's meeting with Palestine Liberation Organization representatives; Jesse Jackson's public embrace of Yassir Arafat; Jackson's characterization of Jews in a private-conversation-made-public as "Hymies" and New York City as "Hymietown" during his 1984 presidential campaign; and the subsequent rise to black mainstream prominence, although not necessarily black mainstream support, of Nation of Islam minister Louis Farrakhan.

By the early 1980s, further flames of division for the black-Jewish coalition on the liberal-progressive left would be fanned by a new, unexpected common ground on the political right. On one side were new-wave conservatives, "neocons," including once-liberal Jews like Irving Kristol, Norman Podhoretz, Gertrude Himmelfarb, and Saul Bellow, whose desire to push Jews away from traditional liberalism meshed remarkably if uncomfortably well with black separatists like Farrakhan, who wanted to push blacks away from whites in general. Toward that end, the separatists targeted Jews with propaganda intended to rob Jews of their status as fellow victims, driving a wedge into the common identity that helped glue the old alliance together.

At the grass roots, the neighborhood level, blacks and Jews pulled apart physically. Many Jews found it easier to assimilate into the upwardly mobile white gentile mainstream than most blacks could. Jewish faith in the fairness of American opportunities was being reinforced, while blacks, in an era of white political backlash, were finding new reasons to question it. This difference in perceptions, based on differing experiences, served to reinforce Jewish impressions of affirmative action as a quota system, a ceiling to put limits on their aspirations, while blacks believed just as strongly in affirmative action as a protective floor, a guarantee, however flawed, that hard-won civil rights gains would not shrivel up into a paper promise, a broken treaty with the only group ever enslaved on American soil.

I used to preach that the "special relationship" between blacks and Jews was like a marriage, a metaphor I appropriated from psychiatrist Price Cobbs, author of *Black Rage* and one of America's foremost experts on interethnic relations. It was a workable and appropriate metaphor, I thought, for it captured the closeness with which blacks and Jews had cooperated, a unique cooperation for two quite dissimilar ethnic groups joined only by a similar, if hardly the same, out-group status in America. Our disputes, I reasoned, served as ironic evidence of how much we had in common. After all, don't married couples inevitably think, after they have toiled in the same vineyard for a long time, that they know each other better than they really do? Doesn't this naive conclusion inevitably encourage them to take each other for granted while tensions build? Then one day the wife storms into the living room, crying, "You don't pay any attention to me anymore," only to hear her husband respond with obvious annoyance, "Of course I pay attention to you. Now please excuse me. It's almost time for the opening kickoff!"

Black Americans and American Jews were taking one another for granted at the time of their mid-1960s split. Each was looking at the other through standards that no longer applied. Jews tended to expect their black compatriots, once the shackles of segregation were relaxed, to follow a similar path to the one most Jews had chosen as an ethnic group: education, entrepreneurship, and assimilation. Some individuals did, but they would exert little influence on the black masses compared to the influence of Malcolm X, Stokely Carmichael, black politicians, and the black power movement, whose course followed more closely that chosen by the Boston, New York, and Chicago Irish: political empowerment, public jobs, and patronage. All we needed to do, I reasoned, was to reintroduce ourselves to each other, like any other couple in marital therapy. We needed to take a fresh look at how far we have come together and how much we still have in common, then decide whether to patch things up or settle for an amicable divorce. I was confident that each community still had enough good hearts and heads to make reunification desirable.

More recent events have made me question the rosiness of

my own outlook. As the anti-Jewish language of some blacks became more intensely nasty in the early 1990s and the reaction from many respected and responsible black leaders stayed ominously silent, I felt suddenly that I had been awakened from a romantic dream by the cold water of reality. As much as we, African Americans and American Jews, have shared experiences as individuals, some of them quite poignant, passionate, and intense, as groups we still live largely separate lives, like two tribes usually at peace, but sometimes warring, feuding over our similarities as much as we fuss over differences.

By the 1990s, relations between us took on a decidedly nasty tone, particularly among the young, particularly in such violent flashpoints as the Crown Heights section of Brooklyn in 1991. America's worst nightmares were realized in the slaying of Yankel Rosenbaum and the beatings of others by a black mob shouting, "Get the Jews." The nightmare flashed anew a year later when a jury failed to convict anyone in the slaying. The riot was ostensibly sparked by the accidental killing of a black child by an out-of-control car in a motorcade hastily carrying the rebbe of the hermetic Lubavitcher sect. Blacks were further enraged by rumors, which turned out to be false, that a Jewish ambulance service had refused to take the boy to a hospital. Charles Dickens could not have imagined a more tragic scenario of urban tensions born of poverty, prejudice, and cultural conflict. The Lubavitchers essentially were being punished for refusing to follow others, including upwardly mobile blacks, who had moved away from the increasingly black and West Indian inner-city neighborhood. Other Jews had their reservations about the Lubavitchers and their almighty rebbe, but all differences evaporated among Jews everywhere as word of the roving bands and their ominous chant—*Get the Jews!*—rolled

out, recalling bitter memories of past victimization—*Pogrom!*
Kristallnacht! Holocaust!—and a long-standing promise to the
dead: *Never again!*

The nasty new edge to black-Jewish relations resurfaced in
November 1993, when Khalid Abdul Muhammad, then
national spokesman for Nation of Islam minister Louis
Farrakhan, attacked "the hook-nosed, bagel-eatin', lox-eatin'"
Jews in a speech at Kean College in Union, New Jersey.
Muhammad cut a broad swatch against many groups and
individuals that day, including Jesse Jackson and other black
leaders who had committed, in his opinion, some affront to
the race. But he came down hardest on the Jews.

His mostly black student audience cheered. A lone black
student, during the question period, politely but firmly suggested that the speech sounded like something Adolf Hitler
might have delivered. Indeed, it also sounded like something
that might have been said by persecutors of the Jews during
the Byzantine era or the Crusades, or under the English in
1290, or the French in 1306, or the Spanish in 1492, or the
Portuguese in 1497, or the Germans in 1614, or the Austrians
in 1670, or the Ukrainians in 1648 and 1768, or the Russians
in 1871 or 1903, or the Germans again in the 1930s and 1940s.

Now here? Jews found the menace inherent in
Muhammad's rant to be exceeded only by that in the subse-
quent ominous silence from prominent black leaders.
Columnist Bob Herbert and professor-commentator Roger
Wilkins spoke out forcefully in the *New York Times* op-ed
pages, as did some black faculty members at the college. But
where, the *Times*'s Abe Rosenthal and the *Washington Post*'s
Richard Cohen asked, were Jesse Jackson or Representative
Kweise Mfume or Ben Chavis? All three had been on stage
two months earlier when Mfume, chair of the Congressional
Black Caucus, embraced Farrakhan in a working "covenant"

at the caucus's annual legislative weekend.

It turned out that, while Jewish leaders were fretting over Khalid, black leaders were coping precariously with a slow-motion holocaust of their own: black kids killing other black kids on American streets. Jackson was hastily organizing an anti-violence conference in the District of Columbia in the aftermath of another Dickensian event, the random shooting of a four-year-old girl at a city swimming pool by an unidentified youth firing from outside a fence. As inured as District residents had become to the horrors of drive-by shootings in crack wars throughout the late 1980s, this killing of an innocent little girl struck a citywide nerve. News media played it up. Mayor Sharon Pratt Kelly showed proper outrage. Jesse Jackson delivered a chilling eulogy at her funeral, pointing out quite correctly that the Ku Klux Klan posed less of a clear and present threat to black life than other black people did. Searching for a course of action to which he, the nation's most prominent black leader, might lead black people, he proposed a national conference on youth violence. Then, once the promise was made, Jackson had to deliver on it, which would not be a simple matter for him to accomplish. As one who has covered Jackson's activities since the late 1960s, I knew his most notorious weakness to be the nuts and bolts of organizing and following through. "I'm a tree shaker, not a jelly maker," he told me in a 1980 interview, and the line had dogged him ever since. Determined to outlive it and do something about black America's biggest internal crisis since slavery, he hammered his youth violence summit conference together—I had to hand it to him—in a matter of weeks. Then, almost on its eve, he received word that the *Times*'s Rosenthal and the *Post*'s Cohen were calling on him and other black leaders to denounce Muhammad's Kean College speech. Annoyed to the point of outrage, Jackson told me later, that he was being asked to put aside his conference preparations to denounce a man and a college that he had never heard of before, he ignored the columns. So did most other prominent black leaders. Some, like Harlem Representative Charles Rangel, expressed open irritation on national television that Jewish leaders would call on blacks, deeply immersed in a vexing life-or-death crisis among their youths—*kids killing kids!*—to drop everything and denounce a nobody demagogue who had decided to run off at the mouth. To many blacks, this temerity by Jews only illustrated further how little Jews differ from any other white people, except that their past victimization affords them a greater license to complain. Then the Anti-Defamation League of B'nai B'rith bought a full-page ad in the *New York Times* in which they ran lengthy excerpts from Muhammad's speech under the bold headline "You Decide." Suddenly bitten by the full venom of Muhammad's words, Jackson and the rest of the black leadership denounced them and called on Farrakhan to do the same. In a lengthy press conference broadcast by CNN, Farrakhan stripped Muhammad of his "national spokesman" title and demoted him, but distanced himself only from the "manner" in which Muhammad delivered his remarks, not from the "truths" of what he said. Farrakhan then went on to reiterate some of those "truths," including the allegation that Jews "controlled" 75 percent of the slave trade.

In fact, the highest estimates reputable historians have been able to attribute to Jewish slave traders—an exceedingly tiny group—is closer to 0.3 percent. A look at the rest shows slavery to have been an equal opportunity exploitation: Europeans, Arabs, Christians, and Muslims, even other black Africans, had a much bigger hand in it than Jews did.

But "demagogues"—a title Farrakhan proudly claims—don't worry about letting facts get in the way of a good scapegoating. Muhammad can take the incidental fact that a

Jew heads the Federal Reserve and inflate that into a general conspiracy of Jews taking over the nation's currency. He can take the coincidental fact that Jews, often forced into self-employment by societies that barred them from conventional vocations, often have offered goods and services black people want or need when no one else would offer them, and twist that to say the Jews are "sucking blood" out of the community, as if by force. He can take the benign fact that Jews founded Hollywood's biggest studios and the less benign fact that Hollywood too often panders to unfortunate stereotypes and use them to imply Jewish conspiracies to undermine the images of blacks in America.

But the demagogue does not have to limit himself to grains of truth. He can take the old lie and recycle it, as in the bogus *Secret Relationship Between Blacks and Jews*. Nation of Islam members also cite *The Protocols of the Elders of Zion*, an anti-Jewish tract of uncertain origin that appeared sometime early this century with allegations of an international conspiracy for Jewish conquest.

Efforts to restore the old relationship are commendable but, if the pessimists are to be believed, doomed. After all, it is reasoned, black and Jewish political objectives, strategies, and success patterns have grown apart. The old civil rights goal of equal justice under law appears in many ways to have been displaced by new conflicting public visions of meritocracy among Jews and group entitlements among blacks. Jews are heavily invested in a vision of America as an open society in which rewards are ultimately available to all who prepare and apply themselves. Blacks have become just as heavily invested in the idea of America as a closed, racist society in which people of color suffer economic disadvantages at all levels in competition for economic and social benefits. Meritocratic strategies have paid off well for Jews. As a group they are richer and significantly more secure than blacks in the professions and in academia and easily as well organized to influence government for their interests, including support for the state of Israel. Blacks, by contrast, have relied heavily on bloc voting, political patronage, and racially targeted government aid programs, justified as redress for historical grievances. Jews did not feel threatened by David Dinkins's 1989 defeat of Mayor Ed Koch. In fact, they turned out in great numbers to help it along. But blacks, by comparison, voiced grievous alarm over Dinkins's loss four years later, seeing Rudolph Giuliani's victory as a giant step backward. Blacks were too deeply invested in city hall as a vehicle for black progress to think otherwise, not to mention too grievously terrified by Giuliani's appeals to white male voters, particularly in one police union rally during which the language turned racially ugly, according to news accounts.

In America, a land where liberal impulses urge us to minimize differences, it is tempting to make much, perhaps too much, of the similarities between blacks and Jews. Among the differences we have to remember are:

1: *"Denunciations" vs. "unity."* The Jewish demand for others to denounce anti-Semitic statements is matched in strength only by black resistance to any outsider's attack on black solidarity. Diversity expert Tom Kochman, author of *Black and White Styles in Conflict* and himself a German-born Jew, notes that history and culture cause African Americans to disconnect words from actions as much as Jews see the two as linked. America's founders, Thomas Jefferson most prominent among them, were not moved to free even their own slaves by their eloquent calls for liberty, justice, and minority rights. Blacks learned to place greater value on their own solidarity, up against white efforts to divide blacks against one another. Jews, by contrast, value words, having seen what early and timely denunciations of Adolf Hitler in the 1930s, among other Jew baiters of the past, might have prevented. As a result, contrary to what ignorant detractors sometimes allege, responsible Jewish leaders were forthright in denouncing racist remarks and deeds by Rabbi Meier Kahane and other Jewish extremists. Jewish unity is less of a concern among Jews than the larger threat of others unified against Jews.

2: *Imbalanced power relationship.* Relationships between unequals, no matter how placid they may appear on the surface, inevitably stir condescension, resentment, and rage. When the Student Nonviolent Coordinating Committee's northern faction led by Stokely Carmichael took over along with his "black power" philosophy, whites were ousted and advised that, if they truly were sincere about wanting to help the "struggle," they should go fight racism as Malcolm X had advised them to, in white community structures, instead of trying to "find themselves" in the black community. Instead, white activists, most of them Jewish, dropped out of the civil rights movement in great numbers and moved to other movements.

3: *Shifting sand.* Blacks and Jews make a mistake when they try to analyze their current or future relationship in light of victimization conditions that no longer apply to either of them. Jews often don't realize how "white" they have become in the eyes of others, we blacks often don't realize how "empowered" we have become.

"I was never called 'white' until I came to America," an elderly rabbi in Chicago once told me. He had survived a Nazi concentration camp in Czechoslovakia. Across Europe he had been oppressed because he was a Jew. But when he arrived in America, he had found to his wondrous surprise that, through absolutely no effort of his own, his status automatically had changed. Suddenly, in the eyes of certain other Americans, he was a member of the "oppressor" class: white males.

At the same time, many blacks feel that, as one Afrocentric argued to me one day, "We aren't strong enough yet to be criticizing each other."

"Speak for yourself," I responded. "As a people, we're not strong enough *not* to criticize each other." As Malcolm X discovered in the final days of his life, self-criticism is itself a sign of maturity and a great, immutable power of a sort that can come not from a unified movement but only from a confident soul within one's self. Denial, by contrast, is the curse of the weak.

In the aftermath of the terror bombing of the Alfred P. Murrah federal building in Oklahoma City, a psychiatrist spoke of the need for local residents to find "points of hope," reasons for optimism that could aid their spiritual recovery. The despair felt by many of us in the wake of the disastrous turn taken by the black-Jewish coalition also cries out for points of hope, blessings to count. The old "special relationship" may never be the same. Times and issues have changed too dramatically. But behind the dreary headlines, hopeful signs abound for the beginning of a new relationship. Sometimes we need to listen less to the news than to our own heads and hearts. News, by its very nature, minimizes history, complexities, and social context, the very elements that can best help us to understand this complicated story about blacks and Jews. It is important to note, for example, that, despite frightening headlines, most black people do not belong to the Nation of Islam, any more than most white people belong to paramilitary militias. In fact, it can be argued

that black anti-Semitism is a big story in the media not
because it is so prevalent, but rather because, under the man-
bites-dog rule of news judgment, it is so unusual. Black hate
deserves attention, but, as the headlines following the terror
bombing of the federal building in Oklahoma City remind us,
so does white hate.

Among the blessings we can count are:

1: *A strikingly similar spiritual heritage.* Blacks, more than
other Christians, traditionally take the Old Testament's witness closest to heart, with its mighty images of enslavement,
liberation, deliverance, and the Promised Land. Our Old
Testament spiritual foundations are evidenced in many ways,
from the writings of James Baldwin to gospel songs like "Go
Down, Moses," "Joshua Fought the Battle of Jericho," and
"Crossin' Over that River Jordan."

2: *Strikingly similar victimization traditions that offer lessons
to the world.* As one friend who used to belong to the Nation
of Islam, but dropped out when Louis Farrakhan took over,
put it, "I think it's a real contradiction for people who call
themselves Afrocentric to embrace a sickness as profoundly
European as anti-Semitism."

3: *Close political ties.* On Capitol Hill, the Congressional
Black Caucus has consistently supported Israel, especially
after the departure of Representative Gus Savage in 1992,
while Jewish legislators have uniformly supported the black
agenda, including affirmative action programs. The "special
relationship" also endures back home among their constituents. Jewish voters tend to support black candidates in
twice the percentages of other whites. Jesse Jackson in the
1988 New York primary was a significant exception when he
garnered a percentage of Jewish voters that was only about
the same as that he received from whites as a whole.

4: *Democratic Party politics.* Despite the urgings of conservatives, Jews remain in the Democratic Party more than other white ethnics do, partly out of misgivings over extremists like Pat Buchanan and the Christian right.

5: *A deeply-imbedded cultural commitment to social justice.* Jonathan Kaufman, author of *Broken Alliance,* writes, "For many of us, a commitment to social justice, to righting society's wrongs, remains a crucial part of our religious ethic, drawn from the Bible and the prayer book and an important secular touchstone, like supporting Israel or making sure the Holocaust is not forgotten. Turning our backs on black America, however temporarily satisfying, will in the long run nag at our consciences too much to allow us to join the neo-conservatives in comfort."

6: *Pragmatic flexibility.* I have heard another specialist in black-Jewish relations, the American Jewish Committee's Murray Friedman, author of *What Went Wrong? The Creation and Collapse of the Black-Jewish Alliance,* advise concerned blacks and Jews to "normalize" relations the way Jews have normalized relations with Catholics. Find areas of common interest where we can work together, Friedman tells fellow Jews, otherwise "get out of the way," and let blacks go their own way on areas like affirmative action where agreement is not as easy.

Friedman's vision of occasional partnerships of convenience centered on specific issues fits the pattern of developments that already are unfolding on various fronts, such as Congress. Such a vision meshes smoothly with traditional American patterns of plurality in ethnic relations. Still, I cling to the view that blacks and Jews have enough in common to make their relationship special, to encourage us to learn more about each other, after years of drifting apart, and offer once again some important lessons to the world on how different ethnic groups can form working partnerships at a time when nonwhite groups are growing faster than white ethnic groups in America. Our communities have grown apart as Jews, by virtue of their whiteness, eased more rapidly into the white mainstream, leaving increasingly resentful blacks behind. Still, as Kaufman says, we share too much to make total divorce any easier than reconciliation. "No question— Farrakhan is a Jew baiter," writes Kaufman, "but Jews do not have to take the bait." Neither, I might add, do blacks.

Many other individuals who share that view continue to come together, often outside the glare of media spotlights. A number of campus Hillels have joined the movement for reintroduction and hoped-for reconciliation. Black-Jewish studies reemerged on the southern black campuses of Morehouse and Dillard universities in the early 1990s. The Anti-Defamation League's World of Difference program encourages the appreciation of ethnic diversity in high schools. The American Jewish Committee also has organized black-Jewish dialogues in major cities such as Washington, where joint projects have included a campaign against hand-gun violence. Martin Luther King, Jr., dreamed of a day when "the lion shall lie down with the lamb and none shall be afraid." Another more secular prophet, Woody Allen, once predicted that "the lion shall lie down with the lamb, but the lamb won't get much sleep."

Let us be, as King asked, "divinely dissatisfied" until we can all sleep more easily. We need the rest.

9

Middleman Minorities

[W]hile whites complain that blacks are too race conscious, the African-American problem has been, in a way, that blacks have never been race conscious enough to stick together in tightly knit economic organizations. The frequent efforts of black community leaders to encourage their members to "buy black" is testimony not to the natural solidarity of the African-American community but rather to its weakness.

—Francis Fukuyama, *Trust: The Social Virtues and the Creation of Prosperity*

One day at a convenience store in my neighborhood a "male youth," as police reports would say, tried to purchase a $3 pack of cigarettes with about $2.85 in change. The two Asian-American youths behind the counter told him he had not given them enough money. The young black man apparently didn't have any more money. But instead of asking them nicely to give him a break, he puffed up his chest and insisted that he had given them enough. When they responded that he had not, he cursed at them for acting like "damn Japs." Standing behind him, I felt sorry, at first, that he had so little money in his pocket. But when he began to curse at the fellows behind the counter, who I happened to know were poor refugees from Southeast Asia, not Japan, as their tormentor's slur implied, I felt my own black machismo begin to rise. Standing behind him, I adopted my brother-man drawl to say, "Aw, cool it, bro'." The two fellows behind the counter didn't say anything to provoke him further. They simply stood their ground and stared back at him with quiet defiance. They were not going to be intimidated. The vulgar would-be customer gave up, scooped his money back into his pocket, and headed for the door, spewing a constant stream of invective against "damn Chinese and Japanese" for "buyin' up all the stores" and flooding America with "yo' damn cars!" It could have been worse. A couple of months later, a black suspect was arrested in connection with a string of cold-blooded killings of Korean merchants in the District of Columbia. Police described the killings as ethnic "hate crimes."

Great shifts of international population come to ground at the corner grocery.

Korean, Arab, and even some black West Indian merchants, riding into town on the wave of post-1965 immigration policies, have restored enterprise to many blighted urban neighborhoods. But they also find themselves caught in the middle, a new class of "middleman minorities" on the urban battleground. Misperceived as an alien force, backed perhaps by evil conspiratorial overlords, they have become targets for killers, shoplifters, and paranoid, occasionally unscrupulous community organizers. Is there hope? Yes, most of the time poor black and middleman minorities need each other. Consumers need the goods and services, and the providers need to make a living. Yet resentments inevitably intrude into relations between unequals. In my wildest dreams, the very qualities that generate the most hostility when we see others exhibit them may hold the key to a new urban peace and prosperity. If we succeed, America can provide, once again, a bright guiding light to a feuding world on how a maddeningly diverse population can "get along," in Rodney King's immortal words. If we fail, we will have compromised this country's best visions of itself.

Such incidents show me how the dreary outlook of the Kerner Commission, President Lyndon B. Johnson's blue-ribbon panel to study the causes of urban riots in the 1960s, has proved to be unexpectedly rosy, compared to our racial reality. It said in 1967 that America was becoming "two nations, one black, one white, separate and unequal." For many urban neighborhoods, it has become several nations, one black, one white, and a few others caught in the crossfire in between. Scenes of rifle-bearing Korean grocers fending off black and Hispanic rioters during the Los Angeles riots of 1992 showed the world how much America had changed since the 1960s. Unlike the Watts riots of 1965, Hispanic arrestees outnumbered black arrestees this time, and, instead of being largely passed over after putting "black owned" or "soul brother" signs in their windows, black businesses often were burned right along with everyone else's. A year earlier Ice Cube had given the world a preview of black vs. Korean resentment in a rap tune that directly attacked Korean businessmen. The lyrics were written after a Korean-American woman received a light sentence in Los Angeles for shooting Natasha Harlans, a black teenage girl, in the head while the two quarreled over whether the girl had shoplifted. Security tapes of the shooting had outraged Los Angeles blacks.

In New York City, similar quarrels between Korean merchants and black customers resulted in pickets and boycotts that drove at least two Korean merchants out of business, while pressure mounted on the city's black mayor, David Dinkins, to do something. A large banner pasted across one of the stores read, "Closed for Murder and Disrespect of Black People."

Elsewhere, a merchant in Fort Worth's Black Stop Six area killed a forty-two-year-old black man. Demonstrations led by

Reverend Michael Bell, of the city's Southeast Neighborhood Interest Coalition, forced it to close. The coalition pushed a seven-point program, including hiring black employees, providing scholarships for black students, and participating in an adopt-a-school program. But, mainly, leaders said they wanted to see day-to-day relations improve. Don't treat every customer like a potential shoplifter, they said. Bell could not help noticing one irony. "They've seen us shoot each other, too," he told *Emerge* magazine (March 1995). "I guess they felt there was a low premium on black lives." If so, the mysteries and misunderstandings only begin there.

In Chicago and Detroit, similar confrontations erupted during the 1980s between black community leaders and Arab merchants. Heavily Palestinian Arab communities in both cities swelled after the 1967 war in the Middle East. Ironically, many occupied storefronts previously occupied by Jewish merchants who were delighted to leave after the riots in 1967 and 1968. By the end of the 1980s, Chicago's human relations department would find itself persuading a black merchant to remove from a front window an enormous sign that read, "American Owned, No Arabs!"

In other bitter, but less publicized, incidents, particularly in New York City and Miami, blacks have shown similar resentments toward other blacks who are immigrants from West Africa or the West Indies.

Behind these public confrontations loom a simmering storm of private resentments centered around a host of aggravating questions. The underrepresentation of African Americans among entrepreneurs has long been an unsolved urban mystery, one that raises baffling questions: Are Arabs and Asians invading the inner city to exploit blacks, as some of the more resentful believe? Why are blacks so resentful? Why don't blacks open their own stores instead of complaining about others? Do Arabs or Asians receive special government subsidies or some other secret benefit that blacks can't get, as many of the black community's more paranoid members believe? Is it a *conspiracy*?

In view of the importance of the small proprietor in other American minorities, the "complete absence of a business class" among blacks is especially perplexing, observed the University of California's Ivan H. Light in his 1972 book, *Ethnic Enterprise in America: Business and Welfare Among Chinese, Japanese and Blacks*, quoting Nathan Glazer and Daniel P. Moynihan's *Beyond the Melting Pot*. The black professional class has grown immensely since then, thanks to civil rights reforms then just beginning to take hold. But, for those left behind in inner-city ghettos, the mom-and-pop stores that flourished for black consumers held captive by segregation have mostly been owned by people of other races. The question of why more blacks don't run their own businesses is all the more puzzling when you consider how vigorous black entrepreneurship used to be. After the Civil War, black people in Baltimore ran their own railroad, dock, and canal company for almost twenty years. Black businessmen from Birmingham to Harlem to Oklahoma and the South Side of Chicago ran their own stores, hotels, insurance companies, newspapers, printing shops, and other businesses. Today black entrepreneurship tends to be mainly in intimate community services: funeral homes, taverns, barbershops, and beauty parlors.

When I was a child growing up in a small midwestern factory town in the 1950s, the merchants in my neighborhood included a few blacks, but most were Jewish, Italian, or Greek, with names like Musberger, Guido, Dubrozzi, and Pantel. Urban America's traditional patterns of ethnic succession have dictated that succeeding generations of various ethnic groups work jobs no one else wants to work or pro-

vide necessary services in locations where no one else wants
to provide them, then they work their way up. When Jews or
Italians no longer felt safe in the inner city, their stores were
taken over in many cases by Arabs or Asians. When native-
born blacks no longer wanted to bus tables or clean homes
for low wages, those jobs were taken over by black and
Hispanic immigrants, legal and illegal.

This process of providing necessary services in deprived
inner-city neighborhoods has spurred economic boomlets in
neighborhoods others had abandoned, which helps explain
why Mayor Rudolph Giuliani in 1994 praised the contributions *illegal*, not just legal, immigrants were making to New
York City, even while California governor Pete Wilson was
campaigning to deny nonemergency services to illegal immigrants. While Wilson, in his pursuit of votes, chose to minimize the contributions immigrants of all sorts had made to
California's economy, Giuliani boldly acknowledged the new
businesses and services that immigrants, legal and illegal,
were providing in a city that, were it not for them, would
have suffered a population deficit in the decade of the 1980s.

Black paranoia has led many to believe the immigrants,
particularly Arabs or Koreans, are receiving some sort of
secret subsidy from the oil-rich Arab states or the Korean
secret police or even our own CIA.

"We know *for a fact* that the government is giving special
tax breaks and other benefits to Arabs, Koreans, Cubans, and
a lot of other people who want to come and set up businesses
in the black community," a militant black Chicago activist
told me in the mid-1980s. The motive was to prevent black
economic development, he said. Yet, when I asked for evidence of what he knows "for a fact," he produced none.

"Check it out," he said, quite indignantly. "You're the
reporter."

I did. I found subsidies for mohair, farm tools, and honey-bees, but none for foreigners who want to open up stores in the ghetto. The real answer to ethnic entrepreneurial success, regardless of skin color or national background, is much less glamorous: thrift, hard work, and trust, particularly when it comes to lending one another money within their own ethnic community.

I found small business loan programs that were, if any-thing, more available to native-born minorities than to any-one else. But, just as it takes more than the presence of water to make a reluctant horse drink, it takes more than access to investment capital to urge people to make use of it. It takes the right values.

Resources help. Berkeley's Ron Takaki, author of *Strangers from a Different Shore: A History of Asian Americans*, points to a New York City study of Korean fresh produce grocers that found more than 70 percent of them had college degrees. Obviously they come to America with greater resources, par-ticularly in education, than most poor inner-city residents have. Since few of their degrees were for areas related to food marketing, Takaki suspects most Korean grocers turned to the produce business as a haven because of language or other barriers to their originally chosen fields.

But education, although crucial, isn't everything. Ethnic groups that are prone to entrepreneurship have cultivated other cultural attributes over time that help them to succeed. They value saving and frugality. They value hard work, often putting family members to work for long hours and below-market compensation. Some of the very qualities that can bring widespread resentment from others, like clannishness, help explain their success: Clannishness is built on trust and helps build trust around which groups build informal net-works to assist one another.

Critical to the rapid growth of immigrant-owned businesses is the *rotating credit association*, an informal money pool that has allowed some ethnic entrepreneurs to bypass conventional, more formal lending institutions that discriminated against them. In a rotating credit association, each investor puts money into the pool, then the association lends various amounts to members who want to use it to start a business, then pay it back with interest. Koreans call it a *"kee"* or *"gae,"* both pronounced "ghay." Chinese call it a *"hui."* The Japanese call it *"tanomoshi"* or *"mujin,"* although they were more popular with the immigrant generation than with the later nisei, especially those with college degrees, who preferred the less personal credit union or savings and loans, says Light in *Ethnic Enterprise in America*.

And, contrary to popular stereotypes, Light also found evidence of rotating credit associations in Africa, including the West African regions from which American slaves were abducted. They included the *"esusu,"* developed among the Yoruba people in southeastern Nigeria, and the *"dashi,"* developed by the Yoruba's northern neighbors, the Nupe. African slaves apparently carried the *esusu* to the Americas, where it showed up in the West Indies, including the British Bahamas as the *"Asu,"* in Trinidad as the *"susu,"* in Barbados as "the meeting," and in Guyana as *"boxi* money." In Jamaica a credit association of "partners" was headed by a "banker" and the membership was composed of "throwers."

In 1920, at the peak of West Indian immigration, particularly to New York City, "West Indians in Harlem distinguished themselves from native-born Negroes by their remarkable propensity to operate small business enterprises," wrote Light. "Whereas native-born Negroes tended only to open noncompetitive service enterprises, the West Indians operated grocery stores, tailor shops, jewelry stores, and fruit vending and real estate operations in which they undertook direct competition with whites doing business in the ghetto."

At the same time, Light notes, West Indians provoked deep resentment on the part of American-born Negroes "who regarded the West Indians as stingy and grasping." Why were West Indian blacks able to hold on to this vital part of African history and culture? Anthropologists suggest it was probably because a much larger percentage of slaves who were brought to the Caribbean were kept with members of their same tribal ethnic groups, keeping much of their language and culture alive, while those who were brought to the mainland United States were interspersed with members of other tribes, accelerating their cultural amnesia.

To succeed in ghetto enterprise, it also pays to be patient and a risk taker. Turnover in these businesses is intense. Contrary to stereotypes of unlimited successes, many fail. Korean leaders estimate that in New York City alone, at least sixteen hundred Korean-owned stores, battered by competition, taxes, crime, and economic downturns, went bankrupt between 1991 and 1994, according to the Manhattan Institute's *City Journal*.

Ethnic differences result in dramatically different rates of entrepreneurship. The self-employment rate for all working Americans was about 11 percent for men and 6 percent for women in 1990, according to the Boston-based National Bureau of Economic Research, up from 10.4 percent for men and 4 percent for women in 1980. But among sixty ethnic or racial groups, self-employment rates ranged from 3.2 percent for Laotians to almost 29 percent for Israelis.

Among Europeans, the French, Portuguese, and Belgian self-employment rates were the lowest, but still almost as high as the national average. The highest European self-employment rates were held by Russians (25 percent for men and 12 percent for women) and Greeks (23 percent for men and 10 percent for women).

The differences were much greater among Asians. Filipinos were the lowest at 5 percent for men and 3 percent for women, and Koreans were the highest, 28 percent for men and 19 percent for women. Hispanics fell below the national averages, as low as 3.6 and 2.3 percent for Puerto Rican men and women, respectively, and as high as 16 and 6 percent for Cuban men and women.

African Americans showed about the same low self-employment rate as blacks from Central America and South America: around 4 percent for men and 2 percent for women.

Significantly, the Boston-based study did not break out black immigrants from the West Indies, even though their high entrepreneurship rate is well known among American-born blacks, particularly in New York City, where a city study in the mid-1980s found that half of the city's black-owned businesses were owned by West Indian blacks, even though they made up only a tenth of the city's total black population. West African vendors proliferate along the streets of Harlem and the District of Columbia. Similarly, Haitian immigrants in Miami have within a generation produced household—although not individual—incomes that are higher than the national average, like Asians.

In short, ethnicity and its cultural luggage appear to be more important than race in determining who succeeds at business ownership. Francis Fukuyama reaches the same conclusion in *Trust: The Social Virtues and the Creation of Prosperity* (1995) on his way to making the book's larger point that some nations succeed better than others because their national cultures encourage higher levels of trust and pass these high-trust values along from generation to generation.

High-trust countries like Germany, Japan, and the United States have high levels of "spontaneous sociability," which lead them to form many civic groups and organize around communitarian models. Societies where trust is low, like Italy, France, and China (including Taiwan), require more contracts, regulation, oversight, and centralized control, which exact higher costs. High-trust societies have more handshake agreements and large enduring corporations with easily recognizable corporate brand names (like Mitsubishi or Mercedes Benz). Low-trust countries have more lawsuits and family businesses (like Fiat) that often fail to last beyond three generations before collapsing in family disputes. Italy and Taiwan have prospered, but mostly with economies based on small family firms. In America, which is sliding nationally from a high-trust society with lots of handshake agreements and bowling leagues into a low-trust society of lawsuits and quick layoffs, we can see similar patterns from one ethnic subgroup's society to another. Immigrant Koreans, Chinese, Arabs, and West Indian blacks are quite enthusiastic and successful entrepreneurs, while most mainland-born blacks are not. The *deracination* of mainland blacks from their native culture and its high-trust values, Fukuyama notes, is "one of the key factors impeding the economic advancement of the African-American community in the United States."

Why do we not trust one another? Slavery robbed our black ancestors of trust and other values of social glue as much as it robbed them of dignity. Light noted the noticeably higher level of social cohesiveness Jamaicans and Trinidadians showed for one another earlier this century. This still can be seen today. Two big reasons: Families and ethnic cultures were kept more intact among island blacks, and whites in the islands were vastly outnumbered by the slaves, unlike on the mainland where whites usually were the majority, except in some local areas.

During Caribbean visits, I have found Jamaicans who are proud to say most of their citizens can trace their roots not only to West Africa but also to the same ethnic tribe. When such deeply rooted islanders move to the United States, it is not surprising to see many of them pull together into tightly knit social and business arrangements, just like Cubans, Greeks, Chinese, and innumerable other American immigrants. On the negative side, the higher the trust within a society, the lower the tolerance for others. Germany and Japan in World War II offer two particularly hideous examples. When this clannish intolerance shows itself within a pluralistic society like ours, it can only inflame the friction that already exists. What is remarkable to me about American ethnic groups is not that we fight so much, but that we fight so little.

Also important to the success of immigrant entrepreneurs are the qualities that lead one to become an immigrant. Surely it is no accident that those who show enough initiative and determination to pack up and strike out for a new home in a new land show the very risk-taking values that lead to success in business.

As important as *how* various ethnic groups are represented is *where*: Russians and Poles tended to concentrate in very profitable industries, such as general building construction, health services, and legal, engineering, and accounting services. Italians and Greeks were overrepresented in eating and drinking establishments. Japanese entrepreneurs were concentrated most highly in horticultural services. Asian Indians and Filipinos were concentrated most highly in health services, and Chinese Americans owned a disproportionate number of restaurants, while Koreans were overrepresented in small retail stores.

Robert Fairlie and Bruce Meyer, authors of the study, found no big mystery as to why self-employment was chosen by various groups: Individuals tended to choose it when it paid better than wage and salary work.

As it happened, the liberalized immigration laws in 1965 that dropped preferences for Europeans coincided with riots and the economic abandonment of inner-city neighborhoods. Contrary to popular myths, the riots failed to revive inner-city ghettos. Instead, old businesses and jobs fled, often to be replaced by immigrant shopkeepers who soon became common fixtures in inner-city neighborhoods nationwide.

Do they exploit the community? Since it is a foolish business owner who deliberately antagonizes the consumer base, other explanations for the high prices, limited selection, and rude service that rankle consumers are more likely. High prices reflect a high cost of doing business. Suspicious "tailing" of customers through the store reflects significant rates of neighborhood crime. Seemingly rude treatment often can result from cultural differences. Insincere smiling, for example, can be viewed as the height of goofiness in Korean culture, I am told, whereas it is routine here in the land of "Have a nice day." Many soon learn the ways of American culture. Some are taught in defensive classes held by Korean business associations. The Korean woman who owns my neighborhood laundry, for example, can say "Have a nice day" with a smile big enough to be seen back in Seoul. In February 1993 the Reverend Al Sharpton, who had led a widely publicized boycott in Brooklyn, gave the invocation at the annual awards dinner of the Korean American Grocers Association of New York. In the early 1990s Korean grocers began to distribute "love turkeys" at Thanksgiving through three thousand churches in minority neighborhoods and sponsored spots on black radio stations to honor black heroes. Still,

Korean community leaders complain that some black leaders will not be satisfied. Community pressures exert an additional tax on them, a resentment tax.

For years anthropologists have recorded similar resentments directed against "middleman minorities," ethnic minorities who cluster in commercial occupations, especially in third-world countries. The largest are the 26 million "overseas Chinese" across Southeast Asia, the Caribbean, and North America. Elsewhere, they also include the Ibo of Nigeria, Armenians of the Ottoman Empire, Tamils in Sri Lanka, Japanese in Peru, and certain religious minorities such as the Jains and Parsees of India, or Quakers in eighteenth-century Britain.

But the most famous middleman minorities undoubtedly are the Jews, the standard by which other middleman minorities are tagged in common parlance: Cubans are the "Jews of the Caribbean"; East Indians (and Pakistanis) are the "Jews of East Africa"; Lebanese are the "Jews of West Africa"; West Indians are the "Jews of Harlem."

Accordingly, many have been brutally persecuted. Chinese have been massacred in Southeast Asia and tragically ousted as "boat people" from postwar Vietnam. Thousands of East Indians, a major entrepreneurial class in East Africa, were ousted from Uganda by Idi Amin and from prewar Burma, and occasionally harassed in Tanzania. Armenians were slaughtered in the Ottoman Empire, Chinese in Indonesia, Ibos in northern Nigeria, and Jews in Nazi-occupied Europe and Russian pogroms, not to mention their mass expulsions from various European countries.

Some anthropologists, like Light, caution against applying the "middleman minority theory" too freely to American cities, since traditional models and American realities differ significantly. America is not a third-world country. Those in commercial roles are lauded here as cultural heroes, not pariahs, as they are in traditional cultures. Finally, middleman theory in the strictest academic sense referred to sojourning minorities, like Jews, Gypsies, and the ethnic Chinese, who were forced to wander because of their pariah status. Koreans, whom Light studied in his 1988 book *Ethnic Entrepreneurs*, like Arabs and West Indians, came here much as other immigrants did, not as wanderers but as settlers.

Others have not been quite as constrained. Thomas Sowell uses the term more freely in his analysis of resentment against middleman minorities in the May/June 1993 issue of *The American Enterprise* magazine, published by the American Enterprise Institute. Among other consistent ironies, Sowell points out, middlemen are most hated where they are most needed—in places where competition has fled and the community is most dependent on them—and are most taken for granted where customers are less dependent on them. He offers the example of Jews in prewar eastern Poland, who controlled 90 percent of commerce, compared to 10 percent in more prosperous western Poland, where anti-Semitism was much less severe.

I think the term "middleman minorities" can apply even more loosely, not only to commercial transactions but also to the role of social and political intermediaries performed by Irish ward bosses in eastern industrial cities such as Boston, New York City, and Chicago, particularly for later-arriving immigrants from non–English-speaking cultures.

I think this broader application helps us understand how it is not accidental that today's conflicts between blacks and Korean, Arab, or West Indian grocers so closely resemble conflicts in recent years between blacks and Jews, another immigrant group whose members often served as intermediaries to help provide important goods, services, and political power for newer groups. When rural blacks moved to northern industrial cities from the rural South, they found Jews prominent among the landlords, merchants, teachers, lawyers, social workers, pawnbrokers, ward committeemen, political activists, and other intermediaries who helped them make the transition to urban life. In Chicago, the American Jewish Committee's ethnic pluralism project has performed similar outreach for the city's large Hispanic immigrant population.

That's how ethnic succession operates in America. As groups work their way into the American mainstream, some find themselves serving as intermediaries for newer arrivals. When I was a child growing up in the 1950s, the merchants in my neighborhood included some blacks but were mostly Jewish and Italian. Today's urban black youths are just as likely to shop merchants who are Koreans and Arabs (particularly in Detroit and Chicago) and Chaldeans, a Middle Eastern minority with a substantial community in Detroit.

But familiarity in such instances also breeds contempt. Plain old-fashioned racial prejudice or ethnic xenophobia does not quite describe the special resentfulness that has built up between black consumers and middleman minority merchants who are Arabic or Korean or West Indian blacks. Prejudice only helps the victimizer feel less guilty. As English essayist William Hazlitt wrote, "There is no prejudice so strong as that which arises from a fancied exemption from all prejudice." He might well have been talking about those poor urban inner-city blacks and their sympathizers who feel their past victimization has conferred on them a certain innocence, an exemption from racism, since they lack the traditional power that enables racists to do real damage. Unfortunately, the Korean merchants who saw their livelihoods go up in smoke in Los Angeles can be excused if they don't see the difference.

The roots of resentment against middleman minorities are a bit more complex and multilayered. Part of it is the resentment felt by any group that sees itself being passed over by opportunity once again. Having been left behind by Jews, other white ethnics, and upwardly mobile blacks fleeing inner-city ghettos, poor blacks fear they will be passed over once again by the Asians, Hispanics, Arabs, and, with a special pain, Haitians and other black West Indians setting up new economic beachheads in their neighborhoods. Miami offers perhaps the clearest example. While blacks in other cities were taking advantage of new opportunities that opened up in the 1960s, Miami blacks saw many of those opportunities snapped up by upwardly mobile Cubans, who, as protected minorities, were eligible for government help, but were better prepared to take advantage of it. Most of Miami's black middle class fled to other growth havens like Houston or Atlanta. Most "Anglo" whites fled to the suburbs. As Miami became increasingly Hispanic, blacks left behind felt increasingly left out.

Then waves of Haitian refugees arrived. Hiring mostly "their own," like most immigrants, they turned the neighborhood of "Little Haiti" into a thriving tourist attraction, particularly on weekends, while even native Miamians were afraid to go into black neighborhoods like Liberty City. When riots broke out in black neighborhoods in the 1980s, they had a sad inevitability. "The difference between riots in the 1960s and riots in the 1980s," a housing activist told me, "is the difference between hope and no hope."

The middleman role is itself enraging. "It is the role rather than the people or their religion, which seems to be crucial,"

Sowell observes. "Prewar Japanese immigrants encountered far more hostility in Peru, where they were often middlemen, than in Brazil, where they deliberately settled in agricultural communities, in part to avoid the middleman stigma."

And, despite Light's minimization of any cultural resentment Americans may have against commercial roles, economic roles like moneylending and retailing have long been stigmatized by the moral teachings of Islam, Confucianism, and early Christianity. Jesus, it must be remembered, threw moneylenders out of the temple. In modern times, Bill and Hillary Clinton's assaults against the "greed" of the 1980s were specifically intended to tap traditional cultural chords that suspect anyone who makes money from money, whether on Wall Street, in savings and loans, or in real estate developments such as, as it turned out, Whitewater, instead of production or services. "Eliminate the middleman" is a common theme even in modern American life. It is also an often futile quest, for the middlemen, contrary to popular perceptions, fill a need in exchange for the profit they make. If the profit is excessive, competitors will enter the market and bring prices down. But such simple economic principles often are lost on those who insist on seeing the middleman as somehow having confiscated goods that rightfully would have gone directly to the consumer, had the middleman not somehow held them hostage. It is just such paranoid reasoning that caused the Chicago activist I interviewed to insist that Arab or Korean merchants must be getting special breaks from the government. Instead of grasping the basic logic that profits come as a reward for hard labor, he insists on precisely the opposite, that they must be the product of cunning, deceit, and grand conspiracies, even while other successful black people prove him wrong. Yet it is precisely this success by some that makes the less successful feel disrespected and resentful and thus obliged to find wild, intricate excuses to soothe their bruised egos, avoid the painful truth, and salvage some semblance of self-respect. One group's ethnic solidarity, a virtue in establishing trust, becomes another group's "clannishness." The paranoid, essayist Richard Hofstadter writes in *The Paranoid Style in American Politics*, fails to develop an essential "intuitive sense of how things do not happen." Circumstances often deprive the paranoid of exposure to events or information that might enlighten, making such a person "a double sufferer, since he is afflicted not only by the real world, with the rest of us, but by his fantasies as well."

Neither African Americans nor any other Americans can afford to be afflicted by fantasies. Economic ignorance and paranoid demagoguery, whether preached by a religious fanatic or by a college professor, need to be ridiculed and rejected, not applauded. We should not confuse our children about this. Today's young inner-city residents lead very public lives. They often live in public housing, attend public schools, eat with public aid, and receive treatment from public hospitals or public health nurses. The only form of free enterprise they may see are pimps, drug dealers, and other entrepreneurs in the underground economy. This, too, is enterprise, ethics aside, but with deplorably high risk and an abysmal retirement plan.

Capitalism works. Our task must be to find ways to make it work for everyone. The biggest "black tax" leveled on inner-city entrepreneurship has been lack of credit. The remedy may be as close as the corner church. Churches and other community groups have a natural base for organizing rotating credit associations. Since the early days of slavery, the black church has been the most vital and effective tool for black progress that black people have had. Today, at the dawn of the twenty-first century, it can once again take the lead in fostering a new era of grass-roots economic progress. Once poor blacks have strengthened the economic and educational base within their own communities, the consumer-provider disparity that breeds friction in middleman-minority relationships can be reduced, along with interethnic resentment. Instead of working to help young people "escape" the ghetto, we can help turn the hostile ghetto back into a welcoming neighborhood. We don't need to "imitate the Asians," as has often been suggested. If that's not "black" enough for us, we can turn to the *esusu* or *dashi* traditions of our ancient West African ancestors. We don't need miracles. We only need trust.

10

A Farewell to Alms

Black Conservatives and "Conservative Blacks"

Why isn't the black community producing leaders worth following? Talk of a "leadership crisis" haunts black conversations. They just aren't making leaders like Martin Luther King, Jr., or Malcolm X anymore, it is said, or movements like the civil rights or black power movement. Even among their admirers, Jesse Jackson and Louis Farrakhan just don't stack up. Call it "movement nostalgia."

"There has not been a time in the history of black people in this country when the quantity of politicians and intellectuals was so great, yet the quality of both groups has been so low," writes Harvard's Cornel West in *Race Matters*. "How do we account for the absence of the Frederick Douglasses, Sojourner Truths, Martin Luther King, Jr.'s, Malcolm X's and Fannie Lou Hamers in our time? Why hasn't black America produced intellectuals of the caliber of W.E.B. Du Bois, Anna Cooper, E. Franklin Frazier, Oliver Cox, and Ralph Ellison in the past few decades?"

Or has the time for black messiahs passed? Leadership rises up from the ranks of people who need it. It also helps to have a rallying issue and organizing principles. Among blacks, as among whites, these organizing principles always have centered around two polar opposite ways of viewing the world, opposites I shall label "outside help" vs. "self-help." When one failed to work for us, we listened with great interest to the other. It is instructive to note, as a tonic for all the media talk of welfare queens and Willie Hortons, that for most of black American history black Americans took care of their own needs: making their own clothes, building their own houses, creating many of their own jobs, and organizing their own churches and other civil organizations.

When government got in the way (slavery, segregation, etc.), black leaders rallied the masses through their civil organizations to change government policy. After years of blacks looking to government and others for help, I think self-reliance is ready to make a comeback, but not in the way many of today's self-proclaimed black conservatives would have us believe. The National Association for the Advancement of Colored People, the Southern Christian Leadership Conference and other traditional civil rights groups still do some good work, but, compared to the national scope of their past glories, since the 1960s they have been suffering from a bad case of what I call "agenda shock."

When I, in my role as a nationally syndicated columnist, took one prominent NAACP leader aside and asked for his personal, off-the-record appraisal of what needed to be done to reach today's violence-plagued, dispirited, and resentful youth, he responded, "Brother Page, I only wish I knew."

His hand-wringing frustration over this fundamental issue of our times confirmed an awful truth. In the current vernacular, our leaders didn't have a clue.

When the *Detroit News* and Gannett News Services conducted a nationwide poll in 1992 (in a project initiated and
supervised, I could not help noting, by a black editor—yet
another sign of how much things have changed since the
1960s) of 1,211 African-American adults, 94 percent said civil
rights organizations were out of touch with changing times.
While they still ranked "civil rights" as an important concern,
they ranked jobs, schools, crime, housing, and economic
development as more important. That sounded to me like a
solid agenda presented up from the streets, the grass roots.
Yet when I asked the Reverend Ben Chavis about the poll
during his brief tenure as executive director of the NAACP,
he responded, "Those other problems are civil rights problems, too! A job is a civil right. Schooling is a civil right.
Housing is a civil right."

Chavis, like other civil rights leaders—Joseph Lowery of
the Southern Christian Leadership Conference, Jesse Jackson
of Operation PUSH and the Rainbow Coalition, and so many
lesser lights—saw no need for his organization to revamp its
civil rights agenda for an age in which the problems plaguing
black America were essentially economic and moral. Instead,
he simply redefined new problems to fit his old agenda.

Suddenly I was reminded of something Robert C. Woodson,
head of the Washington-based National Center for
Neighborhood Enterprise, had said about the folly of civil
rights leaders who insist on seeing an economic world through
civil rights glasses. "If the only tool you have is a hammer," he
said, quoting psychiatrist Abraham Maslow, "all problems
begin to look like nails." When polio was conquered, the
March of Dimes shifted its agenda to take on the problem of
birth defects. Chavis sounded to me as though he would have
us think that birth defects were really polio in disguise.

I distinguish between "black conservatives" and "conservative blacks." The former is a relatively small, if high-profile, movement of avowed conservatives who happen to be black. The latter best describes the black masses who harbor many conservative attitudes, but part company with traditional conservative party lines, especially the line that says black people make too much of racism.

Polls confirm that most black Americans are quite comfortable to be socially conservative, yet politically liberal. Black Americans are acutely aware of how much racism is alive and well, but we also are acutely aware, when we are not too outraged to admit it, that the worst problem facing black Americans today is the failure of so many of us to take advantage of opportunities that already have opened up. As the nature of the problems facing black Americans has changed, so has the need for new strategies to cope with them. At the same time, you must, as the street saying goes, "remember to watch your back."

Woodson is an African American who also proudly calls himself a conservative, a label this era has come to attach, properly or not, to anyone whose thinking parts company with traditional civil rights leadership. In the 1960s, black conservatives had little voice or visibility. Beyond grumpy old men like columnist-author George Schuyler, who died in the mid-1960s without much public notice, or Joseph H. Jackson, then head of the National Baptist Convention, USA, they were hard to find. But times have changed. Black Americans have grown weary of intellectual stagnation on the left and being taken for granted by the Democratic Party. Many have grown weary of the collapse of self-reliance and personal responsibility in too many black households. If ever there was a time when black Americans were ripe for another of our periodic seismic shifts from left to right, or outside help to self-help, this is it.

Woodson offers an example of how it can happen. He had been an NAACP organizer in Harrisburg, Pennsylvania, he says, when his conservative epiphany came after his group had completed a hard-won victory, after much picketing and boycotting, to open up some slots for black chemists at a local plant. But, when he later approached the hired chemists for help, they said, "We got these jobs 'cause we were qualified," Woodson recalls. Suddenly Woodson decided something was out of whack. "I realized then that the poor, grass-roots black people who had worked so hard to win these victories were the last to receive any of the rewards," he said. He determined to turn that around. He had not marched for the privilege of sitting next to white people, he said. He had marched to win freedom for black people. Black people had not depended on white people for their freedom in the past, he said; we need not depend on them now.

Woodson's words struck a long-dormant responsive chord in me. He did not sound like conservatives I had known. He sounded, at different turns, like Martin Luther King, then like Malcolm X; like Fannie Lou Hamer, then like Huey P. Newton. He did not need to wear black berets or African garb. He let his ideas do the talking. In the small southern Ohio factory town where I grew up, conservatives were little old white ladies who wore flowered hats, railed against fluoridated water, thought Eisenhower was a Communist sympathizer, and voted for Barry Goldwater. We didn't have "black conservatives." We only had black Republicans, mostly elderly folk who had hung in with the party of Abraham Lincoln, despite the winning ways of Franklin and Eleanor Roosevelt.

Woodson was different. He was a critic of the civil rights movement, but he did not appear to have sold out. He had paid his dues with the movement, but he was not afraid of change. He spoke knowingly of poor people, not in the abstract as pitiable ghetto residents, but as people with intelligence who had not been "empowered" to take control of their own lives. He criticized government programs but, like Jack Kemp, did not want to do away with them. He only wanted to remove the bureaucratic middlemen, to dismantle what he called "the poverty Pentagon" and give money and power directly to the poor in the fashion of the Community Action Programs of Lyndon B. Johnson's War on Poverty, a war Woodson saw as having considerable merit, before it was corrupted by bureaucrats, professional providers, and machine politicians.

There was just one thing that troubled me about Woodson. For my tastes, he, like other new-wave black conservatives, showed too little respect for the civil rights leaders who remain the black community's frontline defense against racism. But Woodson had answers for this, too. "If racism was to dry up and disappear off the face of the earth tonight, how much would it change the lives of poor black people tomorrow?" he said. Would the street gangs disband? Would bad schools suddenly turn out scholars? Would crack addicts be cured? Would unwed mothers suddenly have husbands?

Here, too, he sounded a note that echoed King's sentiments in the late 1960s, when he shifted his crusade from civil rights to economic justice: What good does it do you to integrate a lunch counter if you can't afford to pay the bill?

The original agenda of the NAACP and the southern civil rights movement was largely achieved in the 1960s, the new black conservatives say, except perhaps for a little mopping-up action here and there. My generation's fleeting fancy with black power, Black Panthers, and revolutionary rhetoric has simmered down. Now the time has come to move on to the other great glory of the movement, which was not the demands it made on white people, but the demands it put on black people. The "We Shall Overcome" generation has spawned the hip-hop generation. Their role models are Ice T and Snoop Doggy Dogg. The age of activism is past, they say. Make way for the *age of accountability*, a time for black people to take stock of themselves, a time to pull themselves up by their own bootstraps, a time to bid a fond but long overdue farewell to what Woodson calls the "alms race."

To which the ringing black liberal reply is: How can we pull ourselves up by our bootstraps when we haven't got any boots? The new black conservatives won't listen to that. We've been through tougher times than these, they point out. Hundreds of years of slavery, lynchings, segregation, subjugation, degradation, and humiliation could not hold us back. "And still we rise," Maya Angelou poetically wrote. We can rise again. We have boots. A healthy two-thirds of black America has risen above the government's official poverty line, mostly since the civil rights revolution of the 1950s and 1960s. Yesterday's mom-and-pop businesses pale in comparison to the multimillion-dollar enterprises run by the likes of Chicago's John H. Johnson, publisher of *Ebony* and *Jet*; Washington's Bob Johnson (no relation), CEO of Black Entertainment Television; or Earl Graves of New York City, publisher of Black Enterprise, or Suzanne de Passe of Los Angeles, producer of television specials—or the multibillion dollar enterprises run by the late Reginald Lewis of Beatrice Foods and the rest of a new generation of black CEOs emerging at the top of traditionally white corporations. Black Americans did not need Ronald Reagan to tell us about self-help.

But those who were left behind in ghetto poverty actually are worse off, sinking deeper not only in income in real inflation-adjusted dollars but also in despair as their brightest lights of hope, their upwardly mobile middle-class-aspiring role models, have mobilized out of sight, out of mind, in a black middle-class flight that has followed "white flight" to the suburbs. Why, the conservatives ask, should we surrender now, simply because the enemy in this age does not always come conveniently cloaked in white? If so many of us have made it, they ask, why not the rest? Why do we not do what Booker T. Washington, the godfather of modern black conservatism, advised: "Cast down our bucket where we are."

For those of us who came of age in the 1960s, Booker T. Washington, America's most prominent black leader at the turn of the century, fell into widespread disfavor. But he is making a comeback on the shoulders of black conservatives. After a decade of high-profile promotion by the Reagan and Bush administrations, they emerged as a real force to be reckoned with when the Senate, by history's narrowest vote, sent federal judge Clarence Thomas to fill Thurgood Marshall's seat on the Supreme Court, with a majority of black respondents supporting him in opinion polls despite relentless assaults from his liberal detractors. The validity of such polls continues to be debated. Many of the black Americans polled undoubtedly supported him on the basis of the color of his skin more than the content of his characterization of government support programs as a modern-day plantation. But one thing was certain. Black conservatives were poised to win converts. Now the question arises, can they succeed in their counterrevolution to win the hearts and minds of black America, or will they, too, implode from their own internal conflicts and contradictions?

First they have to be taken seriously. I have a friend, black like me, who insists that the very term "black conservative" poses an oxymoron, a self-contained contradiction, like "jumbo shrimp," "loyal opposition," or "student athlete." She is not alone. As a political term, "conservative" brings memories—some quite recent—to mind that are not pleasant for blacks. Conservatives tend to stand, as William F. Buckley once put it, athwart history, relentlessly yelling, "Stop!" One would be hard-pressed to find any era of white America's past that offers much appeal to black Americans. Yet today, in the era of crack, drive-by shootings, and gangsta rap, it is not unusual to hear black people recall certain pleasing aspects of black America's past, particularly the days when black businesses thrived in now-abandoned inner-city shopping strips. If you were an unruly child, you might be disciplined on the spot by whatever elder happened to be present. Then you were sent home to be disciplined again by your parents. Our neighborhoods seemed tighter then, more faithful to the finer virtues of the West African tribal teaching that it takes an entire village to raise a child. There were no civil liberties lawyers around to help you then. There were only the eternal verities, fundamental truths that today would be called "conservative."

Contrary to popular belief, black conservatives are not an oddity created in the basement of Ronald Reagan's White House. Anyone who doubts the existence of blacks who happen also to be conservative knows nothing about Martin Delany, Booker T. Washington, Marcus Garvey, George Schuyler, or countless other educators, preachers, journalists, church folk, and entrepreneurs. For that matter, call Malcolm X, Elijah Muhammad, or Louis Farrakhan what you will, but don't call them "liberal."

Black Americans continue to think of themselves as more conservative than media stereotypes allow. Although most have tended to vote Democratic ever since the days of Franklin D. Roosevelt's New Deal, nearly a third of voting-age blacks identified themselves as "conservative" in a 1992 poll by Home Box Office and the Joint Center for Political and Economic Studies, a nonpartisan Washington-based black think tank. Impressive majorities favored such pet conservative proposals as letting tenants buy public housing (91 percent), evicting public housing tenants convicted of using or selling drugs (88 percent), granting parents a choice between public and private schools (88 percent of blacks who were familiar with such proposals), and barring additional benefits for single welfare mothers who have additional children (57 percent).

Since movement leaders always stand on the cutting edge of change, it is not surprising that most blacks stand to the right of most civil rights leaders on many issues. What's more important is to remember, as David Bositis, JCPES research director, points out, that most blacks still stand considerably to the left of mainstream Republicans, too.

He notes that two-thirds called themselves Democrats and big majorities also favored Jesse Jackson (75 percent), affirmative action (79 percent), more spending for education (81 percent), cuts in defense to fund urban programs (76 percent), more Afrocentric education (83 percent), and new government initiatives to help young black men (80 percent). Big majorities also favored national health insurance (91 percent), gun control (70 percent), abortion rights (80 percent), equalization of funding across black and white school districts (86 percent), free condom distribution in schools (78 percent), and free needle exchange programs (53 percent). Not exactly Rush Limbaugh country.

The roots of black conservatism run deep in black community life, but so do the roots of their black intellectual adversaries. Black political thinking has always oscillated between opposing poles of self-help and outside help. Like the "doublethink" described by George Orwell in *1984*, the black mind holds these two contradictory beliefs simultaneously and accepts them both. Most of us want more responsibility and accountability for minorities and the poor, but we also want an active role for government in promoting and protecting rights and opportunities.

In the last days of slavery, the dichotomy was represented by Frederick Douglass and Martin Delany. For Douglass, an ex-slave and pioneer publisher, "outside help" meant working with like-minded whites to promote abolition and equal rights. Delany, an apprentice-trained doctor, advocated separatism and repatriation to Africa so black Americans could build a new homeland, quite apart from their enslavers. Inasmuch as Douglass believed black people already had paid enough dues to warrant their full participation as American citizens, Delany espoused a blunt black moral supremacy and expressed doubts that *white* people were worthy of working with blacks. "I thank God for making me a man simply," said Douglass. "But Delany always thanks Him for making him a *black* man."

The modern black conservative movement tends to trace its roots to Booker Taliaferro Washington, the former slave who, in the late 1800s, founded Tuskegee Institute, which under his direction emphasized industrial training as a means to self-respect and economic independence. He was an able orator who delighted white audiences and became the most powerful and influential black man in America, a confidant of wealthy philanthropists and industrialists like Andrew Carnegie and John D. Rockefeller, and presidents Theodore Roosevelt and William Howard Taft.

His autobiography, *Up from Slavery*, published in 1901,

takes the form of a slave narrative in its opening, but quickly turns into a lesson in the value of using whatever resources one has at hand to build economic power. Don't complain, don't migrate, he said. Just take the best advantage of what you have. "To those of my race who depend on bettering their condition in a foreign land or who underestimate the importance of cultivating friendly relations with the Southern white man, who is their next-door neighbor, I would say: *'Cast down your bucket where you are'*—cast it down in making friends in every manly way of the people of all races by whom you are surrounded," he said in his most famous address, delivered at the Atlanta International Exposition on September 18, 1895. It became known as his "Atlanta Compromise" speech, for in it he stated this compromise with segregation: "In all things that are purely social we can be as separate as the fingers, yet one as the hand in all things essential to mutual progress."

Washington also insisted that whites, too, have a role in treating blacks fairly, but while many whites hailed his positions on the behavior of blacks, they paid little attention to what he had to say about whites. No matter, said Washington. Negroes should not "permit our grievances to overshadow our opportunities."

That accommodationist view drew sharp criticism from Harvard-educated William Edward Burghardt Du Bois. "So far as Mr. Washington preaches Thrift, Patience and Industrial Training for the masses, we must hold up his hands and strive with him," Du Bois wrote in his most famous work, *The Souls of Black Folk*. "But so far as Mr. Washington apologizes for injustice, North or South, does not rightly value the privilege and duty of voting, belittles the emasculating effects of caste distinctions, and opposes the higher training and ambition of our brighter minds,—so far as he, the South, or the Nation, does this—we must unceasingly and firmly oppose them."

Du Bois helped found the National Association for the Advancement of Colored People in 1909 and, working closely with whites, put his highest priorities on attacking segregation, promoting black political empowerment, and stopping the lynchings that were taking black lives with impunity.

"By every civilized and peaceful method," Du Bois wrote, "we must strive for the rights which the world accords to men, clinging unwaveringly to those great words which the sons of the Fathers would fain forget: 'We hold these truths to be self-evident: That all men are created equal; that they are endowed by their Creator with certain unalienable rights; that among these are life, liberty and the pursuit of happiness'."

The self-help vs. outside help dichotomy continued to define black intellectual conversation through the twentieth century. Marcus Garvey, Elijah Muhammad, Malcolm X, and Louis Farrakhan became the chief icons of the separatist, self-help side, and the likes of A. Philip Randolph, Martin Luther King, Jr., and Jesse Jackson rose to supreme prominence on the side of integration, coalition, and direct action.

There were other notable conservatives. Some, like George S. Schuyler, a cultural critic for the black-owned *Pittsburgh Courier* and *The Nation* and a Stanley Crouch of his day, proudly wore the title. Zora Neale Hurston was less vocal in her conservatism, but, like most blacks before Franklin Delano Roosevelt's New Deal, she was a Republican.

In the 1960s, the dichotomy was best exemplified by the integrationist vision of Martin Luther King and the separatist vision of Malcolm X. They continue to define the boundaries of black mainstream thinking today. The genius of Jesse

Jackson, as he struggled mightily to assume King's mantle after the late 1960s, was in combining the appeal of both. He called for self-help among blacks and demanded outside help from whites. He marched for open housing and "our fair share" of jobs and organized Operation Breadbasket and later Operation PUSH to promote black business franchises. He picketed white businesses to get jobs for black workers and franchises for black businesses, but still preached self-help. "No one is going to save us for us but us!" he intoned. He even dressed the part of the changeling, chameleonlike: business suits for white audiences, African dashikis and jeans among blacks.

Significantly, the rise of Louis Farrakhan, first as an ally, then as an adversary over Farrakhan's anti-Jewish comments, subtly repositioned the two into a clear reembodiment of the Martin-Malcolm dichotomy. Jackson reached out to a "Rainbow Coalition" of like-minded activists while Farrakhan picked up Muhammad's call for a separate black nation, which actually was a rehash in Islamic trappings of Booker T. Washington's self-help. Both were falling into opposing sides of the same nostalgia trip.

Then, beginning in the mid-1970s, a swarm of new, self-proclaimed "black conservatives," including Clarence Thomas, took flight. They pointed to the ghettos and announced that the left-liberal-progressive agenda had failed. Like Harvard's Glenn Loury, a product of a black neighborhood on Chicago's South Side, they returned to ghetto streets, asked, "How can they live this way?" and demanded that poor blacks be held accountable for their failures to improve their own condition. They turned the language of the left on itself, blaming liberals for enslaving the poor to new plantations of government dependency. Redistribution of income—"throwing money at the poor"—does no good, they argued, no matter how good

your intentions may be, if you have failed to pass on the values that enable poor people to break out of poverty.

Much of their proselytizing sounded like sloganeering, but
this new generation of black conservatives made up for lack
of originality with boldness and brashness, like the leftists of
the 1960s. "Those who want to share their good fortune can
share the sources of that good fortune—the skills, values, and
discipline that mean productivity," wrote Thomas Sowell in a
1984 column. "Those who want to ease their burden of guilt
should seek professional help, at their own expense—not
make policy at everyone else's expense."

Sowell, who wrote *Race and Economics* in 1975, was soon
joined on the TV, newspaper, and lecture circuit by Walter
Williams, holder of the John M. Olin Chair in Economics at
Virginia's George Mason University. Into the Reagan admin-
istration came the likes of Clarence Pendleton, as Reagan's
chairman of the U.S. Civil Rights Commission, and Clarence
Thomas, as Reagan's head of the Equal Employment
Opportunity Commission.

Reagan declined repeated requests for meetings with the
solidly Democratic Congressional Black Caucus, but on
Martin Luther King's birthday, he met with conservative Bob
Woodson, who brought in a group of black "grass-roots leaders." They included heroic low-income mothers like Kimi
Grey and Bertha Gilkey, who had organized and taken management of public housing developments in the District of
Columbia and St. Louis, respectively, and saved them from
the wrecking ball. They included organizers of independent
schools, black adoption agencies, and neighborhood anti-
crime efforts. The salient fact that most of these grass-roots
leaders still voted Democratic didn't matter. The Reagan revolutionaries and other conservatives had learned something
since Goldwater's landslide defeat in 1964: It was not enough

to stand athwart progress. They also had to offer some alternative to the liberal agenda. Walter Williams offered entrepreneurship. Bob Woodson, an ally of Jack Kemp, offered grass-roots organizing among the poor. It sounded good to me. But was anybody listening?

In the post-Reagan 1990s, a new crop of black conservative showmen rose up in the shadows of Rush Limbaugh: Denver's Ken Hamblin, the "Black Avenger"; Washington's Armstrong Williams, a former staffer for Clarence Thomas; and Baltimore's Alan Keyes, another former Reagan aide. But, to my resounding dismay, most of their notoriety seemed to come from bashing black leaders for the amusement of white audiences. Like Pat Buchanan or Rush Limbaugh, they sounded like what Woodson would call "reactive," not "reflective" conservatives. They made their living by attacking government, not figuring out ways to make government work on behalf of those who needed and deserved "empowerment."

Similarly, San Jose State's Shelby Steele, writing *The Content of Our Character* from an ostensibly liberal perspective, was quickly embraced by the conservative coalition for his therapeutic invitation for blacks to come out from our bunker mentality and take advantage of the hard-won opportunities the civil rights movement has brought. Steele's greatest contribution was to stir up the language of the national debate, demonstrating eloquently that the conventional wisdom about racism had become mightily overblown in an atmosphere of talk radio and urban paranoia. With problems of economic and moral decay mounting and the obvious iron hand of racism becoming more subtle to the point of near-nonexistence, paranoid suspicions of grand conspiracies had rushed in to fill the gap. Polls showed substantial numbers of black Americans were blaming unseen conspiracies for the appearance of crack cocaine, AIDS, and heavy assault weapons on inner-city streets in the 1980s. Steele joined other conservatives in saying that, if this was a conspiracy, black Americans have a hand as coconspirators in their own undoing.

Sounding indistinguishably similar to the self-proclaimed conservatives, Steele made a useful contribution by calling for a shift to economic development as a remedy for inner-city squalor, but he, too, offered little in the way of prescriptions for bringing his remedy about. Yet black Americans hunger for remedies.

In the battle for the hearts and minds of the public, Booker T. Washington was more successful with whites, thanks largely to his accommodation with racial separation, while W. E. B. Du Bois was more successful with blacks, for his emphasis on confronting lynchings and other racial injustices of the era. Washington died in 1915, while Du Bois's influence continued to grow until he died in 1963. By the 1930s, when the Depression caused widespread misery for urban and rural blacks, Du Bois, who was slowly embracing Marxism, also began to express appreciation for Washington's self-help, nation-building theories, a change of heart that resulted in bitter disagreements with his NAACP colleagues.

Today, as we look at the work left undone in the post–civil rights era, Washington deserves a second look, partly to marvel at the parallels between his era and ours, partly to see how his "black economic nationalism" might apply to the multiply segregated world (by race, class, and opportunity) of today's ghetto poor.

In *Up from Slavery*, for example, Booker T. Washington disparages federal help as "cruelly wrong" in fostering dependency instead of education. In fact, he goes further to propose that property and education should have been *required* of blacks *and* whites before they could vote: "During the whole of the Reconstruction period our people throughout the South looked to the Federal Government for everything, very much as a child looks to its mother. This was not unnatural. The central government gave them freedom, and the whole Nation had been enriched for more than two centuries by the labour of the Negro. Even as a youth, and later in manhood, I had the feeling that it was cruelly wrong in the central government, at the beginning of our freedom, to fail to make some provision for the general education of our people in addition to what the states might do, so that the people might be better prepared for the duties of citizenship."

In the late 1960s, the hippie musical *Hair* popularized a song that announced, "This is the dawning of the Age of Aquarius." If anything, the post-1960s era brought the dawning of the *age of accountability*. In 1976, a year after Thomas Sowell's little-heralded *Race and Economics* marked the rise of modern black conservatism, Jesse Jackson launched his PUSH for Excellence program, after calling a civil rights march to an early halt because he smelled marijuana wafting out of the ranks past his nose. PUSH for Excellence was a self-help program designed to pull parents, teachers, and principals together to promote academic excellence with the zeal usually afforded to athletic excellence. The same year, black reporter Barbara Reynolds published *Jesse Jackson: The Man, the Movement, the Myth*, a critical but balanced examination of Jackson and his shortcomings that would be criticized by Jackson's supporters but would stand for many years as the most definitive reference work on the most important black leader after King. If the 1960s marked the zenith of a brief age of progressive political activism, the 1970s marked a new period of picking up the residue and examining it. Every cherished notion would be reexamined in the age of accountability. No one would be spared, not even the poor.

Bashing traditional civil rights leaders helped the new black conservatives get public attention, like walloping the proverbial two-by-four upside the head of a stubborn horse. But while it delighted many white people, it also turned off many black people. Sufferers, whether their pain is real or only perceived, do not like to be told too bluntly that it is all in their head. Nor do they appreciate seeing their heroes pummeled in public, no matter how many private doubts they may harbor. While Ken Hamblin and other black conservative talk-show hosts continued their relentless black-bashing (Hamblin delighted in citing "black trash" more often than Limbaugh attacked "femi-nazis") to win big ratings from predominantly white, male audiences, and Sowell and Walter Williams continued to pummel the "civil rights establishment" in their popular newspaper columns, others who wanted to be regarded as people of ideas, like Woodson and Loury, seemed to be mellowing their appeal. Occasionally they would take fellow conservatives to task for being too reactionary about the ability of government, properly directed, to help poor people improve their lives. "I don't care about what's right or who's left," says Woodson. "I care about what works."

Woodson's grass-roots revolution of local block clubs, public housing residents, independent schools and black churches may show the best hope for picking up where the civil rights revolution left off. Black America in many ways is moving back to its roots, going the way of the rest of America at the end of the twentieth century, toward tolerance for its own diversity of people and ideas. Calls for "unity" and "solidarity" persist in suppressing any opinions that stray from party lines, but their hold is loosening. Young voices, carrying on the time-honored obligation of young people to outrage their elders, are looking for something new. The age of national movements may well be over. Farrakhan and his minions tantalize impressionable, alienated college youths and provide scapegoats and cathartic relief for the deeply frustrated. But the wait for a black messiah seems to be loosening its grip on black America. Weren't many reluctant to recognize even Martin Luther King as one, until he was dead?

Black activism already appears to be moving back to the local level. While the NAACP suffered through feuds, lawsuits, and near-bankruptcy on the national level in the mid-1990s, its twenty-two hundred local chapters remained as dynamic as ever, tackling all manner of local racial eruptions and local issues with a variety of approaches borrowed from the entire spectrum of black thought, including self-help, coalition building, public-private partnerships, and independent schools.

In moving back to the local churches and other grass-roots organizations, the black liberation movement comes full circle, back to where the civil rights movement began, back to where our worst problems continue to fester and grow, back to where young black males kill more young black males every year than the Ku Klux Klan killed in a decade.

Various groups like Washington's Concerned Black Men are organizing black professional men to mentor and provide role models for at-risk young black males, to cross the buppie-to-hip-hop gap. Woodson presents public housing residents like Washington's Kimi Grey, St. Louis's Bertha Gilkey, and Chicago's Irene Johnson as examples of poor people organizing their own clean-up, law enforcement, job training, and "College Here We Come" programs. Like Jack Kemp, Woodson points out that every community has similar "community assets," positive role models and grass-roots leaders

waiting for a chance to show they can succeed where government interveners have failed.

In 1962, the late black journalist Louis Lomax wrote *The
Negro Revolt* about the civil rights movement, while its revolt
was still brewing. Some of today's black conservatives richly
deserve the "sell-out" labels others attach to them, but I think
others are trying to wage, the best they can, a new black
revolt against the hegemony white male power holds over
black life, even when dressed in the velvet gloves of liberal
social programs. Those who call for "empowering" the poor
are calling for nothing short of an inversion of the social
order. Whether they meet their goal or not, the thought
counts.

Why, one might ask, are Black Muslims the only group the
conventional wisdom allows to preach a vision based on self-
help and economic independence? Is it significant that, while
other civil rights groups were bypassing the low-income
underclass, the Nation of Islam was reaching out to the
pimps, prostitutes, drug pushers, and convicts of the neighborhood in the belief that none was irredeemable? Does it say
something about the rest of us that, when the Chicago
Housing Authority invited security companies to bid on providing security guards for Rockwell Gardens, one of the
city's most dangerous public housing developments, the only
bid it received came from a company operated by
Farrakhan's Nation of Islam? We have met the enemy, as
Pogo said, and he is "us," the middle class, having joined
others in abandoning those who need help the most.

When I asked Thurgood Marshall at his final press conference how he wanted to be remembered, he responded quite
memorably, "That he did the best he could with what he
had." With that, the high court's most liberal jurist wrapped

up his extraordinary life with a fundamentally conservative theme, one that resonates well with the way George Schuyler, a conservative voice of the Harlem Renaissance, began his autobiography, *Black and Conservative*: "A black person learns very early that his color is a disadvantage in a world of white folk. This being an unalterable circumstance, one also learns very early to make the best of it."

Liberal, conservative, or in-between, black Americans hold in common the quest to make the best of what we have. I suspect many of those who were slow to condemn Clarence Thomas, despite their disagreements with his politics, appreciated how much he, like they, was just trying to get by the best he could in a land where white men still make most of the important decisions.

Conservatism resonates familiarly with me, as I think it does with most black Americans. We vote liberal, for liberalism has helped us make our greatest gains. But in other areas, we swing conservative. We want to believe that hard work will be rewarded. We want to believe that government will work to help us keep our families together, not force them apart. We want to believe in the promise of America. We want to believe in America.

Yet, when I recently saw on the front page of the *Washington Post* that a District of Columbia public schoolgirl had, despite tremendous odds, scored a perfect score on her Scholastic Aptitude Test, I wondered: Can any of us say confidently that twenty years from now, whatever her chosen profession may be, she will be earning as much annual income as her white counterparts? Yes? No? Not sure? That's how unsure Americans remain over the American promise and its fulfillment, regardless of race, creed, or color.

In its brightest days, it has been said, the civil rights movement took its cues directly from the masses of black people, then lost its moral authority when its emphasis shifted from true self-help to extracting whatever it could from white people. It need not be an either-or proposition. Black conservatives lose the rest of us when they insist, like many white conservatives, that racism is no longer a problem, that government programs and agencies must be trimmed, even when those programs and agencies offer the last slender thread of protection the children of America's black slaves have against further slides back into oppression. But black Americans hit a resonant, resounding chord when they sound the need for all of us to retrieve some of the old-fashioned, old-faithful verities that enabled our ancestors to survive and even prosper in times much tougher and more oppressive than these. We need to do the best we can with what we have. So must the rest of America. The obligation to make America work as a "color-blind society," one in which all will be judged as Dr. King dreamed, by the content of our character and not by the color of our skin, is not up to its people of color alone. White people must also do their part. The big question for the future of American conservatism is whether it can move beyond its feigned racial innocence into a genuine and aggressive assault on racism, beginning with its own ranks. The willingness of *white* conservatives, after decades of benefiting directly from racial division, to meet this obligation will be the true test of their virtue and sincerity at century's end.

11

Supply-side
Affirmative Action

Occasionally I have been asked whether I ever benefited from affirmative action in my career. Yes, I respond. You might say that my first jobs in newspapers came as a result of an affirmative action program called "urban riots."

Most newspapers and broadcast news operations in America were not much interested in hiring black reporters or photographers when I graduated from high school in 1965. Nevertheless, I asked the editor of the local daily if he had any summer jobs in his newsroom. I knew I was good. I was an honors graduate and feature editor at the local high school's student newspaper. I had a regional award already glistening on my short resume. Still, I was not picky. I would be delighted to mop floors just to get a job in a real newsroom.

And it was not as if I did not have connections. The editor had known me since I had been one of his newspaper's carriers at age twelve. Still, it was not to be. He told me the budget would not allow any summer jobs for any young folks that year. Then the very next day I found out through a friend that the newspaper did have an opening after all. The editors had hired a white girl a year younger than I, who also happened to be a reporter under my supervision at the student newspaper, to fill it.

Don't get mad, my dad advised me, just get smart. Get your education, he said. "Then someday you can get even!"

My saintly, interminably patient schoolteacher grandmother, dear old Mother Page, also helped ease my tension. "Son," she said, "just prepare yourself, for someday the doors of opportunity will open up. When they do, you must be ready to step inside."

Little did she know that that very summer, riots would erupt in the Watts section of Los Angeles. More than four hundred riots would explode across the nation over the next three years. Suddenly editors and news directors across the country were actively looking to hire at least a few reporters and photographers who could be sent into the "ghetto" without looking too conspicuous.

Many of the black journalists hired in that talent raid, much of it waged on the staffs of black publications and radio stations, would bring Pulitzers and other honors to their new bosses, dispelling the notion that they were mere "tokens" and confirming the depth of talent that had been passed over for so long. Women soon followed. So did Hispanics, some of whom had worked for years with Anglo pseudonyms to get past anti-Latino prejudices; Asians; and Native Americans.

Times have changed. Twenty-two years after it became the first newspaper to turn me down for a job, my hometown daily became the first to purchase my newly syndicated column. The advice of my elders ("Just prepare yourself") had come to fruition.

You might say that it took me only twenty years to become an "overnight success."

Yet it is significant that I and other "first blacks" hired in the nation's newsrooms felt pretty lonely through several years of "tokenism" before affirmative hiring—or, if you prefer, "diversity hiring"—policies began to take hold at the dawn of the 1970s. The message to us journalists of color was clear: White managers did not mind hiring a few of us now and then, but they didn't want to make a habit of it, not until policies came down from the top stating in military fashion that "you *will* hire more women and minorities."

So, of all the arguments I have heard various people make against affirmative action, I find the least persuasive to be the charge that it makes its recipients feel bad. Stanford law professor Barbara Babcock had the proper response to that notion when President Jimmy Carter appointed her to head the civil rights division of the Justice Department. When she was asked in a press conference how it felt to think that she had gotten the job because she was a woman, she replied that it felt a lot better than thinking that she had *not* gotten the job because she was a woman.

True enough. Most white males have not felt particularly bad about the special preferences they have received because of their race and gender for thousands of years. Why should we? Believe me, compared to the alternative, preferential treatment feels better.

Nor have I heard many express a nagging doubt about their ability to "hack it" in fair competition with others. Quite the opposite, privileged groups tend to look upon their privilege as an entitlement. Whatever guilt or misgivings they may have are assuaged by the cottage industry that has grown up around bolstering the self-esteem of white people. Books like Charles Murray and Richard J. Herrnstein's *Bell*

Curve are intended, at bottom, to answer this deep yearning. Much is made in the book about how whites perform fifteen percentage points higher on average than blacks do on standardized tests and that this may easily explain why whites earn more money than blacks. Little is made of how Asian Americans perform fifteen percentage points higher than whites, yet they have hardly taken over management or ownership of American corporations.

Or, as one of my black professional friends put it, "Since we all know that hardly any of us is really all-black, I want to know how come we only got all the dumb white folks' genes?"

The notion that Babcock should feel bad about her appointment is based on the pernicious presumption that, simply and solely because she is a woman, she must be less qualified than the man who normally would be preferred simply because he was a man.

Charles Sykes, in *A Nation of Victims: The Decay of the American Character* (1993), says that those who insist on affirmative action really are arguing that "minorities" (he speaks little of women) cannot meet existing standards, and that ultimately affirmative action forces all minorities to "deal with the nagging doubt that its policies stigmatize all successful minority individuals."

Another critic of affirmative action, Dinesh D'Souza, resident scholar at the American Enterprise Institute, goes so far as to say in his inflammatory *The End of Racism: Principles for a Multiracial Society* (1995) that most of us middle-class blacks should be stigmatized because we owe our prosperity, such as it is, to affirmative action. He then speculates that middle-class blacks must suffer "intense feelings of guilt" because "they have abandoned their poor brothers and sisters, and realize that their present circumstances became possible solely because of the heart-wrenching sufferings of the underclass."

Yet nothing in affirmative action law calls for the unqualified to be hired regardless of merit. Even "special admissions" minority students are selected from among those who already have met the standards required to do the college's work.

Affirmative action calls only for "merit" standards to be more inclusive. Affirmative action, properly implemented, *widens the pool* of qualified candidates who will be considered. This often benefits qualified white males, too, who would otherwise have been bypassed because of nepotism, favoritism, and other unnecessarily narrow criteria. My favorite example is the University of Indiana Law School's decision in 1969 to broaden its acceptance criteria to open doors to bright, promising applicants who showed high potential but, for the present, had not scored as well as other applicants in a highly competitive field. The goal of the program was to offer a second chance to disadvantaged students like those who could be found in abundance in Gary and other urban centers, but the program was not limited to them. Several white students got in, too. One was a well-heeled De Pauw University graduate named J. Danforth Quayle. He later became vice president of the United States. He apparently had not scored well enough to qualify for the law school under existing criteria, but, like him or not, he did have potential. Some people are late bloomers.

Despite America's new "atmosphere of tolerance" cited by Sykes, white skin still has its privileges. Sociology professor Andrew Hacker of Queens College recounts in his book, *Two Nations*, that he has posed to his white students the hypothetical proposition of being turned black overnight. When he asks them how much compensation they would ask for whatever inconvenience they might suffer, they tend to ask for millions of dollars for every year of their life expectancy. Who wouldn't? We all love money. The point is that none of the students presumes he or she would *not* be penalized in some fundamentally significant way by nonwhite skin.

Most debates about affirmative action remind me of the old television commercial arguments over whether Certs is a "breath mint" or a "candy mint" or whether Miller Lite is "less filling" or simply "tastes great." Affirmative action can be many things. It can be an anti-poverty program or an equal opportunity program. It can be a means to diversify a workplace or make a college's student enrollment more representative of the larger society. It can be a form of group reparations for historical patterns of discrimination or a program to impose group remedies for specific class-action grievances. How you see its purpose affects how well you evaluate it.

Arguments against affirmative action fall under the following general categories:

"We don't need it anymore." The work of early feminists and the civil rights movement did their job, but now it is time to move on. The nation has outgrown employment and educational discrimination. Nonwhite skin may actually be an advantage in many businesses and schools. The market is ultimately color-blind and would be fair, if only those infernal lawyers and government regulators would get out of the way.

Comment: Americans hate intrusions into their marketplace, unless the intrusions benefit them. I would argue that bias is as natural as xenophobia and as common as apple pie. Until opportunities are equalized enough to encourage women and minorities to have more trust in the free marketplace, there will be a glaring demand for extraordinary measures to target what is actually only a quite modest amount of jobs, scholarships, and contracts to minorities.

"Racism has reversed." This is David Duke's claim. Whites, particularly white males, now suffer a distinct disadvantage in the workplace and in college applications. Affirmative action sets racial "quotas" that only reinforce prejudices. Besides, two wrongs do not make a right.

Comment: Not anymore. Conservative court decisions in the 1990s actually have shifted the burden of proof in hiring, promotions, publicly funded scholarships, and contract set-aside cases from whites and males to minorities and women. If women and minorities ever had a time of supremacy under the law, it is gone. Conservative court opinions have worked hastily to restore white male primacy.

"It cheats those who need help most." The biggest beneficiaries of affirmative action have been, first, middle-class women and, second, advantaged minorities. It misses the less qualified "underclass."

Comment: It is easy to criticize a program that fails to reach goals it never was intended to achieve. The argument that affirmative action benefits those who need help the least falsely presumes affirmative action to be (1) an anti-poverty program and (2) a program that forces employers and colleges to accept the unqualified. It is neither. It is an equal opportunity process that, by that definition, helps most those who are best equipped to take advantage of opportunities once they are opened. I find it ironic that many of the same critics who argue that affirmative action is anti-competitive and bad for business can so quickly spin on a dime to complain that it also is uncharitable.

For example, the biggest black beneficiaries of affirmative action have been working-class blacks who had skills but were shut out of slots for which they were fully qualified in higher-paying blue-collar semiskilled, service, craft, police, and firefighter jobs because of restrictive unions and other discriminatory policies. Before President Nixon signed an executive order in 1972 calling for vigorous affirmative action among federal contractors, few black carpenters, plumbers, and other skilled building tradesmen were allowed to receive union cards. Only when construction boomed high enough to hire all available whites were skilled black tradesmen given union cards, and then only temporary cards, on a last-hired, first-fired basis. Significantly, within months of signing the executive order, Nixon was campaigning for reelection against racial "quotas." His executive order had come not so much out of his best intentions for blacks as out of a keen desire to drive a political wedge between minorities and labor-union whites.

Other examples can be found in the southern textile industry, which, under government pressure in the middle and late 1960s, finally hired blacks into their predominantly female workforce as laborers, operatives, and service and craft workers. "As a result, these black women—many of whom had spent their working lives cleaning other people's homes for a few dollars a day—tripled their wages, an enormous improvement in the quality of their lives," Gertrude Ezorsky, a Brooklyn College philosophy professor, wrote in *Racism & Justice: The Case for Affirmative Action* (1991). "I conclude that affirmative action has not merely helped a 'few fortunate' blacks."

"Be like the model minorities." Behave more like Asians and, for that matter, hardworking immigrant African and West Indian blacks who appear to get along just fine despite racism and without affirmative action. In one notable screed, backlash journalist Jared Taylor's *Paved with Good Intentions: The Failure of Race Relations in America*, asks the question:

Why do blacks continue in spite of civil rights reforms and outright preferential treatment to bring so much trouble on themselves and others with family failures, violent crimes, and drug abuse? Black leaders are no help, says Taylor, for they have become "shakedown artists" who encourage excuses, handouts, and self-pity that generate a "denial of individual responsibility." Why, oh why, asks Taylor, don't blacks simply behave more like Asian immigrants in "taking possession of their own lives"?

Comment: Opponents of affirmative action invented the "model minority" myth to stereotype Asian-American success in misleading ways that don't benefit Asians or anyone else. According to the myth, Asians succeed better academically and earn higher household income than whites despite racial discrimination and without the benefit of affirmative action. Quite the contrary, goes the myth, affirmative action sets quota ceilings on Asian participation, much like those that once limited enrollment of Jews in the Ivy League. So, therefore, affirmative action actually is harmful, both to minority initiative and to Asian success.

It's an attractive myth, but reality is a bit more complicated. There is a significant difference, for example, between *household* income and *individual* income. Asian household income, like the household income of immigrant blacks from the West Indies, exceeds white household income because more individuals in the house are likely to be working. Asian individual income still lags behind whites at every income level, from the bottom, where low-income Hmongs and many Filipinos, in particular, suffer poverty not unlike that of poor blacks and Hispanics, to the upper levels of corporate management, where a new set of myths continue to stereotype Asians as "not quite American" or "good at rational skills, but not 'people skills.'" Asian-American friends whose families have been here for several generations speak of being asked routinely, "You speak such good English; how long have you been in this country?" More ominous to many Asians are the horror stories like that of Vincent Chin, a Chinese-American who was beaten to death one night in the early 1980s by two disgruntled Detroit auto workers who were angry at competition by Japanese automakers.

As Ron Takaki details in *Strangers from a Different Shore* (1989), Asian-descended Americans have struggled against stereotypes since the early 1800s, stereotypes that characterized them as underachievers, subversives, or overachievers. In the 1800s anti-Irish bigots compared Irish immigrants unfavorably to "the industrious Asians" as blacks often are compared today. While every ethnic group has something to teach others in the American salad bowl, it is not helpful to the progress of our diverse society for anyone to turn one against the other. Affirmative action works best when it downplays "preferences" and emphasizes "inclusion."

"We have many Chinese business leaders who flatly oppose affirmative action in academia, but are very much in favor of it when they are trying to get city contracts," a pro-affirmative action Chinese-American activist told me in San Francisco.

"Give meritocracy a chance." Free market zealots like University of Chicago law professor Richard Epstein, who believes all "irrational discrimination" would disappear in an unfettered marketplace, have called for the elimination of anti-discrimination laws, saying the market will punish those who turn aside talented workers or customers with money in their pockets just because of race or ethnicity. D'Souza agrees with Epstein's bold assertion that anti-discrimination laws actually get in the way of women and minorities who would prefer to hire family members. He calls for an end to all anti-

discrimination laws except those that apply solely to government.

Comment: "Merit" by whose standard? Market forces do count, but so do culture and personal prejudices. Segregation cost white businesses valuable consumer business, yet, even in the North, where it was required only by local custom, not by government, many refused to serve blacks anyway.

Any intrusions into the marketplace trouble free-market conservatives like Epstein and D'Souza, but the larger question we Americans must ask ourselves is this: What kind of country do we want? There is no neutral "color-blind" approach to the law that has for centuries been tilted against women and minorities. It either defends the status quo, which is imbalanced by race and gender, it shifts some benefits to certain groups, or it shifts benefits away from those groups. Do we want rampant irrational, completely unfair discrimination reminiscent of the Jim Crow days that dehumanizes large numbers of Americans while we wait for the vagaries of the marketplace to catch up? Or do we want to shape law and social practice to encourage people to mix, get to know each other better, and ultimately reduce tensions?

"It encourages balkanization." Affirmative action opens social wedges that threatens to replace the basic American melting pot creed with a new "balkanization."

Comment: Anyone who thinks American society was *less* balkanized in the 1950s and 1960s was not only color-blind but also quite deaf to the complaints of people of color. If there was less racial or gender friction in major newsrooms, campuses, and other workplaces, it is only because there was no race or gender in them except white men.

Racism and sexism have not disappeared, it is widely agreed, they have only become more subtle—"gone underground"—making them less easy to detect, harder to root out.

Most of us tend to ignore our own prejudices unless someone points them out. If individuals wish to discriminate in their private social world, that's their business. But discrimination in hiring and promotional practices is everyone's business. With the courts already jammed and the complaint mechanisms of the Equal Employment Opportunity Commission suffering backlogs of two years or worse, especially after Americans with Disabilities Act cases were layered onto its already overtaxed, underfunded enforcement mechanisms, promises of enforcement of individual complaints were simply not enough to make up for cruel realities. Even when the courts do reach guilty verdicts, they often impose racial or gender quotas onto the plaintiffs as part of the penalty and remedies. Such court-ordered mandates are, by the way, the only real "quotas" that are allowed under civil rights law and only as a last resort to remedy particularly egregious cases of historic discrimination, such as the police and fire department hiring and promotion practices in cities like Chicago, Memphis, and Birmingham. Yet even these quotas have been quite modest, used sparingly, and, beginning in the 1980s, steadily rolled back by the courts, even while the numbers showed modest progress in the face of the enormous problem.

What most people call rigid "quotas" are actually quite flexible goals and timetables, a distinction that has diminished in the public mind in recent years as conservative politicians have, with remarkable success, attacked flexible goals and timetables with as much vigor as they once reserved for attacking rigid quotas.

"Focus on class not race." In attempts to salvage some rudiments of affirmative action in the face of a conservative onslaught, some centrists have argued for programs that reach out to the most needy, regardless of race or gender. If such programs are conducted equitably, a preponderance of

minorities will be brought in anyway, without the dubious air of unfairness.

The ghetto "underclass" has not benefited from affirmative action, University of Chicago sociology professor William Julius Wilson writes in *The Truly Disadvantaged* (1987) because this group is "outside the mainstream of the American occupational system." For this group, Wilson advocates macroeconomic policies aimed at promoting economic growth to replace inner-city manufacturing jobs lost since the 1950s and on-the-job training programs.

Each of these arguments has some merit and much myth. Left to our own devices, most of us unfortunately will discriminate, often in ways too subtle for us to notice even when we do it. Either way, such irrational discrimination occurs and is not healthy for a diverse society.

Is there less prejudice today? It is certainly less obvious, and what remains of it is mostly denied. If the words "racism" and "sexism" have lost their sting with white America through overuse, so has the phrase "I'm not prejudiced" for those who have been victims of prejudice, for it is inevitably followed by a qualifier—"I'm not prejudiced, but . . . "—that prepares listeners to brace themselves for an announcement of the speaker's prejudices. A page-one *Wall Street Journal* feature in June 1995, for example, described the reluctance of many immigrant entrepreneurs to hire blacks, even when their clientele is black. One Chinese-American owner of a Los Angeles toy company "says he isn't prejudiced," but nevertheless expects to fill his next job opening with a Mexican immigrant, probably recruited by his workers, because blacks have a "negative image" and "don't mix well with workers of other backgrounds," the story reported. Not prejudiced? Right. He's not prejudiced. He just doesn't like black people.

The wrongs committed by affirmative action are constantly overblown. At the newspaper where I work, I have received mail from people who allege episodes of reverse discrimination. Since I have experienced the sting of racial discrimination in jobs, housing, and public access, I sympathize with them, but not by much. After all, if they have a legitimate complaint, they can do the same thing I would do. They can file a complaint with the proper federal, state, or local authorities. Many white males do, and many win. Many receive sizable judgments. Some even have famous Supreme Court cases like "Bakke," "Weber," and "Crosson" named after them. So I called my readers' bluff. I challenged them to send me examples they have *personally* experienced. The mail fell to a trickle, all of which came from white males who described job interviewers who had turned them down saying something like, "Too bad you're not a woman or a minority." Why, I wondered, had they not filed a complaint? More important, if the company had not been looking for women or minorities, would this particular complaining individual have stood a ghost of a chance of getting the job instead? Or would some other white male have gotten it? Was the complainer really certain the company had any jobs available anyway? Was the job interviewer just trying to let the applicant down easy by passing the buck? I called my letter writers who included their telephone numbers and asked. They did not know. I think the worst foes of affirmative action have not been Ronald Reagan, Jesse Helms, or David Duke. They have been job interviewers. Hesitant to tell applicants the awful truth that they are not going to be hired, some job interviewers use affirmative action as a scapegoat. Some actually have been told by their superiors to keep an eye out for more women or minorities because, in many cases, their own year-end bonuses depend on showing improvements in their hiring numbers. This is not a bad thing, since the companies that do this tend to be companies that have dismally low numbers in the first place. An *affinity impulse* drives most of us, when given a chance, to prefer hiring people who look and sound like us. Sometimes the best way to break through the affinity impulse is to put somebody's paycheck in the balance.

Nor does it settle the argument to say affirmative action is unfair to "meritocracy," America's cherished traditions of rewarding effort by "deserving" individuals. Americans have always had a wide array of exotic standards for determining "merit." For example, I have a blond-haired, blue-eyed friend of Scandinavian descent who is a Washington lawyer; he told me, jokingly, that he "got into Harvard thanks to affirmative action for Nebraskans."

Another, who happens to be a Greek-American college professor, tells me he is "convinced I got into Dartmouth because I was the only application they got from Albuquerque that year. I'm sure some talented Jewish kid from New York was kept out so I could get in."

Indeed, geographic diversity was practiced by college and university admissions officers long before affirmative action came along. Few people would deny Harvard the right to choose from a broader pool of qualified applicants than just Philips Exeter graduates from New England. Nor have I seen valiant efforts put forth to dismantle preferences for promising athletes or the children of alumni or major contributors. But let a university's admissions criteria take race or ethnicity into account, and suddenly the alarms are sounded.

Then again, I have been asked, "Would you want to be treated by a doctor who got into medical school through affirmative action?" As I once heard Yale's Stephen Carter argue back, "I would care less about how that doctor got into medical school than how he or she came out." Contrary to what some critics say, affirmative action, when it works properly, guarantees only equal opportunity, not equal results.

A Georgetown University law student, for example, kicked off a scandal there in the late 1980s by revealing to the student newspaper confidential files that showed most of the law school's black students had scored lower on their admissions tests than some qualified white applicants who had been turned down. Horrors, exclaimed conservative critics in a high state of dudgeon. The critics gave little attention to some other relevant facts. For one, admissions tests have never been and probably never will be the sole criterion on which colleges' admissions are based. Experts agree that their ability to predict performance drops off sharply after the first academic year. For that reason, as well as the simple enriching virtues of diversity, colleges use many criteria to select their students, including geography and areas of interest. Most important, no one could argue that the black students, despite having scored lower than the white students who were accepted, were not qualified to enter the school. The critics conveniently overlooked the fact that the black students who were accepted still scored higher test scores than most other white students who applied. Despite myths to the contrary, affirmative action is not intended to promote people who are not qualified. It is intended to widen the criteria for those who are chosen out of the pool of the qualified.

Affirmative action is, at bottom, intended to do what its advocates say: level the playing field. Unfortunately, government inevitably does a pretty heavy-handed job of it, especially in a country as diverse as this one is, and heavy-handed enforcement of any kinds of laws, regulations, or guidelines always raises the threat that innocents will be penalized. White men are not accustomed to feeling racially vulnerable. Affirmative action has given them a taste, a tiny taste, of it. They don't like it, they want to get rid of it, and they don't want to feel it again.

Recruitment, retention, and promotion of women and minorities leads to lowered standards only when cynical managers resort to "bean counting" and impose quotas *of their own* without regard to individual merit. For example, the biggest political enemies of affirmative action are job interviewers who don't want to admit to white male applicants that there are no jobs, so instead they say something like, "Gee, it's too bad you aren't a woman or a minority. I could hire you right now."

They could, but would they? In most cases, they wouldn't. But it doesn't matter. Every applicant who hears that excuse feels cheated about what might have been, if not for that darned pesky affirmative action.

In fact, affirmative action properly conducted asks nothing more of interviewers than a widening of the criteria and the search pool by which companies do their hiring. An excellent example is offered by Clifford Alexander when he was secretary of the army under President Carter. Sent a list of candidates for promotion to general, he sent it back with a demand for more women and minority candidates. One of the names added to the second list, and a name that he approved, was Colin Powell.

President Bush also boldly promoted diversity in his Cabinet and set high numerical goals for female and minority hiring at the Pentagon, among other agencies, despite his public protestations against "quotas." Bush promoted Powell over other generals with higher seniority to make him the first black chairman of the Joint Chiefs of Staff. Was that an affirmative action decision? No one could say for sure, since he obviously was qualified, judging by, among other criteria, his performance during Operation Desert Storm.

I sympathize with those whites and males who feel they have been or might be victimized by affirmative action. Even though I think their fears are overblown, I sympathize because I can empathize. Long before there was affirmative action for women and minorities, there were racial and gender preferences for white males. This fundamental preference for white males in the employment marketplace may have diminished in these more enlightened times, but they have not gone away. None of us is immune from the fundamental affinity impulse that causes us to prefer the company of people who are as much like us as possible.

The major corporation managers and chambers of commerce who have invited me to speak have not asked me how they can get out from other cumbersome and costly government regulations. Rather, they want to know how to find, recruit, hire, train, retain, and promote more of the nation's best qualified women and minorities. They are not doing it out of the goodness of their hearts or because the government told them to. Few CEOs can operate for very long out of the goodness of their hearts before they operate themselves out of a job, and government pressure has been easing since the early Reagan years. Yet affirmative action efforts by big corporations have been growing, largely so they can stay competitive in a world where often there are, quite simply, not enough white guys to go around. Women and minorities are increasing in the workforce at a much faster pace than white males, and the most talented among them are being attracted to companies whose workplaces appear to be the most hospitable. *Workforce 2000*, a Department of Labor study, expects only 10 percent of the projected increase in the workforce in the 1990s to be white males. This should not, by any means, be viewed as a threat to white males. Quite the opposite, companies that persist in giving preferences to white males will find themselves paying a premium to get the talent because that particular talent pool is shrinking. They also will pay a premium in high turnover for their women and minorities who decide they can find a more hospitable work environment with greater potential for upward mobility elsewhere. Plus, consumer profiles are diversifying, too, leading to even more reasons that it pays to have a workforce inside that is in tune with the diverse customers you are trying to reach.

By the mid-1990s it had become commonplace for upper managers' annual bonuses to depend on their maintaining or improving their hiring and promotions of women and minorities. "Diversity management" training seminars for managers and, in some cases, workers became a booming industry. Industry-sponsored job fairs, targeted internships, and other special minority recruitment efforts reached out.

I, too, am troubled by the possibility of overreliance on affirmative action or of versions of it that amount to excess and cast a shadow over other, more legitimate efforts. Some universities, for example, have gone so far as to offer special economic incentives that can only be called "bounties" to lure high-achieving minorities to their schools. I once criticized the University of Illinois for offering a minimum of $500 to all black or Hispanic applicants who had graduated in the top 10 percent of their high school classes, *whether they needed the money or not*. If they needed it, they could qualify for more. But I thought it was sinful to offer $500 to my son, for example, when the money could have been pooled to help a far more needy child in one of Chicago's teeming ghettos. No one was more amazed than I at how little negative response the college received. One university official did call me for suggestions I might have for dealing with the vexing problem of attracting more minorities to the university, particularly when they were competing for high achievers with Harvard and the rest. I also received a call from a University of Illinois sophomore who told me he was black and the son of a doctor mother and a lawyer father in prosperous suburban Du Page County. I braced myself for an argument, but instead, he said he was calling to spill his soul. He had been offered $500 to come to the university and, like me, he felt awkward taking it. Nevertheless, I noticed that he still took it. He might feel guilty, but he was not nuts.

It is such excesses of affirmative action, excesses that either decline to take need as well as race into account or try to guarantee results as well as opportunity (like the California bill Governor Pete Wilson vetoed that would have set racial quotas on *graduation* from state universities as well as admissions to them) that drive much of the opposition to all affirmative action programs. Such excesses, on top of the myths, have fueled opposition that, in turn, has generated new concern among affirmative action defenders for how the programs might be saved.

Is there another process that can reassure all candidates that equal opportunity is being made available and everyone will be judged fairly? Even the most learned critics of affirmative action have a difficult time answering that question.

The "class, not race" argument is attractive, but not applicable to all cases. How does one choose, for example, a business contractor based on "class"? How many poor contractors are there? Would you want to hire one to build your bridge?

The experience of America's military, a traditional model for corporate culture, offers valuable lessons. In the 1940s, the conventional wisdom held that black and Asian-American troops should be kept separate from whites. Then, in 1948, while Jackie Robinson was breaking baseball's color bar, President Harry Truman ordered the military's color bar to be dropped. Yet, contrary to popular belief, his executive order was not immediately carried out. Actual racial desegregation did not come until the Korean War broke out and the generals, in accordance with the ancient combat wisdom that says there are no bigots in foxholes, ordered troops to be desegregated at the battlefront, where white casualties were replaced by blacks and black casualties were replaced by whites. By the end of the Korean War, the military was well on its way to desegregation. But it still did not have equal opportunity. By the mid-1960s, when civil unrest in America's streets spilled over into the military's hermetic world, friction over racial inequities, real and perceived, boiled over into fights, mutinies, and riots at a variety of outposts and ships at sea. The Pentagon, after careful study, responded by 1967 with a policy that ordered aggressive action against discrimination from the top down, orders that were followed in the military's unique, unquestioning way.

Today we can see the results. By leveling the playing field, the military, particularly the army, turns away more qualified women and minorities than most private industries ever see. Yet America's military has never been better educated, per capita, in its history, and its runaway success in the Persian Gulf War should put any questions about its effectiveness to rest.

It is significant that General Dwight Eisenhower's passionate arguments against the prospect of racial desegregation—hazardous to "morale, discipline and good order"—sound virtually identical to the words used by General Powell to argue against Clinton's wish to drop the military's ban against homosexuals. Was he offering a subtle hint that deep down he thought the ban against gays made no more sense than the military's earlier ban against racial integration did?

Regardless, whether the group in question happens to be blacks, Asians, women, or gays, defenders of the status quo inevitably argue that the military "is not a laboratory for social change." But of course it is. The military offers an excellent model of what I call "supply-side affirmative action." Instead of forcing diversity from the top down, it scouts, enlists, trains, and promotes everyone on an equal basis. The result: more talent than it can take. Level the playing field, and the world will beat a path to your door. Operation Desert Storm showed the payoff. America's military has never been better trained, better educated (more high school graduates than ever before), more diverse, or better qualified.

Most affirmative action attempts to push change from the demand side, forcing private companies, agencies, and institutions to seek out women and minorities and lure them in. Some do a better job than others. Supply-side affirmative action works from the side of increasing educational and training opportunities and, as a result, the talent pool.

It does not set quotas. It does not hold white males back at the door while ushering women and minorities inside. Instead, it works to improve the supply of qualified talent from which to choose. It opens its doors to everyone, but makes a special outreach effort to women and minorities who may not have felt welcome in the past. Instead of sitting back and waiting for women or minorities to appear at the door, practitioners of supply-side affirmative action take a hard look at their own companies or agencies. Assisted by diversity consultants or simply by employees, they look for signs of racism and sexism that might not have been immediately apparent to the white males who traditionally dominated the workplace.

I came to this conclusion while watching the advances made by women in my own profession. When opportunities opened up for women in America's newsrooms, there was a bountiful supply of overqualified, underutilized female talent, long penned up in research and secretarial ghettos or the "women's page," suddenly quite ready and able to rush through the door. Unfortunately, the same was not true for blacks and other minorities who had not even been able to get in the door. (Some did, through subterfuge. Guillermo Martinez, a former editorial writer at the *Miami Herald* and a Cuban American, once told me that he used to pronounce his name "Bill Martin-NEZZ" until the late 1960s to find reporting work in south Florida despite local prejudices.) As helpful as affirmative *recruitment* efforts have been, you cannot recruit people who are not available or, yes, qualified.

In the absence of a strong liberal response between the 1960s and the 1990s, opponents of affirmative action have had the luxury of having their argument both ways: Some say affirmative action has failed, therefore it should be ended, while others argue that affirmative action has *succeeded*, therefore it should be ended. Here, again, the truth runs somewhere down the middle. Affirmative action has succeeded, but not enough to say it should remain unchanged. It has also failed, but not enough to say it should be eradicated. Andrew Hacker offers the example of his alma mater, Amherst College, where his own graduating class of 250 had only two black members, "not even 1 percent," he notes in an essay for *The Nation*. Today, Amherst classes tend to be about 8 percent black, at least partly because the college has adjusted its admissions criteria to create a more diverse student body. The eight Ivy League schools together have 5,471 black students out of their total enrollment of 95,204. Without affirmative action, will these schools return to their

old 1 percent days? At least one study Berkeley conducted forecast a two-thirds drop in its black enrollment if affirmative action was ended, a possibility that caused one conservative black member of the state university system's board of regents to concede that perhaps some affirmative action should be retained.

The good effects of efforts to improve IQ have been only temporary, Murray says with a note of sadness in interviews. But that simply is not true. Focused IQ-improvement efforts in various communities around the country have shown remarkable results. Claude Steele's Michigan experiment, among others, begs for further study. Cultural context can make enormous differences in a minority's performance. For example, the Ainu, an indigenous ethnic minority in Japan, it is worth noting, score fifteen points behind other Japanese on IQ tests in Japan, where they are regarded socially as second-class citizens. But when they move to the United States, they soon perform *at the same level* as other Japanese immigrants, which is fifteen points higher than whites, who, in turn, perform fifteen points higher than the average for blacks, America's pariah class. Meanwhile, as I mentioned earlier, neither Japanese Americans nor other Asian Americans have risen to the *power* elite in numbers that come anywhere near matching their prevalence in the cognitive elite.

America will not have racial equality until opportunities are equalized, beginning at the preschool level, to build up the supply of qualified applicants for the new jobs emerging in information-age America. The American ideal of equal opportunity still produces rewards, when it is given a real try. It needs to be tried more often. Affirmative action is not a perfect remedy, but it beats the alternative, if the only alternative is to do nothing.

12

Politics

The "Race Card" vs. the "Class Card"

Today I see more clearly than yesterday that back of the problem of race and color, lies a greater problem which both obscures and implements it: and that is the fact that so many civilized persons are willing to live in comfort even if the price of this is poverty, ignorance and disease of the majority of their fellowmen; that to maintain this privilege men have waged war until today war tends to become universal and continuous, and the excuse for this war continues largely to be color and race.

— W. E. B. Du Bois, *The Souls of Black Folk*

The effort to calculate exactly what the voters want at each particular moment leaves out of account the fact that when they are troubled the thing the voters most want is to be told what to want.

—Walter Lippmann, "The Bogey of Public Opinion"

Virginia Governor C. Douglas Wilder's 1992 presidential campaign appeared to be progressing well. Then the voters saw him.

One particularly telling example occurred in a conference room in New Hampshire, where a group of uncommitted voters had been assembled into a "focus group" by Wilder's campaign team to test their candidate's viability a few months before the 1992 presidential primary in that state.

Their candidate stood up very well when he was described to the groups. After all, he had an impressive resume. He struggled out of a tough childhood to graduate college and earn a Bronze Star for valor on Pork Chop Hill in Korea. He became a lawyer, a state legislator, and then governor of his medium-sized state. He also took the right stand on the issues, as far as New Hampshire Democrats were concerned. He won national acclaim for closing a $2 billion shortfall in the Virginia state budget without raising taxes or putting a strain on public services.

Then they got a chance to see him. David Petts, the Washington-based political consultant, played a television ad from his candidate's successful gubernatorial campaign. Suddenly the expressions of the group members changed to surprise, disapproval, and dismay.

"He's black," one woman said to another.

Suddenly the wind was knocked out of Wilder's sails. When the voters had presumed Wilder was white, they could vote for him. When they found out he was black, suddenly there was no way. Yet the offenders in this case were reluctant to come clean. The post-1960s has been the age of racial denial. Accordingly, no one would admit to personal prejudices, but all had excuses based on someone else's prejudices. It was not they as individuals who could not fathom voting for a black man. It was "my neighbors" or "the state's voters" who wouldn't go for him. Racial denial shows itself most glaringly in America's politics. The quest for racial innocence never ceases.

The sad irony of Wilder's early rejection was that he had worked so diligently to identify himself in the minds of voters not as a "black candidate," but as a candidate who *hap-*

pened to be black. His winning issues, low taxes and abortion rights, crossed racial lines. He deliberately asked Jesse Jackson to please campaign for someone else, somewhere else, thank you very much. His staffs and appointments were well integrated. His election as the nation's first black governor since Reconstruction had buoyed national hopes that the nation was outgrowing its grim racial past at last. But voters in New Hampshire were not ready yet to make similar breakthroughs. They were not blind to his color, instead, his color made them blind to him. Wilder would be the first of the six Democratic candidates to drop out.

Wilder's experience in New Hampshire prominently illustrates the critical interplay between race and class in modern American politics: When white focus groups viewed Wilder in terms of his economic issues, they tended to like him. It was only when they viewed him through the prism of race that they turned sour. Here we see a salient truth in American politics since the 1960s: When race is the issue, Republicans win. When class is the issue, Democrats win.

Race always has been a powerful force in American politics. The compromise that allowed slaves (or "others," as the document put it; the Framers somehow could not bring themselves to put the word "slaves" in their document to liberty) to be counted as three-fifths of a person for purposes of reapportionment held up the ratification of the Constitution. When Abraham Lincoln emancipated the slaves, blacks would vote overwhelmingly Republican until the New Deal, and southern whites would vote overwhelmingly Democratic until the Harry Truman era. Pressures in favor of civil rights grew in the Democratic Party and exploded in 1948, when the party's first strong civil rights platform plank "to eradicate all racial, religious and economic discrimination" led to a walkout by Strom Thurmond, then governor of South Carolina, who took with him his own state delegation, the Mississippi delegation, and half of the Alabama delegation. The "Dixiecrat" party that resulted nominated Thurmond for president and carried Mississippi, Louisiana, South Carolina, and Alabama and formed the beginning of a new Republican South.

John F. Kennedy, Catholic and pro–civil rights, failed to carry the South. Neither did Texan Lyndon B. Johnson, also pro–civil rights. When Johnson signed the 1964 Civil Rights Act, he confided to an aide, Bill Moyers, that this action had "delivered the South to the Republican Party for a long time to come."

And the South would not be alone. The demonization of blacks through racially coded appeals to white fears became a standard feature of the Republican Party's comeback after Barry Goldwater's landslide 1964 defeat. Alabama governor George Wallace's 1968 third-party assault on "forced busing" and "pointy-headed liberal intellectuals" would help show the way. Richard Nixon won that year with his attack on "crime in the streets." Ronald Reagan beat Jimmy Carter in 1980 by attacking "welfare queens." George Bush would win in 1988 attacking the Willie Horton issue.

A poor white, unmarried, rural Louisiana mother offered an excellent example of how the racial code worked during David Duke's 1989 gubernatorial race. A *New York Times* reporter spotted a poster for the former Ku Klux Klan leader in her window and asked her why she was voting for Duke. She said she was pleased that he wanted to do something about all the people who were collecting welfare. But, the reporter reminded her, *you're* on welfare. Yes, she agreed, "but the blacks get more."

Despite denials by Duke and other more genteel Republicans that their attacks on crime, welfare, and affirmative action were racial codes, this particular woman was hav-

ing no trouble reading between the lines. In an age-old pattern for American politics, she was willing to ignore the interests she had in common with poor blacks when she could,
instead, use blacks as a scapegoat for her misery.

By the early 1990s, Democrats appeared to be catching on.
After years of enduring deep Republican-driven wedges
between them, the party's many component factions were
learning how to reach out and work together again. Bridges
destroyed by divisive national "code word" politics began to
be rebuilt. Pioneers like Virginia's Doug Wilder and Illinois
senator Carol Moseley-Braun, the nation's first black woman
senator, made history by appealing to their prominently white
constituencies with nonracially based issues. Black mayors
won elections in cities like Cleveland, St. Louis, and Detroit
by appealing to multiracial coalitions, breaking patterns of
black-oriented campaigns set in the 1960s. Delegates to the
1992 National Democratic Convention effectively smoothed
over their usual factional disputes to present a grand show of
unity on national television. Bill Clinton bridged the "wedge"
issues of race that year by appealing to the "forgotten middle
class" through such issues as taxes, crime, welfare, and "family values" issues, which Representative Barney Frank of
Massachusetts dubbed the "notsapostas" because so many of
his fellow liberal Democrats had avoided them as issues they
were "*not supposed to* talk about." Clinton tackled them head-
on and famously drew robust cheers and "amens" from,
among others, black church congregations, rebuilding a cen-
ter-left consensus that Republicans had ripped apart by turning such issues into racially loaded code words.

The single most significant moment in a campaign that
was full of significant moments probably was Clinton's televised admonishing of Jesse Jackson's Rainbow Coalition for
giving a forum to Sister Souljah, a little-known rap star who

appeared, in an earlier *Washington Post* interview, to approve of black attacks on whites during the Los Angeles riots. The rapper, who claimed rather weakly that her comments had been taken out of context, had been only one member of a sixteen-person interracial panel discussion on how the civil rights movement might improve its outreach to young people. Moreover, Jackson himself had admonished her during the session to reconsider her strident militancy. If she would study the movement's history of multiracial coalition-building, she would be less pessimistic about white people, he said.

But Clinton, who needed strategically to reassure white voters that he was not in the pocket of the party's left wing, turned the little panel into a major issue of the moment. It worked. His speech received far more coverage than the panel session did (only Black Entertainment Television taped the panel discussion, then declined to air it), and his approval rating among white voters immediately soared. In the battle for middle America, Clinton won. Despite Jackson's espoused desire to build multiracial coalitions, white voters approved of Clinton's putting Jackson in what they felt was his place.

Unlike Walter Mondale in 1984 or Michael Dukakis in 1988, Clinton would not vacillate ambiguously with Jackson. Instead, Clinton protected his political base by surrounding himself with other, more moderate black leaders like Ernest Green, one of the nine students who integrated Little Rock High School in 1958, and Bobby Rush, a former Black Panther leader who would be elected to Congress from Chicago that November. Clinton was doing what others thought might be impossible, hanging on to his black support while winning skeptical white "Reagan Democrats" back to the fold. Just as helpful was President Bush's declining to use the subtle race card he and his supporters played so well in 1988 by using the black face of Willie Horton. For a bright and shining moment, before affirmative action returned as a major issue in the mid-1990s, racial hostility appeared to be in retreat. A new generation of pragmatic centrists and racial crossover candidates was beginning noticeably to address directly the sources of division that had broken up the traditional winning Democratic coalition.

But then came 1994. Clinton's failure to ease white middle-class anxiety led to a Republican landslide in both houses of Congress. This became known as an "angry white male" revolt after two-thirds of white male voters turned out to be the election's biggest group of Republican voters. And, sooner than you could say "affirmative action," Republican candidates Pete Wilson, Phil Gramm, Bob Dole, and Patrick Buchanan, knowing what issue had paid off with surefire success for Republicans in the past, were putting the volatile issue of race back on the front burner for the 1996 election campaign.

Centrist Clinton advisers pleaded with Clinton to adopt a more "class-based" approach to affirmative action, targeted to those who show economic need, not merely the right skin color. Again, just as Republicans had lined up with race, traditional Democrats almost instinctively clung to class.

But Clinton preferred not to. He came out fully in favor of affirmative action, coining a bumper sticker slogan of his own: "Mend it, don't end it." Polls showed he had guessed right. Most Americans were uncomfortable with the idea of "quotas," but still felt the need for some sort of race and gender-based remedies and diversity "inclusion" programs. Americans were ambivalent about affirmative action. All this issue needed, one side or another, was some bold leadership. Republicans had a dilemma, too. They could put their money and efforts behind wooing blacks away from the Democratic Party, as House Speaker Newt Gingrich and others said they wanted to do, or they could continue to play the race card as Nixon aide Pat Buchanan had suggested in the late 1980s: Divide the country along lines of race and take the larger piece.

> *The rich get the gold mine and the middle class gets the shaft. It's wrong and it's going to ruin the country.*

> —Democratic presidential nominee Bill Clinton, 1992

I am amused whenever Republicans denounce Democrats for waging "class warfare," for their complaint only acknowledges the power class holds as a strategic issue for Democrats, comparable to the power of race for Republicans. Both are delicate issues. Yet effective appeals to class consciousness, suspicions, and resentments win elections.

It only shows that the GOP knows what the game really is. It is particularly amusing to hear them claim, "Class warfare never works," like a mantra. Didn't it work for Harris Wofford? He won an upset in the 1991 Pennsylvania Senate race against cocky former governor Dick Thornburgh, President Bush's former attorney general, by selling the issue of health care with a populist, class-conscious zeal.

"If every criminal can have a lawyer, why can't every working American have a doctor," he said repeatedly on the campaign trail, offering faint echoes of the anti-liberal rhetoric that fueled Bush's Willie Horton campaign. Wofford's victory reenergized morose Democrats in the months after Bush's Desert Storm victory. His campaign adviser, James Carville, would organize Clinton's victory march the following year. Showing himself to be a tireless campaigner and an excellent student of what wins, Clinton appealed directly to the "forgotten middle class," the big group in the middle that was feeling left out of Reagan-Bush era bonanzas for the wealthy and Democratic reforms for minorities and the poor. Then, even before his inauguration, Clinton rapidly began to lose that same bloc's support when he allowed his lenient position on gays in the military to take the spotlight away from the rest of his agenda. Republicans, reading from the same populist playbook, would further neutralize his appeal by casting him and his First Lady as either Yale-educated Washington elites or, when it suited them, country bumpkins who couldn't handle the Washington Beltway sophisticates.

For better or worse, effective politics is often nothing more than an effective appeal to the resentments of those who vote in large numbers, directed against a target group that doesn't. A reputation for soaking the poor doomed Republican hopes in elections in which the poor, or those who view themselves as poor, outnumbered those who saw themselves as rich. In fact, polls show 90 percent or more of Americans view themselves as middle class, giving America the largest middle class the world has ever known. Here, as in most issues, politics is a manipulated interplay of perceptions. The realignment that has occurred since the 1960s is attributable, more than anything else, to perceptions that Democratic programs, according to Nixon adviser Kevin Phillips, in *The Emerging Republican Majority*, had moved from "taxing the few for the benefit of the many [the New Deal] to programs taxing the many on behalf of the few [the Great Society]."

If white middle-class voters failed to see Democrats as caring about them anymore, even though the largest share of federal spending continues to go to middle-class entitlements like Social Security and Medicare, it was largely because conservatives persuaded numbers of whites that government spending was generally being wasted, mostly on blacks.

The voice of the "angry white male," who would constitute the decisively pivotal vote in the Republican landslide of
1994, could be heard in the voice of Dan Donahue, a Chicago
carpenter interviewed at the campaign headquarters of a
GOP state senator in 1988 and quoted in *Chain Reaction*
(1991), by Thomas Byrne Edsall and Mary Edsall:

> You could classify me as a working-class Democrat, a
> card-carrying union member. I'm not a card-carrying
> Republican, yet. . . . We have four or five generations of
> welfare mothers. And they [Democrats] say the answer
> to that is we need more programs. Come on. . . . It's well
> and good we should have compassion for these people,
> but your compassion goes only so far. I don't mind
> helping, but somebody has got to help themselves,
> you've got to pull. When you try to pick somebody up,
> they have to help. . . . Unfortunately, most of the people
> who need help in this situation are black and most of
> the people who are doing the helping are white . . . We
> [white Cook County voters] are tired of paying for the
> Chicago Housing Authority, and for public housing and
> public transportation that we don't use. . . . They hate it
> [the school board levy] because they are paying for
> black schools that aren't even educating kids, and the
> money is just going into the Board of Education and the
> teachers union.

It was a voice that echoed across the nation, and soon
would be picked up in the early 1990s by a wave of conservative talk radio programs, spreading the word that whites
were always giving and the blacks were always taking and
the liberal elites were overseeing it all.

By 1993, Kevin Phillips, who helped orchestrate Richard

Nixon's battle against the "liberal elites" who had taken over the Democratic Party, was railing against the Wall Street elites in his book *Boiling Point: Democrats, Republicans and the Decline of Middle-Class Prosperity*. Republican policies, Phillips reported, had resulted in the biggest concentration of wealth during the 1980s among the upper 5 percent of income earners since the great income-leveling actions of the New Deal and World War II. "Class warfare" apparently was okay as long as it was waged against the lower classes.

Today it is easy to see more clearly than ever that, behind middle-class anger, whether it is directed against blacks or taxes, is a greater problem afflicting the group Secretary of Labor Robert Reich called the "anxious class." They are the vast numbers of Americans who see and feel a growing divide between rich and poor, skilled and unskilled, the secure and the insecure in post-industrial America. They have been feeling increasingly nervous about the trend, which appears to be irreversible, and about the weak responses both major parties were making to it.

This middle-class anxiety explains why party loyalty shrunk to record lows by the mid-1990s and the urge to find alternatives soared. In the midst of it all, three years after Doug Wilder's rebuff in New Hampshire, America had a new great black hope. His name was Colin Powell.

The retired army general, first black chairman of the Joint Chiefs of Staff, high commander of the Persian Gulf conflict, two-tour Vietnam veteran, and self-made son of Jamaican immigrants to Harlem and the South Bronx, emerged as the front-runner in all demographic, political, and ideological groups—male, female, white, minority, liberal, conservative, Democrat, and Republican—well ahead of the declared field.

Powell's emergence benefited mightily from a national

yearning for heroes and "outsiders," as most pundits put it, but more significantly, he embodied more than any other black hero or celebrity the nation's yearning to transcend its agony over race.

Unlike Jesse Jackson, Powell was introduced to the public eye without mention of race. Media stories played down his race and played up the popular *universals* in his life, images that touched on cherished all-American values: born to an immigrant household in a poor ethnic neighborhood; a poorly motivated high school performer who found himself in ROTC; excelled in the army, served *two tours* in Vietnam; studied a year as a White House Fellow during the Nixon years, and eventually was introduced to the world as a key national security adviser to the Gipper himself, Ronald Reagan.

For years he is seen conferring confidently, authoritatively, and (and this was important) *nonthreateningly* in the inner circle of advisers to Presidents Reagan and Bush. Not only did he walk, talk, and behave like one of the boys—no dashikis, confrontational talk, or appeals to white guilt here—but he also looked, in his high-*gravitas* way, like the *smartest* guy in the room.

Then there's Desert Storm, where General Norman Schwarzkopf led the forces in the field but Powell confidently led the nation through press conferences that acted to restore whatever lost confidence the nation had in its military forces and, by subtle connection, in the competence of black Americans to hack it with the opportunities we had, at long last, been given.

Even the fact that Powell came to the public eye through the army had important cultural significance, since the military is the first and, for many, the last time many white American males can recall making a genuine friendship, *Forrest Gump*–style, across racial lines.

Blacks, women, the disabled, and other oppressed and alienated people yearning to feel *rehumanized* after years of dehumanization could find a lot to like about Powell, too. He embodied the desire all oppressed people have to be seen as people first.

Americans became so invested in the notion of Colin Powell as a black man who had made it on merit and merit alone despite his racial assignment to American society's lowest caste, confirming the durable goodness of the American Dream, that he actually appeared to have turned his race into an *advantage*.

National polling on racial attitudes, conducted by Paul M. Sniderman, a Stanford University political scientist, for the National Science Foundation, supports that point. Sniderman found that Powell's race, in some polls, actually "magnifies his political strength," he said. When whites of all ideological stripes encounter an individual black person whose character refutes negative racial stereotypes, he said, "their response is to respond *even more positively* to him." In other words, white voters will vote for a black who is not *too black* in the sense of their stereotypes about blackness. Powell fit that bill.

But I did not believe for a minute that Powell's popularity showed that Americans suddenly had outgrown their racial hang-ups. On a less sanguine note, the army also plays to another white ideal: It is a place that has a reputation, although somewhat overblown, for whipping rebellious youths, particularly poor youths of color, into line and teaching them *their place*. In some ways, Powell may have benefited from the ancient notion that black people could do a better, more economical job of overseeing other blacks and keeping them in line than white people could.

Few were eager to say Powell was not *qualified for the job* in the way so many blacks had been blocked in the past. Quite the opposite, he offered an image, an icon, an ideal, a *role model* for what so many whites had been saying they had been looking for in a qualified black all along.

In short, Powell was a beneficiary of the *Bill Cosby effect*. He was so famous and so widely admired that white people quickly forgot he was not white, while black people delighted in remembering that he was black. I first began to experience this firsthand in the early 1980s while working as a television reporter in Chicago. I was astonished to find working-class white ethnics in neighborhoods that once greeted Martin Luther King with rocks, bottles, and bricks treating me like a celebrity. "You're not black anymore, Clarence," said a seasoned white producer back at the studio. "You're on television now."

So it was for Colin Powell. Like Bill Cosby, Oprah Winfrey, or the two Michaels, Jordan and Jackson, he had *crossed over* in the minds of white America to the larger white audience. It was Powell's good fortune to emerge at the right time to capitalize on a little-recognized but deeply felt American yearning for "positive" black role models. Americans by the 1980s might have been too hip, too cynical, too disbelieving of the old verities to accept "Ozzie and Harriet" or "Father Knows Best" as anything better than quaint nostalgia. Yet many of those same cynics eagerly embraced "The Cosby Show," making it the nation's number-one show for several years in a row. Americans, it appeared, would accept "Father Knows Best" or "Ozzie and Harriet" after all, as long as it was played with a black cast in an ostensibly urban neighborhood.

The same may have been true for Powell. Maybe American voters were looking for Oprah Winfreys and Bill Cosbys in politics, too. The age of the Eisenhower-style leader was over, according to the prevailing wisdom. Americans in their post–cold war isolationism were not wildly enthusiastic about scouting out any new ones, until they were offered an Eisenhower who happened to be black. Wilder, with much hard work, filled the bill in Virginia. But he couldn't get out of the starting gate in New Hampshire. Race had something to do with it, but so perhaps was his appearing to be too obviously a *politician*. Powell coyly and cleverly insisted that he was not, even while he clearly was politicking.

Wilder also was black and a Democrat, a combination that Republicans had cleverly and thoroughly demonized in the minds of many voters since the 1960s when Lyndon B. Johnson's strong support of civil rights and Richard M. Nixon's racially coded conservatism sent whites scurrying away from the Democratic Party like rabbits from a prairie fire.

All of this worked in Powell's favor as the right man at the right time. For many Americans, he helped confirm that America's fabled meritocracy still works. After all, had Powell's Jamaica-born parents decided to go to England under British Commonwealth laws instead of to Harlem, he might have risen to sergeant-major, at best. Instead, he had risen to this country's top military post and might become the nation's commander-in-chief, a full confirmation of the American ideal and a signal to all those other promising young men and women out there that all you have to do is to work hard, dress well, speak good English, play by the rules, and *fit in* with the standards of the mainstream, which is to say the white world, and you will get your reward. If he had benefited from affirmative action at any point along the way, it was by no means obvious, which is just how such programs should work. The prospect of a Colin Powell presidential campaign offered the prospect of blessed relief, a welcome oasis on a political landscape that had turned into a dust bowl of racial rancor and competing resentment. Inasmuch as whites once held blacks down to feel good about themselves, today's whites could feel good about themselves by lifting up at least this one black.

Americans deeply value such good feelings, deeply enough to award bonus points to a likable black candidate whose race can help them feel good about how open-minded they have always imagined themselves. Many of the white suburban Republicans who crossed over to make Carol Moseley-Braun the Senate's first black woman member told pollsters the wish to "make history" figured strongly in their decision, which is another way of saying they felt good about voting for a black woman. Voters like to help make history in ways that move America forward. As long as his sparkling image remained pristine clean, America needed to know that Colin Powell could succeed. Or, to put it another way, if he could not succeed, could any person of color? Would his failure not be unwanted confirmation of a terrible truth, that there really truly is something fundamentally wrong with America's sense of fairness? America needed Colin Powell to assuage white guilt. He made it possible for white Americans to say confidently, *No, I am not opposed to all black candidates; I am only opposed to those black candidates who are not like Colin Powell.* He became a Rorschach inkblot test of whatever or whomever we wanted him to be, a direct reflection of our best vision of ourselves.

There was a lesson here for crossover candidates everywhere. White people are more open to voting for a black candidate than ever before. But, to win white votes, it still is necessary, first of all, to ease white guilt.

It is not essential to be so conservative that you alienate much of the black mainstream, but it doesn't hurt. It is not insignificant that the only two black Republicans in

Congress, Connecticut's Gary Franks and Oklahoma's J.C. Watts, both came from districts that were predominantly white. (It also did not hurt Watts's popularity that he was a former University of Oklahoma football hero. If anything counts as much as military heroism in our culture, it is athletic "heroism.") It is a telling development of this, the age of the crossover black candidate, that they win by first becoming a perceived ally to the interests of their white constituents.

By contrast, Carol Moseley-Braun, like Wilder in Virginia, won white support not so much *because* she was black as *despite* it. Her race became incidental in a campaign that focused on women's issues, particularly the incumbent Democratic senator Alan Dixon's crucial vote for controversial Supreme Court Justice Clarence Thomas's confirmation. Angered by Thomas, scores of white suburban women crossed over from the Republican column, according to exit polls, to vote for Moseley-Braun and provide her margin of victory. White women gave Wilder a similarly crucial margin of victory (a much narrower margin than exit polls indicated he would get) based on the issue of abortion. His anti-abortion opponent waffled, costing him valuable support from Virginia's Christian fundamentalist voters, while pro-choice Wilder stood firm and won.

Can a black candidate who has been elected by whites effectively represent blacks? Lani Guinier was criticized as a "quota queen" for bringing up such questions for discussion in her scholarly papers on voting rights. In writing the Supreme Court's five-to-four decision to ban race as a "predominant factor" in drawing congressional districts, Justice Anthony Kennedy denounced the "racial stereotyping" that expects blacks to vote differently from whites. Yet blacks do tend to vote for blacks and whites for whites, and the gulf between their political attitudes as groups is wide and deep. For example, one 1986 poll* found that 74 percent of blacks thought federal spending on programs to assist blacks should be increased, compared to 17 percent for whites. Kennedy would have blacks and whites work harder to campaign for each other's votes, which is a noble goal and one that conservative critics of Voting Rights Act enforcement have called for. Ironically, it may result in the restoration of substantial black populations to the districts of staunchly conservative white Republicans like Newt Gingrich, forcing a moderation in their racial messages. That already happened with black representative Gus Savage, a virulently anti-Israel firebrand whose far South Side Chicago district was extended after the 1990 census into the suburbs, picking up more suburban white voters. Savage was replaced in the 1992 primaries by a more moderate black and former Rhodes scholar named Mel Reynolds, who later would be forced to resign after being convicted of having a sexual affair with an underaged girl in his district.

As long as race remains an American dilemma, as Gunnar Myrdal famously declared it to be in the early 1940s, it will play a salient role in American politics. Americans of all races need to learn who their real enemies are. It is not the members of other races. It is those who use race as a smokescreen to hide the nation's deeper agonies over class and a dream of upward mobility that for too many members of all races appears to be rapidly slipping away.

---

*Cited by Donald R. Kinder and Lynn M. Sanders, "Pluralistic Foundations of American Opinion on Race," paper presented at American Political Science Association, Chicago, September 3–6, 1987.

13

We, the Indigestibles
The Campus Culture Wars

The forgetting of race in the university, which was predicted and confidently expected when the barriers were let down, has not occurred. There is now a large black presence in the major universities, frequently equivalent to their proportion in the general population. But they have, by and large, proved indigestible. *[Emphasis mine.]*

—Allan Bloom, *The Closing of the American Mind*

Call me "indigestible." Allan Bloom did have a gift for the colorful metaphor. I have often heard America's vast ethnic diversity compared to a melting pot or a salad bowl or even a stir-fry. Bloom, a distinguished classical scholar at the University of Chicago at the time of his death, was the first I ever heard compare it to a gastrointestinal system. Perhaps it is not altogether inappropriate to compare students to food, since students do bring life, energy, and nutrients to the university, along, alas, with some waste. Bloom merely saw some students and, for that matter, faculty as more nutritious to the academic organism than others.

Bloom's *Closing of the American Mind*, from which the above quote is lifted, caused a major sensation in 1987, soaring to the *New York Times*'s best-seller list, a surprising stroke of good fortune for a book about academic life by a scholar of the classics. Bloom's eloquent and wide-ranging critique of "careerism" and intellectual fascism in students and the capitulation by faculty and administrators struck a nerve, making him something of a Paul Revere in a looming culture war, a harbinger of backlash against a growing left-progressive dominance of the thinking, particularly in the liberal arts, in our principal incubators and disseminators of culture, our colleges and universities. Bloom struck a nerve. Other conservative backlash books, like Dinesh D'Souza's *Illiberal Education* (1991) would follow, along with reams of editorials and commentaries that would make campus jargon like "political correctness" and "deconstruction" into household terms. On the battlefront of social relations, there are self-segregated dining tables, social and service clubs, and ethnic "theme dorms." In academic studies there are scuffles over what reading, if any, should be required of all students, reading also known by the loftier terms the "canon" or "core curriculum," dominated, much to the dismay of the progressives, by history's great deep-thinking "DWEMs"—dead white European males. Covering all of these and more was the emerging and often-pejorative label of "political correctness" to describe the array of speech codes and less formal strictures on free expression that attempt to squelch any offense to women or minorities. As D'Souza, under the subheading "The New Racism," quoted S. Frederick Starr, president of Oberlin College, as saying, "It is common in universities today to hear talk of politically correct opinions, or PC for short. These are questions that are not really open to argument. It takes real courage to oppose the campus orthodoxy. To tell you the truth, I was a student during the days of McCarthy, and there is less freedom now than there was then."

That's pretty strong stuff from the president of a traditionally progressive college, especially since no one had lost a career, a job, a house, or a scholarship for writing or uttering

anything that upset the left the way many lost their livelihoods and reputations for upsetting Senator Joe McCarthy
and his fellow Red-baiting witch hunters in the 1950s. Quite
the opposite, professors and students who were hauled
before student tribunals in the 1980s and 1990s for offending
well-intended but often benighted speech codes tended to
receive widespread media attention and support from a variety of free speech defenders. Charges inevitably were
dropped and the worst of the codes were tossed out in court,
as well they should be. I think our colleges suffer from too little free speech, not too much.

Bloom spots some of this, but, curiously, only among the
black students whom he singles out for special rebuke for
their indigestibility. They have stranded themselves outside
the vital life of the university, he says. He praises the way
most modern students tend to revere individualism, but relations between blacks and whites are the one "eccentric ele-
ment" in this portrait, the one "failure" and "a particularly
grave one inasmuch as it was the part most fraught with
hope."

"[M]ost keep to themselves," he says of black students.
While white students relate in ways that are as "immediate"
and "unself-conscious" to blacks as to anyone else—"including Orientals," Bloom adds parenthetically—but the atmosphere seems to be "one of effort rather than instinct." Only a
few "perfectly integrated black students" are exceptions, "but
they are rare and in a difficult position." Bloom returns our
attention to the blamelessness of the whites: "I do not believe
this somber situation is the fault of the white students." No,
they have "made the adjustment, without missing a beat . . .
It would require a great deal of proof to persuade me that
they remain subtly racist." No, the real problem to Bloom is
that blacks hijacked the "programmatic brotherhood of the

sixties" and turned off its course bound toward integration onto one of separatism—"just at the moment when everyone else has become a 'person,' blacks have become blacks."

As one of those few "perfectly integrated black students" who were "rare and in a difficult position," I understand what Bloom was talking about. I was called "Oreo" (black on the outside, white on the inside) a time or two for having too many white friends, but I managed. I also was called a "militant" and "unreasonable" once or twice for declining to be "integrated" on somebody else's terms. But when Bloom speaks of the "forgetting of race," I detect he has made a common error. He confuses integration with desegregation. The black movement of the 1960s asked for desegregation, the removal of barriers to free choice, and the law provided that. Idealists called for integration, which often meant assimilation, and whenever the law tried to force that, it often failed. Forced busing, which has since been rejected by many black parents as well as whites, is a prime example.

On the other hand, when Bloom writes of whites having "made the adjustment, without missing a beat," I wonder: Adjustment to what? How have their lives been changed by the ability of blacks to choose whether to integrate? Whites have had that right all along. To what did they have to adjust?

Yet Bloom's lamentations live on. Other anguished analysts bemoan the "balkanization" of campus life, comparing ethnic pluralism on campus to the notorious ethnic rivalries in the Balkans.

"Racial Balkanization at Cornell" shouts a headline over a grumpy Wall Street Journal editorial in the summer of 1995. The Journal's editorial page has become something of a daily bulletin for the rear guard in the campus culture wars, alerting the corporate elites to where their foundation money and alumni donations are going. This particular editorial blasted the New York State Board of Regents for having "recently proved once more that balkanizing students on college campuses according to race or ethnicity has the endorsement of too many government authorities, no matter what the law says about avoiding discrimination. That is, as long as the students seeking self-segregation are not white."

Specifically, the *Journal* worked itself up into high dudgeon over a ruling by the state's education commission that the university's black-theme dormitory, Ujamaa College; its Hispanic-theme dormitory, the Latino Living Center; and its Native American–theme dormitory, Akwe:kon, don't violate the Board of Regents rule of open-living facilities.

After all, any student could apply to live in the dorms, and a state investigation had concluded that no student had been excluded from the dorms because of race or national origin. Still, the *Journal* was upset because "self-segregation got official sanction." The *Journal* also was upset that "two-thirds of the university's minority students lived on North Campus," while West Campus "has always been overwhelmingly white." Efforts to change that through a random housing program were voted down by a student referendum. Apparently the students have little quarrel with the housing situation. But that was not good enough for the *Journal*. "The fact is," said the *Journal*, "if you believe in racial integration, Cornell's campus is fragmented beyond repair."

Still, it is curious that the *Journal*, which vehemently opposes forced integration in school busing or affirmative action cases, is so vigorously angry about "de facto segregation" at Cornell. That editorial cites no cases of anyone who has been turned down for housing because of race or ethnicity. Even the Ujamaa dorm had "only" one white student in it the previous year, the editorial mentions. It does not mention how many other whites applied to get in, if any. Everyone agrees that Cornell has been desegregated. Students have the opportunity to mix or not mix as they choose. Why do born-again integrationists like Bloom and the *Journal* so often put the burden to mix on the black students and other non-whites?

Social Segregation

"We have a campus of 25,000 students and there is no mixing across cultural and racial lines," a student editor at Iowa State University told a survey by *U.S. News & World Report* in 1993. After a racial skirmish on campus, she said, "they had a rally for unity, but all the blacks clustered together and all the whites clustered together." The magazine's survey of 550 student editors found nine out of ten editors at the larger schools (75 percent overall) reported that self-segregation among blacks was common on their campuses; 53 percent at the larger schools (37 percent overall) agreed that blacks on their campus feel "white students are hostile and aloof"; 33 percent at the larger schools (24 percent overall) said that white students are physically afraid of blacks; and 85 percent of the respondents at the larger schools (71 percent overall) reported that there had been at least one incident on campus that could be characterized as "racial" during the year.

Racial divisions on campus are a worthy cause for concern. What concerns me most is the approach embodied in Bloom's remarks that places so much of the burden for easing the digestion of blacks on the blacks. Why, it is often asked, do all the black students sit at separate dining tables? Why do they hang together at basketball arenas and football stadiums? "They all hang together" is an ancient complaint made against ethnic groups that are seen as too clannish. Yet seldom does one hear a complaint about the seven or eleven tables full of *white* students one had to pass before reaching the black table. White people are quick to notice whenever black people are getting tribal. They are slow to notice that white people are still tribal, too. White students were segregating themselves long before I came to campus in the 1960s and continued right through these times that, by contrast, are far more openly conservative. Black students sitting with one another is called "self-segregating" or "balkanizing." White students sitting together is called "normal." If self-segregation is not a virtue, it also must be remembered that, alas, students of color didn't invent it.

In fact, a visitor from another planet might easily believe at first glance that it is the white students who are shunning the students of color, not vice versa. After all, are there not more of them?

A study by the School of Education at the University of Michigan documented this paradox. After surveying six thousand students at 390 colleges in 1987 and 1991, it found white students were more guilty of failing to integrate with other students than nonwhite students were. Students of color were more likely to study with, dine with, and go out on dates with individuals from another racial or ethnic background.

The survey found that:

• Nearly 69 percent of Asian-American, 78 percent of Mexican-American, and 55 percent of African-American students frequently dined with someone of a different ethnic or racial background, compared to only 21 percent of white students.

• Almost 42 percent of Asian-American students, 24 percent of Mexican-American students, and 13 percent of

African-American students said they dated someone outside their own race or ethnic category, compared to only 4 percent of whites.

• Less happily, about 53 percent of African-American students said they felt excluded from social activities because of their race, compared with 24 percent of Asian Americans, 16 percent of Mexican Americans, and only 6 percent of whites.

• Some 30 percent of Asian-American students and 32 percent of African-American students reported being insulted or threatened by other students because of their ethnic backgrounds, compared to only 10 percent of Mexican Americans and 9 percent of whites.

Bloom wrote that "it would require a great deal of proof" to persuade him that whites remain subtly racist enough to bear the blame for lingering racial separation on campus. I don't know if the University of Michigan study would be proof enough for him that, at least, something is seriously wrong on both sides of the racial fence. Nevertheless, it shows how only the simplistic and the naive would blame black separatists who somehow hijacked the "programmatic brotherhood of the sixties." If students of color have proved to be less "digestible" in campus life, it may be because some other social arbiters somehow have found them hard to swallow.

The "forgetting of race" is not easily accomplished on the campus when it is so uneasily accomplished in the world off campus. Instead it becomes a liberal fantasy based, I believe, on a misreading of Martin Luther King's invitation in his "I Have a Dream" speech for "the grandchildren of slaves and the grandchildren of slave owners" to "at long last be able to sit down together at the table of brotherhood." That noble dream will not become a reality by rendering black life invisible, by "digesting" blacks in a way that denies their humanity and tells them that their 350 years of history and life in America count for nothing. Inequality breeds distrust, resentment, and contempt. To sit down together at the great table of brotherhood in peace and comfort, we must do it as equal partners, not as dominant and submissive.

In my travels to campuses across the country, I have found many of today's students of color struggling to find a comfortable place for themselves in a situation many feel was not made for them, yet that they feel eager to transform into an environment that will welcome others like them. A twenty-year-old black woman at Harvard tells me she is tired of serving as resident "defender of the race" in classrooms and conversations with whites. Black students late one night in Stanford's Ujamaa ethnic theme dorm tell me it makes them feel good to have a place where they are "not in the minority" and that whites seldom want to enlarge the conversation between the races beyond their own "narrow white world." A nineteen-year-old black male at Florida International University in Miami tells me his organization has invited Minister Louis Farrakhan to campus because they are tired of feeling "invisible" on the predominantly Hispanic campus. I hear similar comments from black students at Northern Illinois University and the State University of New York, Brockport. Black students at the University of Iowa complain that white social life on campus tends to be centered around beer kegs while black social life tends to be centered around music and dancing, and never the twain shall meet.

It is not just the black students who raise these concerns. As the nonwhite population on campus has grown, so has the rainbow of complaints. I have heard Latino students in Texas and California and Native American students in Arizona, New Mexico, and South Dakota speak across almost identical culture gaps. A twenty-year-old Inuit Eskimo woman at the University of Alaska in Fairbanks told me she felt torn between the need to make it in the white man's world and to preserve the rich, yet dying language and visual arts of her people. Why, asks the chorus of voices from students of color, don't the whites want to meet *us* halfway?

As a result, many nonwhite students turn inward and establish little cultural enclaves and inevitably build walls of apprehension around themselves. The Michigan study found that students tend to self-segregate to grasp a sense of community on a campus where they felt alienated from the white mainstream of campus life.

Conservatives often blame self-segregation by blacks, Hispanics, Asians, and Native Americans on affirmative action. Somehow, they reason, it has packed onto the campus too many underqualified students who turn to one another for support and consolation. I think self-segregation is more apparent on campus in recent years largely because there have been more blacks, Hispanics, Asians, and Native Americans on campus. Their proportion and visible presence has more than doubled since the 1960s. Students have always balkanized themselves. It just appears more visible today because greater numbers of students of color are enrolled. Ironically, this happy development has led unhappily to the visual impression that things have gotten more balkanized when actually American campuses have never been more integrated, nor options and opportunities more open. At Stanford, for example, I visited and chatted with black and white students, liberal and conservative, in Ujamaa House, an ethnic theme dorm that, like the campus's other theme dorms, must be at least half-populated by students who are not from the dorm's theme group. As minority presence on campus grows, so grows the need for many to have their cultural *com-*

fort zones on campus, but so also do opportunities to have contacts with whites, positive and negative. Unfortunately, it is only the negative contacts that make news, often as "hate crimes." Some of the worst examples have occurred at the University of Massachusetts at Amherst, where a white visitor beat a black residential adviser, who also had feces smeared on the door of his room, in the fall of 1992, an incident that sparked a rampage by black students through a twenty-two-story dormitory.

But hundreds of other examples, most of them much less violent, have erupted across the country. In today's atmosphere of heightened sensitivity, even the hanging of a Confederate flag in the window of a Berkeley fraternity house on Martin Luther King's birthday is recorded as a "hate crime," indistinguishable from more serious offenses. It does a disservice to the cause to lump vicious assaults together with minor slights, but the science of analyzing ethnic tension on campus is a new one. Sorting out the big offenses from the little ones takes time. So does meaningful comparison of incidents that have taken place since the late 1980s, when such record keeping began, with the many years of unrecorded affronts that preceded them.

My own experience at Ohio University, a large racially integrated campus, in the seemingly enlightened 1960s includes several such unrecorded episodes. My overall experience was memorably pleasant and rewarding, but being "one of the guys" was not always easy in a dormitory where most of the guys were working-class or lower middle-class white guys from Cleveland and other similar bastions of urban and rural tension. Ethnic slurs were part of the landscape, tossed around liberally at everyone, including me. Among the mildest were insensitive remarks like, "Smile, Clarence, so we can see you," whenever the lights went out.

Male bonding in dorms is partly a process of determining how close insults can cut without drawing blood. For putting up with it in good humor—for giving as good as I got—I was awarded a mock "Official White Man's Card," after the cards black Americans received, according to legend, when visiting South Africa. "Thanks, guys," I said with feigned humility. "But if this means I have to marry any of your ugly sisters, I'm not taking it."

On the flip side, white guys were not my only social challenge. So was the "community," the tightly knit network of black students on campus. Nonconformity and a free exchange of ideas were stridently discouraged in the name of "unity," much as high school children suppress their individuality so they can be "popular." Public disagreement or self-criticism was frowned on as providing ammunition to the "enemy," the white people who, by their very omnipresence and omnipotence, were guilty of making us feel uncomfortable. Black students on a campus with very many other black students might find themselves suddenly pinched under the thumb of a social fascism that forbids their making white friends, sitting at any but the "black tables" in dining halls, or presenting anything to the rest of the world but a "united front" in the cause of blackness. The irony is that the black movement formed around demands for respect, tolerance for difference, and a love for dissent—black difference and dissent from the standards of white racism. As a student, I, like others, was put on notice for failing to conform to the narrowest "black community" standards. While struggling out of one plantation, I was being roped into another.

Why, one might ask, should race be forgotten so quickly and casually in the university when it is so ruthlessly and relentlessly remembered in the day-to-day world off-campus? Is it not counterintuitive for human beings to view one another suddenly as equals after centuries of viewing one another through the prism of race and social caste? It would be an unnatural act for human beings in only a generation to suddenly cleanse themselves of the residual effects of hundreds of years of slavery, segregation, degradation, and humiliation.   •

But, then, is not integration itself an unnatural act? 'Tis human to follow the natural *affinity impulse* that lures us into cliques and associations with others who are as much like ourselves as possible. Although we urge our children not to run with the crowd to such a degree that they sacrifice their individual good sense, they only repeat the actions of their elders and generations past. It is a tribute to the indomitable human inclination for risk, adventure, diversity, and self-searching that in our diverse society we Americans cross the lines as often as we do. ("There is a place where Serbs and Croatians get along peacefully," Michael Barone, editor of *The Political Almanac*, once quipped. "It is called Chicago.") We humans draw many such lines. Race is only one small set of them. Color blindness comes naturally to children, who have not been taught the many ubiquitous lessons of racial life, values, and etiquette in America. It does not come so naturally to adults who have been long separated from one another along racial lines. Integration that does not spring from natural occurrence must be carefully cultivated.

This is particularly true for many African-American students on campus. In candid moments, they sometimes often speak of a self-doubt imposed early by society and culture and brought with them as excess baggage to the campus, where many, thrown into a predominantly white environment for the first time, detect a palpable curiosity or sense of superiority, at best, and a hostility or resentment, at worst, from white students and professors. All it takes is one racial

epithet, spoken or painted in bathroom graffiti, to offer what
James Baldwin called "evidence of things not seen" that con-
firms the grand conspiracy many see afoot to undo them and
black progress. This racial discomfort may help explain why
historically black colleges and universities have, since the
1960s, graduated 37 percent of black college students, even
though they have only 16 percent of the enrollment.

Media also have failed quite often to distinguish between
active and *incidental* racial self-segregation. Upon entering a
school dining hall, a professor at a West Coast university was
surprised and delighted to find a table full of black, white,
Hispanic, and Asian students happily eating and socializing
together. As at most integrated colleges and high schools, students usually clustered at dining hall tables according to race,
blacks here, whites there, et cetera. The professor was delighted
to see one table, at least, where the racial barriers had disappeared. Then, as he came closer, he realized he had judged too
quickly. The students at this racially mixed table were not talking to one another in the conventional way. They were "signing" to one another by hand. The seemingly "mixed" students
actually were part of the community of the deaf. Suddenly the
professor realized his error. There are many ways for humans
to segregate themselves. Race is only one of the most obvious.

Since that day when he was so abruptly reminded of how
communities form around a wide array of commonalties, the
professor says, he sees student self-segregation in a different
light. Look around the dining halls and, yes, you will see students divided by race, but you also will see they are divided
by interest. Art students sit with other "artsies." Jocks sit
with cheerleaders. Fraternity brothers sit with sorority sisters.
Hippies sit with hippies. Rap fans sit with rap fans.
Sometimes interests align with race. When they do, it attracts
the eye, especially when it is a new sight.

So goes the affinity impulse that attracts us to others who are as much like us as possible. Students, especially students far from home, always seek social comfort zones with other students who share similar backgrounds and tastes. Part of it is a natural result of the identity formation period known as adolescence, with all its usual social rebellion. Walk into any high school cafeteria and you are likely to find hard rock fans at one table, greasers at another, and jocks and cheerleaders at another. Preppies, punk rockers, art students, and auto fans congregate with one another. Why is it only upsetting when black students (or others of color) do it? Why is it always presumed that it is blacks who should want to meet the standards of whites and not the other way around? Why is it so hard, one might ask, for white Americans to think of integration as a two-way street, a process of sharing, not just a one-way assimilation—*digestion*—of blacks into the world of whites?

Blatant prejudices—the "subtly racist" of whom Bloom writes—are only part of the problem of modern race relations. The other part is perceptions. Even the sophisticated observers at "60 Minutes" were seduced in the spring of 1993 by the need to simplify it in "Equal but Separate," a report on self-segregation at Duke University. The program showed students ostensibly splitting off into separate parties, separate apartment complexes, separate outdoor benches, and, most dramatically, separate buses for Duke's famous football team. The report also traveled across country to interview Shelby Steele, who said essentially that there was no excuse for the most privileged generation of black youngsters America ever had to be withdrawing from white campus life and asking for special privileges. How sad, said "60 Minutes" reporter Lesley Stahl, that a campus once closed to blacks now was being segregated by them.

But the week after the report, "60 Minutes" issued a cor-
rection. The football team, it turns out, was not segregating
by race after all, but by musical tastes. On game trips, they
played heavy metal music on one bus and rap on the other.

That wasn't all that was misleading about the report,
according to Hardy J. Vieux, Duke student body president
that year. Vieux pointed out that black students gravitate to
Central Campus apartments not so much because of race as
because the East and West Campus apartments tend to have
beer parties, and black students tend to prefer parties where
"kegs of beer are not staples." Nevertheless, the Central
Campus parties that blacks hold are not exclusive. In fact, he
noted, the so-called black party shown during the television
report actually took place in the apartment of two *nonblack*
students. As further evidence of how well the races try to get
along at Duke, Vieux offered the fact that the predominantly
white student body elected him, an African-American, to be
its student body president.

But neither "60 Minutes" nor any other national media
found much news in that. News, as an older and perhaps
therefore more cynical colleague told me during my younger
reporting days, is what is happening when things are *not*
going the way they are supposed to be going.

For those of us who genuinely believed in Martin Luther
King's integration dream, it is no small tragedy to see voluntary lines of racial division replace those once decreed by law.
But a greater tragedy is the tendency by those who should
know better to have blacks bear the entire burden of
improved race relations. In this, the campus offers a
metaphor for poor race relations in the larger society. Perhaps
Dr. King spoiled white America. The sacrifices he and the
early southern civil rights movement made to save white
America from its own worst impulses seem to have made it

easier for whites to keep asking us to make more sacrifices.
King never intended for black men and women to bear the
burden of desegregation alone.

The Canon

Conservatives, whipped up by former Secretary of Education
William Bennett, the *National Review*, and the *Wall Street
Journal*'s editorial page, among other battlefield coverage of
the campus culture wars, were alarmed nationwide when
Stanford students in a rally attended by Jesse Jackson in the
1980s chanted, "Hey, hey, ho, ho, Western Civ has got to go!"
The "canon" or "core curriculum," a fancy term, as Robert
Hughes has put it, for "required reading," was under attack
and was being defended even by those who had never read
its "great books."

Bloom, a scholar of Shakespeare, Plato, and Rousseau,
writes in *The Closing of the American Mind* how he opposed
Cornell's dismantling of its core curriculum in the late 1960s,
amid student and faculty uprisings for socially "relevant
studies." During faculty meetings on the matter, Bloom con-
ceded that students were bored by the core curriculum, but
he felt it should be kept if only because it represented the last
rudiments of a core knowledge all collegiates should have. It
might not be much and most students might forget it shortly
after they learn it, but something is better than nothing. My
question is: "Why must the 'something' be boring?"
Excitement follows the connection of teaching to the lives of
students.

Let us agree that the "great books" are, indeed, great. Let
us agree that the dead white males who wrote the European
and American classics are still very much worth studying.
Let us agree that one would be hard-pressed to find a great

black writer who has not at one time or another been positively influenced by a great white writer, just as the reverse is
increasingly and happily true.

At the same time, let us note an ironic similarity between
conservative defenders of the canon and left-progressive
advocates of extreme Afrocentrism: They all share what *Time*
art critic Robert Hughes describes in his *Culture of Complaint*
(1993) as "the sturdy assumption that works of art are or
ought to be therapeutic."

"Imbibe the *Republic* or *Phaedra* at nineteen, and you will
be one kind of person," Hughes writes, "study *Jane Eyre* or
Mrs. Dalloway or the poetry of Aphra Behn, and you will be
another; read Amiri Baraka or *The Color Purple* or the writings
of Wole Soyinka, and you will be a third. This happens, or is
supposed to happen, because the author, whether it's Plato or
Alice Walker, becomes a 'role model' for the reader, whose
imitative faculties are roused by the writer's imaginative
ones. If you read Evelyn Waugh before Frantz Fanon you
may become a racist (if white), or (if black) suffer an attack of
the bends through sudden decompression of self-esteem. For
in the literary zero-sum game of Canon talk, if you read X it
means that you don't read Y."

The zero-sum view of classical studies is a zero. Susan
Sontag got it right when she said in a 1975 interview: "All . . .
forms of consensus about 'great' books and 'perennial' problems, once stabilized, tend to deteriorate eventually into
something philistine. The real life of the mind is always at the
frontiers of 'what is already known.' Those great books don't
only need custodians and transmitters. To stay alive, they also
need adversaries. The most interesting ideas are heresies."*

**Salamagundi interview by Robert Boyas and Maxine Bernstein, April 1975, *Salmagundi* (Fall
1975–Winter 1976); reprinted in Susan Sontag, *A Susan Sontag Reader* (New York: Farrar,
Straus & Giroux, 1982) pp. 329–346.

Author Charles Johnson put it in simpler terms during an interview on ABC's "Sunday Morning with David Brinkley." Columnist George Will, noting that Johnson's prize-winning novel *Middle Passage* displayed echoes of his affection for Mark Twain, Joseph Conrad, and Herman Melville, asked the author what he thought of the current campus assault on "DWEMs." Johnson responded that he had, indeed, read the great works of Euro-American authors of the past two or three hundred years, but he also had read the great books of Asian authors of the past couple thousand years, as well as great books from African and Latin American authors. He went on to say that the arguments over the literary canon were based on a false premise that college is about four years of reading great books. In fact, he said, "college should be four years of preparation for a lifetime of reading great books."

For this reason, I reject Afrocentrism, Hispanocentrism, Asiacentrism, feminocentrism, and any other line of study when its placing of one group at the center of its universe results in a bending of history and reality to suit the cause of ethnic or gender therapy or cheerleading. Multiculturalism, it has been said, is pluralism without walls. It is a call for inclusion. It is a blow against the culturally imposed barriers that impede the ability of groups to learn about one another. It is not necessarily a rejection of all that is produced by dead white males. Multiculturalism should be and increasingly will be considered an integral part of one's education in the coming multicultural century.

Political Correctness

In the drive by many campuses to make a more hospitable environment for minorities, some overdo it. Instead of finding ways to make students feel more comfortable with one another, they impose speech codes, "sensitivity sessions," and special orientation sessions that try, in effect, to suppress any possibility of offense to women or minorities on campus. In response have come howls of outrage over "political correctness." Conservatives have waged a culture war against speech codes, orientation days, "sensitivity sessions," and any other activity that contributes to a sense described aptly by the Wellesley senior who said mournfully, "You have to be a victim to fit in at Wellesley." Yet, somehow, the academy survives. Efforts by well-meaning progressives to "protect" us people of color and other perennial victims from objectionable words or ideas tend to fold rather quickly under the heat of public scrutiny and ridicule. As new-wave "censors" or academic "McCarthyites," they tend to have paper teeth compared to the armor of those who have real power in America. While there have been occasional excesses and idiocies, it is still true, as British journalist Katharine Whitehorn said in 1991, that "there are a lot more places where you can say 'spic' and 'bitch' with impunity than places where you can smoke a cigarette."*

A greater calamity is the array of actions students take upon themselves to squelch ideas or speech they don't like. In one case, for example, students at the University of Maryland woke up one autumn morning in 1993 to find that at least half of the copies of their campus newspaper, the *Diamondback*, had been lifted from their distribution points around the campus and dumped into the trash. In their place were leaflets saying, "Due to its racist nature, the Diamondback will not be available today. Read a book."

With that, the *Diamondback* joined more than two dozen other campus newspapers that would be trashed that school year. The most famous incident involved the trashing of stu-

The Observer (London, August 25, 1991).

dent newspapers at the University of Pennsylvania, an occurrence that became an issue in the confirmation hearings of National Endowment for the Humanities head Sheldon Hackney, Penn's president at the time. Conservatives charged Hackney had let the black perpetrators off easy.

Elsewhere, Asians were offended by a cartoon in the Johns Hopkins University weekly that used the word "chinks," and feminists have been affronted by a variety of offenses, real or perceived, to women.

I have long believed that episodes of racial friction on campus are never about the issue that ostensibly touches them off. The most obvious incident provides only a spark for less apparent kindling that has been building up over time. At Maryland, for example, black students' complaints about the student newspaper sounded painfully trivial at first glance. For example, it showed only white models in a fashion supplement; it misreported Frederick Douglass's name as "Franklin Douglass" in a black history month tribute, and it mistitled W.E.B. Du Bois's *Souls of Black Folk* as "The Sales of Black Folks." Ironically, the newspaper's efforts to reach out and include black life in its pages had backfired painfully. It had done badly in trying to do good.

But at an open forum organized by the campus chapter of the National Association of Black Journalists, a litany of abuses, affronts, cruelties, and insensitivities, big and small, came out that touched almost every department on campus. But the biggest overall complaint was a common one heard across the country: They were tired of invisibility. They wanted to do more than assimilate on white men's terms. They also wanted respect. Since universities are not in the market of dispensing respect, they try shortcuts. Some, like speech codes, can be unnecessarily draconian.

The destroying of campus newspapers strikes a personal

chord with me. As an editor and columnist on my campus
daily, I usually had to defend myself against white conservatives. Today's campus press is just as likely to find itself faced
down by black left-progressives.

Typically, campus newspapers do not have many black
staff members, even at colleges that have a substantial number of black journalism majors. Yet campus newspapers and
broadcast stations provide some of the most valuable experience a job-seeking student can have in our profession. Editors
will typically tell you they are short-staffed, since they usually have little or no money to pay. Yet when I ask black journalism majors why they are not beating down the campus
daily's door looking for work, they usually tell me that the
"white kids" who run the paper are "spoiled" and "self-centered," that they "don't want to listen," that they're "unfair"
and "out of touch," that they "don't know and don't care
about the black community," that they run the paper "like a
tight little clique" and "give all the good assignments to the
same people all the time."

What, I respond, makes you think it's going to be any different in the real world? Campus newsrooms are a micro-
cosm of real-world newsrooms, with all the same social
dynamics and personnel miscues. Journalism majors who
plan to work in professional newsrooms might as well get
used to it. Talking to editors does not guarantee that they will
listen, but it works better than silent rage.

As an African American who made it my task to comfort
the afflicted and afflict the comfortable, as the old quotation
goes, it annoys me to hear the authors of speech codes say
women and minorities are such sensitive souls that we need
special protections from the idiotic statements of the ignorant. The University of Maryland, after careful study and,
one presumes, agony, came up with a student-approved

speech policy that others should take as a model. It cautions everyone to "consider the hurt which may result from the use of slurs and epithets," but it does not limit speech. Instead, it says, the educational mission of the university requires "the need for freedom, the right to think the unthinkable, discuss the unmentionable and challenge the unchallengeable."

Let worthy ideas drive out the bad. It is no accident that the creative spirit of black America has flourished at the frontiers of struggle, hardship, and risk. Safety stagnates the intellect. The real life of the mind flourishes at the frontiers of conventional thinking, flouting protected borders. The proper answer to objectionable speech is more speech, not less. The intellectual lives of women and people of color need more than baby-sitters and bodyguards. They also need adversaries. As Sontag said, the most interesting ideas are heresies, whether they come from outside the community or well up from within.

What to Do?

Garry Trudeau's syndicated "Doonesbury" comic strip stepped into the campus culture wars in September 1993, with two weeks of strips that showed a college president struggling with empowerment-hungry students pressing their pluralistic wishes. Alarmed that various ethnic and gender enclaves had "managed to produce a fully segregated campus," the college president thought things couldn't get worse. Then he found out they could. The campus black students were at the door demanding separate water fountains.

It was the type of fiction that, in many minds, was more true than facts. Many believe the resegregation of America's campuses is just that severe, but I caution, before we throw around the word "resegregate," the campuses must first desegregate.

Students can begin by talking to one another more often across racial lines. Black students, having heard one too many curious questions about how they do their hair and the like, tell me wearily, "I'm tired of trying to educate white students about black folks." White students just as wearily complain, "I'm tired of being called a racist every time I try to talk about it."

These are not new complaints. I heard the same complaints expressed in precisely the same words a generation ago in the 1960s, a decade that has since become far more romanticized as a paragon of brotherhood and understanding than it deserves to be. Judging by some critics, it is now theoretically possible for a student of color to pass through four years without having to communicate on more than a superficial level with anyone who comes from another ethnic group. That's not new. It's just more formalized.

Those who hark back to some halcyon time when students of color seemed to be more content on predominantly white campuses are expressing a nostalgia for a place and time to which they never have been. Just ask the alumni. Alumni of color have shunned conventional alumni organizations so thoroughly that desperate alma maters have consented, often with great reluctance, to encourage special minority-focused chapters and fund-raisers. The results have been mixed, largely because of enduring hard feelings for colleges where they had not been made to feel particularly welcome as students, according to the February 23, 1994, issue of the *Chronicle of Higher Education*.

The Hispanic Alumni Club of the University of Arizona, for example, had raised $300,000 in its nine years by holding annual black-tie dinners and developing special newsletters for Hispanic graduates. Unfortunately, the university, whose alumni were about 4 percent Hispanic, had hoped to reach closer to $1 million. The Colgate University Alumni of Color Organization had raised only $10,000 in its eight-year life by sponsoring various fund-raisers. "We're just trying to wear down the bitterness," the group's president told the *Chronicle*.

The bitterness was illustrated by the Reverend Ladell M. Flowers, of Kansas City, head of the University of Missouri's Black Alumni Organization, who was quoted as saying he had refused to give money to the university for many years after receiving a bachelor's and two master's degrees there in the 1970s. Among his memories were fistfights between whites and blacks in his dormitory, racial slurs scrawled on bathroom mirrors, nights when campus security officers questioned him and other black students—but not whites—about where they were walking, and a white professor "who did not understand the hardships that black people faced in society, but lectured as though he did."

Episodes like that drive many students, particularly those whose backgrounds left them largely unacquainted with white college life or white people, to seek their own ethnic brethren and sistren as a campus comfort zone. But, for their own good, they should avoid treating their comfort zone as anything more than a temporary expedient, a strategic base of operation from which they can go forth and deal with the larger world. Just as changing demographics require white students to learn more about the diversity of other cultures, so must students of color learn how to work in an increasingly multicultural America. No amount of name calling or "unity" checks is going to change that. Black students, in particular, cheat themselves when they pass up golden opportunities to socialize with whites and learn more about America's dominant culture. Before you can change the world, you need to know how it works. There is no better place to begin than in the world as it is represented in the diversity of a multiethnic campus.

In my travels to campuses across the country, I have found that the real victims of the culture wars tend not to be the activists of either the right or the left, righteously armed with their ideology, organization, and, particularly in the case of conservative student groups, financial backing from conservative foundations, media, and alumni. The real victims tend to be the vast majority of students who merely want to get a diploma and get out. It is they who stand on the sidelines of free inquiry rather than engage in candid discussion and debate across racial, ethnic, or gender lines, for fear of offending someone, either on the right or on the left. It is they who, in my opinion, are being cheated out of the very mind-broadening experience that campus life should be. They are not indigestible, these students in the middle. It is campus life that has become indigestible to them. They come in all colors and genders. Who will speak up for them?

14

What Is Race For?

I foresee a day when racial and religious differences will be of no importance whatsoever, and people will hate one another for completely personal reasons.

—Caption on cartoon of man speaking to woman at cocktail party, *Wall Street Journal*, August 3, 1995

Back in the 1960s, Woody Allen used to tell a joke about a paranoid man who married a schizophrenic woman, then argued over how they were going to raise the children. That question—*how to raise the children?*—came back to me in a curious way years later when I was between marriages and dating a young Irish-American woman who grew up in rural Wisconsin. She told me she could never marry a black man because she didn't know how she could raise the children. Her reason sounded cryptic.

"I would feel alone in the house," she said.

Alone? It took me a few microseconds to figure out what she meant. She believed in the "one-drop rule," the ancient and peculiarly American standard for racial categorization under which just "one drop" of black blood makes you black, whether your skin is as light as Lani Guinier's or as dark as Clarence Thomas's. I had no intentions of having children with this woman before and I was certainly not entertaining them now. Still, her statement annoyed me.

But they would be *your children*, I reminded her.

Yes, she agreed, "but *they wouldn't be white.*"

No, not under the one-drop rule. Our relationship was headed up a blind alley toward a dead end, thanks to one of white America's most powerful tools of social control, a legacy of slavery that in recent years ironically has been embraced just as fiercely by blacks. On some level she knew that she, as a mother to "black" children, would suddenly be brought down to something less than the first-class status her white skin usually afforded her. She would be thrust suddenly into a new world, a black world quite different from the white Irish-Catholic world in which she was raised in Wisconsin, and she wanted no part of it. She didn't mind crossing over temporarily to dabble in a little cross-racial adventure with me. But she had no plans to stay. Those battles would have to be fought without her.

It probably was just as well. She knew her limitations. Biracial children are quite special people with special needs in a society that is more obsessed with race than its members usually care to admit. They are white, but not quite. They are black, but not all-black. In some less-enlightened black circles, they find themselves envied and ostracized, exalted and defiled, all because of a genetic accident in which they had no say. They live, like their parents, on the edges of tribal life, on the margins of America's historical racial contradictions. By their very existence, they flout both the immutability of the one-drop rule and the purity of Africa-descended Americans as a "race."

But times are changing. Interracial marriage and reproduction are on the upswing, and a new generation of post-1960s multiracial children is demanding recognition, not in the margins of society but as a mainstream of their very own.

My temporary girlfriend's attitudes are a product of America's racial past. To get a glimpse of its future, look at Eldrick "Tiger" Woods, the golf prodigy. His mother, from Thailand, is half Thai, a quarter Chinese, and a quarter white. His father is half black, a quarter Chinese, and a quarter American Indian. Yet, since age six, when he first was profiled in *Ebony* magazine, he has been called a "black" golf prodigy. On his first day in kindergarten in Cypress, California, Tiger was tied to a tree and taunted by older white kids who were not happy with the first "black" family in the neighborhood. Years later at Shoal Creek, a Birmingham club that once refused black members, he was picketed by black protesters for playing in a college tournament there. That was the story of Tiger's life; either he was too black or he was not black enough. But in the spring of 1995 when he became, at age nineteen, the fourth "black" golfer to play the Masters Tournament in Augusta, Georgia, while still enrolled in Stanford, he refused to settle for that label. It was an injustice to all of his other heritages, he said, to call him simply "black." He was not ashamed to be black. But it was not all that he was proud of, either.

What does he put on forms? "Asian," he told *Sports Illustrated*.

The future of race in America increasingly will sound out the question a *Newsweek* cover asked in 1994, "What Color Is Black?" What color is white? What is race? Such questions always have nagged at the rigid underpinnings of America's racial order, but never more urgently than today, on the brink of a new century in which the standards of a new generation pose the greatest challenge yet to the curse of the color line.

The future of race in America is the focus of a current political and social movement by mixed-race children and their families. They don't seek much, just recognition. They want the government to create a new "multiracial" category on census and school forms. Their organizations and support groups across the country include the Atlanta-based Project RACE, the San Francisco–based Association of Multiethnic Americans, the Chicago-based Biracial Family Network, and the District of Columbia–based Interracial Family Circle, among others.

The future of race in America is being covered by new media, like *Interrace* and *Biracial Child*, two magazines based in Atlanta, and *New People*, based in Oak Park, Michigan.

The future of race in America is Candy Mills, the editor and publisher of *Interrace* and *Biracial Child*. Mills is of black, white, and Indian descent. Her husband, Gabe Gross, who handles the marketing, is white. Circulation quickly grew from 300 to 25,000 within a few years of their founding in 1990. "We admit it's a limited market," says Gross, who assists his wife in editing *Interrace* and *Biracial Child*. "A lot of interracial couples are reluctant to buy it [*Interrace*] from a newsstand. Like a lot of gays are reluctant to let people see them buy gay publications. People don't want to be identified by picking it up. Even with mail orders, we get a lot of requests for plain envelopes. There is still a stigma in society. I see their point. Candy and I don't look on ourselves as an interracial couple. We just happen to be one."

The future of race in America will see the growth of a new culture and community distinct from their larger ethnic communities.

The future of race in America is changing. The Supreme Court struck down the last of the nation's anti-miscegenation laws in the ironically named case of *Loving v. Virginia* in 1967, appropriately at the tail end of the civil rights era. Since then, changed laws and relaxed attitudes have resulted in skyrocketing mixed-race marriages and births. From 1970 to 1991, census figures show the number of mixed-race married couples more than tripled, from 310,000 to 994,000. Between 1968 and 1989, children born to parents of different races increased, from 0.7 percent of total births to 3.4 percent, or from 22,100 to 110,500.

Patterns vary widely from one race to another. Births for black and white parents were the largest group, having increased rapidly from 8,700 in 1968 to 45,000 in 1989. Children with one Asian and one white parent were the next largest group at 38,900. Another 5,000 births that year involved one parent who was black and one parent who was Asian, Hispanic, Native American, Indian, or "other." More Japanese-Americans married outside the Asian race than within it. For every 100 births in which both parents were Japanese, there were 139 in which the parents were racially mixed. A similar pattern emerged among those who checked Native American Indian on their census forms. For every 100 children born to two Native American parents, 140 have one parent who is white and one who is Native American. Chinese-white births almost quadrupled from 1,000 to 3,800 during the same period, but so did Chinese-Chinese parents, from 4,600 to 17,100.

Although the percentages still sound small, experts say the statistics dramatically undercount the number of interracial births, partly because the father's race isn't always on the birth certificate and partly because government forms often allow just one racial designation.

The future of race in America is the two groups of mixed-race students on the campus of the University of California, Berkeley. Similar groups had formed on more than a dozen other campuses across the country. The future of race in America is being studied in a class called "People of Mixed Race Descent" that was initiated in 1981 at the University of California at Berkeley by Terry P. Wilson, son of a Potawatomi

Indian father and a white mother. Soon it had a waiting list.
Many waiting to sign up were the products of mixed-race marriages or were themselves involved in mixed-race relationships.
One of his students, he told the *Chronicle of Higher Education*,
has grandparents who were white, Japanese, American Indian,
and black. Now her graduation was in danger because she did
not want to pick a conventional racial designation on university forms.

The future of race in America will see blacks and whites
wondering anxiously, as many Japanese Americans and
American Jews do today, about their survival as a race. As
one friend put it when I asked whether multiracials should
be recognized as a separate category, "How far back do you
go?" He was a walking illustration of the dilemma posed by
his question. His complexion was light. His hair was sandy-
brown. Like most African Americans, he was "mixed," if you
go back far enough.

Most of American history's greatest black leaders were
white to some extent. Booker T. Washington and Frederick
Douglass had white fathers. W.E.B. Du Bois, Malcolm X,
Martin Luther King, Jr. (who had an Irish grandmother and
some American Indian ancestry), and Jesse Jackson also had
some white ancestry, as does, judging by his physical features, Louis Farrakhan, the son of West Indian immigrants.

The future of race in America could be glimpsed at the
1990 National Association of Black Journalists convention in
Los Angeles, where a call for recognition and cooperation
between self-identified "blacks" and "multiethnics" was
openly hissed and booed by a predominantly black and professional audience. As recounted by Itabari Njeri in the
September 1991 *Essence* magazine panelist Charles Stewart
asked the crowd, "If you consider yourself Black for political
reasons, raise your hand."

Most raised their hands.

Then Stewart, chief deputy to California state senator Diane Watson, asked how many people in the audience believed they were of "pure African descent, without any mixture."

Nobody raised a hand.

"If you advocate a category that includes people who are multiracial to the detriment of their black identification, you will replicate what you saw—an empty room," he said. "We cannot afford to have an empty room. We cannot afford to have a race empty of black people—not so long as we are struggling against discrimination based on our identification as black people."

> Color is not a human or personal reality; it is a political reality.

> —James Baldwin

But a growing chorus of voices among those of mixed race resent being told the black community "cannot afford" to allow them to have a distinct identity that is anything other than purely, devotedly black. Njeri, a product of African, French, English, Arawak, and East Indian bloodlines, writes of other melting-pot ethnics like Velina Hasu Houston, an award-winning Los Angeles playwright and executive director of the Amerasian League, who happens to be of Japanese, African-American, and Native American ancestry. "The sushi-and-grits generation of multicultural diversity," says Njeri.

Houston is upset that "African Americans want us to be their political slaves." She has seen much of the "brother and sister love" others profess evaporate when her organization has sought help for Amerasian refugee children who have

African-American fathers: "I just saw a boy who is seventeen years old, who is half African American; his mother is Vietnamese. He can't speak English very well and he needs help. . . . But the people who make the most fun of him, give him the hardest time, are African Americans."

The future of race in America is in Mexico today. "Mexicans, especially, regard themselves as mestizo—part Spanish, part indigenous," Carlos Fernandez, president of the San Francisco–based Association of Multi-Ethnic Americans, told *American Demographics* (June 1994). "The large majority of Mexico is multiracial. It's almost the official culture. Mexico hasn't asked a race question on its census since 1921. So on the U.S. census, people who put Mexican for race know full well what it means. It's mestizo, and that is a racial designation, not a nationality."

The number of people who checked the box marked "other race" on census forms increased 45 percent between the 1980 and 1990 censuses, to 9.8 million people—about 1 in 25 Americans, according to *American Demographics*. Out of that group, 98 percent claimed Hispanic origin on the ethnicity question, which means more than 40 percent of the nation's 22 million self-identified Hispanics are not willing to identify themselves as black or white.

Even in the 1920s, when Mexico was removing race from its census forms, the United States Census Bureau was estimating three-quarters of African Americans could claim at least some white blood.

The future of race in America is in South Africa today, where it is said that the first "Coloured" was born nine months after the arrival of the Europeans.

The future of race in America is in Brazil, where a national survey of visibly "black" Brazilians, by American standards, turned up four dozen different words for what they called themselves.

The future of race in America is the Latino-American woman whose great-great-grandmother was black, but she passes for white, while she describes her dark-skinned sister to *American Demographics* magazine as *trigueña*, which she translated as "brown."

The future of race in America might be seen in the family of Shirley Morris Taylor Haizlip of Los Angeles. She chronicles in her family biography, *The Sweeter the Juice* (1994), that her family went from being "black" to "mulatto" to "white" within twenty years, thanks to the census taker's pen.

In 1900 a white census taker knocked on the door of the Washington, D.C., home of Shirley's great-grandfather, Edward Everett Morris, born in slavery to a Virginia federal judge and a slave. Under the United States government's criterion for judging race at the time, the "eyeball test" and the one-drop rule, all but one of the light-skinned Morris family was recorded as "B," for black. Only Morris's Irish wife, Margaret, was recorded as "W," for white.

But by 1920, some of the Morris children, including Shirley's grandfather, William, had "passed" into the ranks of white America. After William's wife died, he sent his youngest daughter, Margaret, to live with "black" relatives. More than seventy years would pass before Margaret's daughter, Shirley, would reunite the "black" and "white" branches of the Morris clan through diligent detective work recorded in her book, much to the surprise of the "white" side of the family, which had not known until then that they had any African ancestry.

Who knows how many other white people have black blood in them? Nobody does, partly because for most of this country's history it was technically illegal for them to have been conceived. Only in America did one find the one-drop rule that one drop of black blood in your family line made you black, as if one drop of ink had tainted the entire milk glass. American slaveholders held to the one-drop rule to create more slaves and distance themselves from direct familial responsibility for their mulatto offspring. Black Americans, embracing these children into the community's extended family, also embraced the one-drop rule as fiercely as if they had invented it, to increase black solidarity and community clout.

Color Consciousness

Black people, in my experience, have seldom been very sophisticated or tolerant about fellow blacks who don't want to be, as a college roommate of mine used to say, "black, the whole black, and nothing else but black." Few are willing, in the face of what appears to be omnipotent, omnipresent white racism, to split hairs or chromosomes over the one-drop rule.

Much of the black backlash against blacks who want to be identified as "mixed" or "multiracial" stems from ancient resentments in the black community over not just color but complexion and even deeper self-loathing that reaches the boiling point at the suggestion that some other black person does not want to be black.

Like any other tribe, African Americans have an ambivalent relationship with those who show the most visible signs of white ancestry. Along with the nicer names for them— mulatto, mestizo, biracial, multiracial, Eurasian, Afrasian— street vernacular produces others that are not so nice: "Yellow people." "High yella." "Half-breed." "Zebras." "Redbones." "Mixed nuts."

These resentments date back to the antebellum days when

light-skinned blacks served more often as the more privileged "house slaves" while their darker-skinned brethren worked in the sweltering fields. The privileged mulatto class formed the core of America's later emergent black bourgeoisie and the color-conscious snobs who founded the "brown paper bag" clubs, where no member could have skin darker than a brown paper bag, or the "blue vein" societies, whose members' skin was light enough to show their veins beneath the underside of their wrists.

Biracial children sometimes carry the stigma from that notion in the black community. Hollywood's representations of Dorothy Dandridge, Lena Horne, and other light-skinned black women as the "tragic mulatto," simultaneously a tragic figure and an object of desire, in films of the 1930s and 1940s taps deep-rooted impulses in white patriarchy and black self-hatred, writes black feminist bell hooks: "Stereotypically portrayed as embodying a passionate sensual eroticism as well as a subordinate feminine nature, the biracial black woman has been and remains the standard other black females are measured against." White men have regarded the biracial female as a "sexual ideal," hooks writes, and "black men have taken their cues from white men."

Small wonder, then, that the desire of many of today's new mulattos to go off on their own, now that the coast is clear, does not sit well with many other blacks. The "wannabes" who want to be "better" than black, by their actions, demean, however unintentionally, the trials and pride of those who have no choice.

So at a time when the one-drop rule should be most thoroughly discredited and put to rest, it is instead being most relentlessly enforced by law, customs, traditions, and habits of mind. Yet its arbitrariness undermines its usefulness and the viability of race-based remedies that grow out of it. I have

known biracial students who put "white" or some cute alternative like "b/w" on a college application form, only to be
told they were nuts to throw away an opportunity for preference in admissions or scholarships. Similarly, I also have
known at least one Latino woman whose decision to use her
husband's non-Hispanic surname enraged her white boss by
"ruining my affirmative action numbers."

Originally designed to rope blacks into subservience, the
one-drop rule since has helped expand and unify the black
community as a political and social force. Now, just when
black Americans are beginning, however marginally, to turn
the curse of race to their advantage, through the machina-
tions and manipulations of white guilt and black political
empowerment, suddenly the new "mixed" Americans
threaten to minimize it, if not obliterate it entirely. It is not
surprising, then, that the new biracialists often are seen particularly by other Americans of African ancestry as some sort
of traitors, a marginally privileged group willing to torpedo
affirmative action programs and other race-based remedies
just to soothe their own individualistic inclinations.

Census Politics

The future of race in America is being determined in the
Office of Management and Budget in Washington. Since 1977
the seemingly bland, unexciting OMB has been a hotbed of
raging controversy. That was the year it was given the thank-
less task of determining the categories of racial classifications
used in each census. The census determines congressional
redistricting, federal funding, and entitlements. It also determines which races will be counted and how.

It is not biology that determines race. It is bureaucrats.
Nearly every census since Thomas Jefferson conducted the

first one in 1790 has measured race differently. For most of the nineteenth century, the color of slaves was specified as "B" for black and "M" for mulatto. In the 1890 census, mulattos were further broken down into quadroons and octoroons. But the Census Bureau gave up on such distinctions after 1920, when three-quarters of all blacks appeared to be racially mixed, and pure black Americans looked increasingly like an endangered species.

The future of race in America became the subject of congressional hearings in the obscure House Subcommittee on Census, Statistics and Postal Personnel in 1993 to help determine who will be counted as what at the millennium. They were deluged as never before with requests to add a variety of categories or subcategories to the current four general racial groups: black, white, American Indian or Alaskan Native, and Asian or Pacific Islander. One group wanted to add Cambodians and Lao to the nine different nationalities already listed on census forms under the heading of Asian or Pacific Islander. Senator Daniel K. Akaka wanted his people added as "Native Hawaiian." Another group wanted Arabs to be counted among races to be protected by civil rights laws.

Others want government to get out of the business of racial categorizations and record keeping. It's inaccurate, capricious, and leads to the "balkanization" of Americans by race and ethnicity, says a remarkable coalition of political conservatives and members of the multiracial movement. Much to the delight of conservatives, it would destroy the underpinnings of affirmative action.

Unfortunately, it would also eradicate all of the yardsticks, however flawed they may be, by which the government measures racial progress. Those who oppose government record keeping by race remind me of those who oppose government-funded studies of possible links between genetics and behavior: They fear what such studies might find or how they might be used even before they have been conducted. Conservatives who criticize the imprecise way government and the courts level playing fields conveniently overlook how much it is the legacy of a period when conservative politicians and voters made sure government and the courts were black America's only recourse. Would they replace it now with nothing more than the good graces of those very souls whose *bad* graces put America into this predicament?

In 1967, the same year the Supreme Court was striking down America's last miscegenation laws, Sidney Poitier starred with Spencer Tracy and Katharine Hepburn in the Oscar-winning *Guess Who's Coming to Dinner?* Its interracial marriage theme was considered a breakthrough. Yet it already was considered hip among my generation, then in college, not to be shocked or even impressed by the idea of interracial marriage, even as onlookers cast furtive glances at interracial couples who dared hold hands in public. Some were horrified by it. Others delighted in it as a revolutionary act. No one, it seemed, was allowed to be neutral about it.

Today, if white people don't like the idea of intermarriage, it is considered outright racist to say so, while black people remain a bit more openly divided. Some, particularly black women, even write essays about it. In an essay published in *Wild Women Don't Wear No Blues*, author Bebe Moore Campbell wrote amusingly and poignantly about how tight her jaw and those of her black girlfriends became when, while dining in a restaurant, they saw a black male movie star they all knew walk in followed by . . . *his blond date!*

I've been on the other end of that scene. Hell hath no fury like the glare of a black woman at a black man who is walking arm-in-arm with a white woman. As my friend Larry the

Barber says, "They look at you like you just killed your mama." Every race in America has its politics. White men in this seemingly enlightened era may date whom they please, but black men who cross the line are viewed by many other blacks as having placed some cancer on their entire race.

"To the ordinary white American the caste line between whites and Negroes is based upon, and defended by, the anti-amalgamation doctrine," wrote Gunnar Myrdal in *An American Dilemma* (1944), his magisterially influential eight-year study of American race relations. "Would you like to have your sister or daughter marry a Negro?" The stereo-typed and hypothetical question is asked in the North and the South alike, "regularly raised without any intermediary reasoning as to its applicability or relevance to the social problem discussed . . . This is an unargued appeal to 'racial solidarity' as a primary valuation. It is corollary to this atti-tude that in America the offspring of miscegenation is related to the Negro race," wrote Myrdal.

From the 1940s, when Myrdal wrote, to the 1980s, when my temporary girlfriend shuddered at the notion of bearing "black" children, the anti-amalgamation doctrine holds, not only among whites but also, perhaps even more rigorously, among blacks.

In the past, intermarriage has been a bigger concern for whites than for blacks. When Myrdal surveyed southern whites and blacks to rank which discriminations against blacks were most important to them, they listed an order of importance that paralleled the priorities of the anti-amalga-mation doctrine:

1. The bar against sex and intermarriage with white women.

2. Segregation in personal relations (dancing, eating,

socializing, etc., together; peculiar etiquette in greetings, hat lifting, titles, back door entering, etc.).

3. Segregation in public facilities, such as schools, churches, and transportation.

4. Political disenfranchisement.

5. Discrimination by police, law courts, and other public servants.

6. Discrimination in securing jobs, land, credit, and other means of earning a living or claiming social welfare activities.

But, just as revealing as "the white man's rank order of discrimination," as Myrdal called it, was "the Negro's own rank order"—it was the same as the white man's but in exactly opposite order. "The Negro resists least the discrimination on the ranks placed highest in the white man's evaluation," he wrote, "and resents most any discrimination on the lowest level." This was in accord with the African American's most immediate interests. They needed jobs, housing, and credit most desperately, even more than equal justice in the courts. They needed social integration and intermarriage with whites the least.

In recent years it has become more obvious and urgent to blacks that, just as whites traditionally used the anti-amalgamation doctrine as an "unargued appeal to racial solidarity as a primary valuation," so do blacks have a deep investment in the one-drop rule as an inarguably fundamental appeal to black racial solidarity. In this sense, African Americans want what other Americans want, roots in another land to call their own. But we traditionally have wanted them more, for we are America's only racial-ethnic group to have been robbed of our history through brutal relocation, reeducation, and resocialization.

Myrdal again: "The Negroes do not, like the Japanese and

the Chinese, have a politically organized nation and an accepted culture of their own outside of America to fall back upon. Unlike the Oriental, there attaches to the Negro an historical memory of slavery and inferiority. It is more difficult for them to answer prejudice with prejudice and, as the Orientals may do, to consider themselves and their history superior to the white Americans and their recent cultural achievements. The Negroes do not have these fortifications for self-respect. They are more helplessly imprisoned as a subordinate caste in America, a caste of people deemed to be lacking a cultural past and assumed to be incapable of a cultural future."

Who, then, after centuries of having the offspring of miscegenation relegated to the Negro race, can blame African Americans for feeling an additional and exceptionally strong claim to today's mixed kids? Still, one cannot claim someone else's identity against his or her wishes and, as old lines of racial caste fragment around rapidly changing attitudes, it will become more difficult to claim that everyone who carries black blood should share the same racial label.

My former lover's attitudes, widely held, are products of the past. The future of race in America will prove her wrong. The future of race in America will make the one-drop rule obsolete.

The future of race in America can be seen in the "WURE"— the Woman of Unidentifiable Race or Ethnicity—who is selling gym shoes, mineral water, yuppie furniture, or long-distance "collect" telephone service to the MTV generation perhaps at this very moment. Advertising executives and producers of rock videos who in the 1960s and 1970s rejected light-skinned black models because they didn't instantly "read black" to consumers were relishing the same models in the 1980s and 1990s *precisely because* they were not quickly or easily identifiable as ethnically *anything*, thus enhancing their universal appeal. The "Universal Other" is how *Chicago Tribune* fashion writer Teresa Wiltz describes this generic multiethnic product of the modern marketing age. Look at her light brown eyes! Look at her light brown complexion! Look at her graceful little nose, lips, and cheekbones. What is she? Black? Latino? Turkish? Italian? Arab? Hawaiian? No way to tell. She is simply what Wiltz, a young African-American woman who is fair-skinned enough to have been mistaken on occasion for Italian or Arab, calls the Universal Other!

Whatever she is, you really can't tell, so it really doesn't matter, and isn't that the real point? The very fact that you can't tell and shouldn't care shows her to be truly contemporary, the ultimate in the fashionable, the trendy, the *new, hip, and with-it!* She has yet to displace the blue-eyed blond as the perennial American beauty standard, but she has won a place firmly perched in the public mind and, one imagines, in America's future. If there is a living embodiment of the next American century, she may be it. She is imposed color blindness, rendering race virtually meaningless until, of course, she is called upon to fill out a form—a college admissions form or a census form or any other form that asks upfront, "What is your race?" What is it? What, indeed?

> *When I discover who I am, I'll be free.*

> —Ralph Ellison

If black Americans of whatever color cannot be freed to be appreciated as individuals, one wonders, what is freedom worth when it is a freedom limited by the tyranny of small community minds dressed up in the trappings of cultural nationalism?

Perhaps, then, the future of race in America is captured at the end of a handy list of "Coping Tips" for biracial teens published in *Biracial Child* magazine: "Don't try to befriend people who won't accept you for whom you are." It is the easiest advice for parents to give. And the most difficult for teens, still forming a sense of their own individual identity while also yearning to be part of a crowd, to follow.

Multiracial children bear a special burden. They hear black people instructing them to identify strictly as black because that is the way society will view them. Whose society? At bottom, it is the society of those very same black people. Black Americans who have internalized white supremacist attitudes and values become agents of those attitudes and values, enforcing them in others and passing them on to new generations more effectively than the Ku Klux Klan ever could.

Biracials point out that they are running away from nothing. I believe them. They cannot run away from race any more than any other American can, as long as they remain in America. They are still people of color, still evoking all the responses that people of color evoke. They cannot run away. They can only turn, as W.C. Fields once said, take the bull by the tail, and face the situation.

"I want to be black," Harvard's Henry Louis Gates, Jr., who happens to have biracial children, once said, "to know black, to luxuriate in whatever I might be calling blackness at any particular time, but to do so in order to come out on the other side, to experience a humanity that is neither colorless nor reducible to color."

The future of race in America will win a freedom not only to be black but also to discover and appreciate one's own individual humanity. It will include not only our obligation

as black Americans to the Africa-descended community that
culturally nurtured us, whether others accept us or not, but
also our obligation to be true to ourselves. Black self-determination is an empty victory if it is not accompanied by one's
individual ability to control one's own fate. America will
have to go through race to get beyond race.

Selected Bibliography

Following are works that either are cited in this book or helped inform its arguments:

Anderson, Elijah. *Street Wise: Race, Class, and Change in an Urban Community.* University of Chicago Press, 1990.

Anson, Robert Sam. *Best Intentions: The Education and Killing of Edmund Perry.* New York: Random House, 1987.

Auletta, Ken. *The Underclass.* New York: Random House, 1983.

Baldwin, James. *The Price of the Ticket: Collected Nonfiction 1948–1985.* New York: St. Martin's/Marek, 1985.

Berman, Paul, editor. *Blacks and Jews: Alliances and Arguments.* New York: Delacorte Press, 1994.

Branch, Taylor. *Parting the Waters: America in the King Years, 1954–63.* New York: Simon & Schuster, 1988.

Comer, James P., M.D., and Alvin F. Poussaint, M.D. *Raising Black Children.* New York: Plume, 1992.

Cone, James H. *Martin and Martin and America: A Dream or a Nightmare.* Maryknoll, N.Y.: Orbis, 1991.

Connor, Marlene Kim. *What Is Cool? Understanding Black Manhood in America.* New York: Crown, 1995.

Crouch, Stanley. *Notes of a Hanging Judge: Essays and Reviews, 1979–1989.* New York: Oxford University Press, 1990.

Cruse, Harold. *The Crisis of the Negro Intellectual.* New York: William Morrow/Quill, 1984.

———. *Plural But Equal.* New York: William Morrow, 1987.

De Beauvoir, Simone. *The Second Sex.* New York: Alfred A. Knopf, 1952.

Du Bois, W. E. B. *The Souls of Black Folk.* New York: New American Library, 1982.

Edsall, Thomas Byrne, and Mary D. Edsall. *Chain Reaction: The Impact of Race, Rights and Taxes on American Politics.* New York: W.W. Norton, 1991.

Edwards, Audrey, and Dr. Craig K. Polite. *Children of the Dream: The Psychology of Black Success.* Garden City, N.Y.: Doubleday, 1992.

Fanon, Frantz. *Black Skin, White Masks*. New York: Grove Press, 1967.

Fogel, Robert William, and Stanley L. Engerman. *Time on the Cross: The Economics of American Negro Slavery*. New York: W.W. Norton, 1974.

Frazier, E. Franklin. *Black Bourgeoisie: The Rise of a New Middle Class in the United States*. New York: Collier Books, 1962.

Gates, Henry Louis, Jr. *The Signifying Monkey: A Theory of African-American Literary Criticism*. New York: Oxford University Press, 1988.

George, Nelson. *Buppies, B-Boys, BAPS & Bohos: Notes on Post-Soul Black Culture*. New York: HarperCollins, 1992.

Glazer, Nathan, and Daniel Patrick Moynihan. *Beyond the Melting Pot: The Negroes, Puerto Ricans, Jews, Italians, and Irish of New York City*. Cambridge, Mass.: MIT Press, 1963.

Goldman, Peter, Thomas M. De Frank, Mark Miller, Andrew Murr, and Tom Mathews. *Quest for the Presidency 1992*. (A *Newsweek* Book.) College Station, Tex.: Texas A & M University Press, 1994.

Hacker, Andrew. *Two Nations: Black and White, Separate, Hostile, Unequal*. New York: Scribner's, 1992.

Hernton, Calvin C. *Sex and Racism in America*. New York: Doubleday, 1965.

Higginbotham, A. Leon, Jr. *In the Matter of Color: Race and the American Legal Process: The Colonial Period*. New York: Oxford University Press, 1978.

Kaufman, Jonathan. *Broken Alliance: The Turbulent Times Between Blacks and Jews in America*. New York: Scribner's, 1988.

King, Martin Luther, Jr. *A Testament of Hope: The Essential Writings of Martin Luther King, Jr.* New York: Harper & Row, 1986.

Kochman, Thomas. *Blacks and Whites Styles in Conflict*. Chicago: University of Chicago Press, 1981.

Kotlowitz, Alex. *There Are No Children Here: The Story of Two Boys Growing Up in the Other America*. Garden City, N.Y.: Nan Talese/Doubleday, 1991.

Kozol, Jonathan. *Savage Inequalities: Children in America's Schools*. New York: Crown, 1991.

Landry, Bart. *The New Black Middle Class*. Berkeley, Cal.: University of California Press, 1987.

Lincoln, C. Eric. *The Black Muslims in America, Third Edition*. Trenton, N.J.: Erdsmans/Africa World Press, 1994.

Lind, Michael. *The Next American Nation: The New Nationalism and the Fourth American Revolution*. New York: Free Press, 1995.

Lomax, Louis. *To Kill a Black Man*. Los Angeles: Holloway House, 1968, 1987.

Loury, Glenn C. *One by One from the Inside Out; Essays and Reviews on Race and Responsibility in America*. New York: Free Press, 1995.

Majors, Richard, and Janet Mancini Billson. *Cool Pose: The Dilemmas of Black Manhood in America*. New York: Lexington Books, 1992.

Malcolm X. *The Autobiography of Malcolm X* (with the assistance of Alex Haley). New York: Grove Press, 1965.

Massey, Douglas S., and Nancy A. Denton. *American Apartheid: Segregation and the Making of the Underclass*. Cambridge, Mass.: Harvard University Press, 1993.

McClain, Leanita. *A Foot in Each World: Articles and Essays of Leanita McClain*. Edited by Clarence Page. Evanston, Ill.: Northwestern University Press, 1984.

Myrdal, Gunnar. *An American Dilemma: The Negro Problem and Modern Democracy*. New York: Harper & Row, 1944; reprint, 1962.

Parenti, Michael. *Democracy for the Few*. New York: St. Martin's Press, 1995.

Quarles, Benjamin. *The Negro in the Making of America*. New York: Collier, 1987.

Rivlin, Gary. *Fire on the Prairie: Chicago's Harold Washington and the Politics of Race*. New York: Henry Holt, 1992.

Rodriguez, Richard. *Hunger of Memory: The Education of Richard Rodriguez*. New York: Bantam, 1983.

Schlesinger, Arthur M., Jr. *The Disuniting of America: Reflections on a Multicultural Society*. Knoxville: Whittle, 1991.

Steele, Shelby. *The Content of Our Character: A New Vision of Race in America*. New York: St. Martin's, 1990.

Styron, William. *Darkness Visible: A Memoir of Madness*. New York: Vintage, 1992.

Takaki, Ronald. *A Different Mirror: A History of Multicultural America*. Boston: Little, Brown, 1993.

————. *Strangers from a Different Shore: A History of Asian Americans*. Boston: Little, Brown, 1989.

Terkel, Studs. *Race: How Blacks and Whites Think and Feel about the American Obsession*. New York: The New Press, 1992.

Van Deburg, William L. *New Day in Babylon: the Black Power Movement and American Culture, 1965–1975*. Chicago: University of Chicago Press, 1992.

Wallace, Michele. *Black Macho and the Myth of the Superwoman*. 1978; reprint, New York: Verso, 1990, 1991.

West, Cornel. *Race Matters*. Boston: Beacon Press, 1993.

Wiley, Ralph. *Why Black People Tend to Shout: Cold Facts and Wry Views from a Black Man's World*. New York: Birch Lane Pres,1991.

Wilson, William Julius. *The Truly Disadvantaged: The Inner City, the Underclass and Public Policy*. Chicago: University of Chicago Press, 1987.

Woodson, Robert L., editor. *On the Road to Economic Freedom: An Agenda for Black Progress*. Chicago: Regnery Books, 1987.